Workbook/Laboratory
Manual for

Puntos
de partida

Workbook/Laboratory
Manual for

Alice A. Arana
FORMERLY OF FULLERTON
COLLEGE

Oswaldo Arana
FORMERLY OF CALIFORNIA
STATE UNIVERSITY, FULLERTON

**María Francisca
Sabló-Yates**

Amy Uribe, Ph.D.
LONE STAR COLLEGE

Puntos
de partida

Tenth Edition

Volume 1
Capítulo 1–Capítulo 9

Mc
Graw
Hill
Education

WORKBOOK / LABORATORY MANUAL FOR PUNTOS DE PARTIDA VOLUME 1, TENTH EDITION

Published by McGraw-Hill Education, 2 Penn Plaza, New York, NY 10121. Copyright © 2017 by McGraw-Hill Education. All rights reserved. Printed in the United States of America. Previous editions © 2012, 2009, and 2005. No part of this publication may be reproduced or distributed in any form or by any means, or stored in a database or retrieval system, without the prior written consent of McGraw-Hill Education, including, but not limited to, in any network or other electronic storage or transmission, or broadcast for distance learning.

This book is printed on acid-free paper.

3 4 5 6 7 8 QVS/ 22 21 20 19 18

ISBN: 978-1-259-63309-6
MHID: 1-259-63309-8

Senior Vice President, Products & Markets: *Kurt L. Strand*
Vice President, General Manager, Products & Markets: *Michael Ryan*
Vice President, Content Design & Delivery: *Kimberly Meriwether David*
Managing Director: *Katie Stevens*
Senior Brand Manager: *Kim Sallee*
Director, Product Development: *Meghan Campbell*
Product Developer: *Misha MacLaird*
Director, Marketing: *Craig Gill*
Senior Faculty Development Manager: *Jorge Arbujas*
Marketing Managers: *Mike Ambrosino / Chris Brown*
Executive Market Development Manger: *Helen Greenlea*
Editorial Coordinator: *Sean Costello*
Senior Director of Digital Content: *Janet Banhidi*
Senior Digital Product Analyst: *Sarah Carey*
Director, Content Design & Delivery: *Terri Schiesl*
Program Manager: *Kelly Heinrichs*
Senior Content Project Manager: *Erin Melloy*
Buyer: *Susan K. Culbertson*
Design: *Matt Backhaus*
Content Licensing Specialists: *Shawntel Schmitt / Beth Thole*
Compositor: *Lumina Datamatics, Inc.*
Printer: *Quad/Graphics*

Photo credits: Page 1 (top): © GoGo Images Corporation/Alamy RF, p. 1 (bottom): © Tom Fowlks/Getty Images, All other photos in the book: © McGraw-Hill Education/Wray Media.

The Internet addresses listed in the text were accurate at the time of publication. The inclusion of a website does not indicate an endorsement by the authors or McGraw-Hill, and McGraw-Hill does not guarantee the accuracy of the information presented at these sites.

Printed in the USA

www.mhhe.com

CONTENTS

TO THE INSTRUCTOR

Welcome to Volume 1 of the combined Workbook/Laboratory Manual for *Puntos de partida*, Tenth Edition!

INTEGRATION AND ACTIVITY FLOW

- The Workbook / Laboratory Manual for *Puntos de partida* consists of two volumes of integrated activities. The first volume corresponds to material covered in **Capítulos 1–9** and the second corresponds to **Capítulos 10–18**, with **Capítulo 9** offered as an appendix. The aural, speaking, and writing activities for each grammar and vocabulary point in the text appear together and are meant to enrich and enhance the students' learning.
- Each **Vocabulario** and **Gramática** subsection contains a progression of carefully structured and organized activities. For example, in **Capítulo 4: De compras,** the **La ropa** vocabulary subsection starts with written exercises, progresses to a listening and speaking activity, and then moves to a final audio activity. This culminating audio activity, as well as other audio activities throughout this supplement, feature different characters, many of whom are recurring, and expose students to language in a natural and authentic context in the form of interviews and conversations.

AUDIO ACTIVITIES

- The *Puntos* Audio Program is available as streaming audio at www.mhhe.com/puntos10.
- Audio activities in the Workbook/Laboratory Manual are easily identified by this headphones icon ⌒.
- Students will hear a variety of native speakers in the audio activities, allowing them to become accustomed to some of the different accents, voice types, and vocabulary found in the Spanish-speaking world. The rate of speech will start out slower than native speed in the earlier chapters and will gradually increase to a moderate pace. As mentioned, many of the audio activities feature recurring characters, who will become familiar to students as they progress through the program: Miguel René (from Mexico), Karina (from Venezuela), Tané (from Cuba), and Rubén (from Spain).

ORGANIZATION/CHAPTER STRUCTURE AND FEATURES

- Each chapter of this Workbook/Laboratory Manual is based on the corresponding chapter of the textbook so that students may practice and review on their own what they are learning in class. For ease of identification, most exercises appear under the same headings as in the main text. Once a section from the textbook has been introduced, students can complete the same section in the Workbook/Laboratory Manual with the assurance that any new vocabulary or structures from later sections of that chapter will be glossed.
- The structure of **Capítulo 1: Ante todo** of the Workbook/Laboratory Manual parallels that of **Capítulo 1** in the main text.
- **Capítulos 2–9** are organized as follows.
  - **Vocabulario: Preparación** allows students to practice the thematic vocabulary in both written and aural/oral forms in a variety of contexts.
  - The expanded **Pronunciación** section contains activities that are almost entirely based on auditory cues, with, in most cases, immediate confirmation of the correct pronunciation or answer. In early chapters, these sections correspond to the section in the main text. Though Pronunciación sections in the main text end in **Capítulo 5,** the Workbook/Laboratory Manual has Pronunciación sections in every chapter.

- **Gramática** presents a variety of written, listening, and speaking exercises on each grammar point in the corresponding section of the main text. Many of these grammar points are introduced by a **¿Recuerda Ud.?** activity, which focuses on similarities between a previously learned grammatical item and the new structure being introduced.
- The **Un poco de todo** section starts with a cloze activity—a narrative with blanks to be filled in by the student—and provides a good opportunity for review of structures and vocabulary of the current chapter as well as previous chapters. This section also contains a culturally based Listening Passage activity. Most Listening Passage activities begin with a pre-listening activity (**Antes de escuchar**) and conclude with a post-listening activity (**Después de escuchar**). The final activity in **Un poco de todo** is an audio activity in the form of an authentic conversation, narration, or interview that features the use of language in a natural context and provides students with additional listening and comprehension practice. This activity is frequently followed by one that gives students the opportunity to create and participate in a similar conversation based on the theme or topic of the primary audio activity.
- The **Cultura** section consists of two activities: a map activity and a reading comprehension activity. The map activity, based on the country or countries of focus of a given chapter, provides the students with another opportunity to visualize the chapter's country of focus in relation to neighboring countries. The reading comprehension activity, based on the cultural reading in the **A leer** section of the main text (**Lectura cultural**), allows the student additional contact with the chapter theme and country of focus.
- **Póngase a prueba** is a short quiz that focuses on some of the most mechanical aspects of the language-learning process: vocabulary, verb structures, and syntax. By taking this quiz, students can evaluate their knowledge of the more basic aspects of the language before they move on to the **Prueba corta.**
- In the **Prueba corta** section, students will complete a test based on more contextual sentences. Audio activities follow the written ones and check students' abilities to listen and respond to various situations. Immediate confirmation of the students' answers to these audio activities is provided.
- The final section, **Puntos personales,** consists of personalized activities. In most cases, no answers are given for these activities due to their nature. The Guided Composition includes questions and/or suggested vocabulary to help students organize their thoughts before writing. **Mi diario** provides a prompt related to the theme and/or grammar in the chapter and encourages students to write freely about their own experiences. Instructors should not grade or correct **Mi diario,** but rather merely react to the content of what the student has written. It is recommended that students keep their **Mi diario** entries in a journal that is easy to carry, as this way the students can easily view their language progress. As the semester progresses and students acquire more language and vocabulary, it is expected that their entries will become more lengthy and complex. **Puntos personales** concludes with **Intercambios,** an audio activity in which students are asked to respond to thematically based questions about themselves. Although brief, this activity contains key elements of the vocabulary and grammar introduced in the chapter. All of the activities in **Puntos personales** allow students to demonstrate their ability to use in a meaningful way what they have learned in both the current and previous chapters.

OTHER NEW FEATURES OF THE TENTH EDITION

- In this edition of *Puntos*, an effort has been made to make the audio exercises less dehydrated and easier for students to process.
- In this edition, students are gradually introduced to Spanish direction lines in **Capítulos 1–4.** The direction lines appear entirely in Spanish starting with **Capítulo 5;** the only exception to this is the Listening Passages, where the complexity of the direction lines for this activity dictates that they remain in English.

ACKNOWLEDGMENTS

- The authors would like to express their deep appreciation to Thalia Dorwick and Ana María Pérez-Gironés for their continued leadership and guidance in this edition. We could not have done this Workbook/Laboratory Manual without their wise and perceptive comments. Thanks also to Kim Sallee (Senior Brand Manager), Sadie Ray (Senior Product Developer), Kelly Heinrichs (Program Manager), and Erin Melloy (Senior Content Project Manager) for managing every aspect of the project, from conception to development and production. Last, but definitely not least, we would like to thank Jessica Becker, Misha MacLaird, Lorena Gómez Mostajo, and Lynne Lemley for their tireless efforts in the content development and editing of this Workbook/Laboratory Manual.

TO THE STUDENT

Welcome to the Workbook/Laboratory Manual for *Puntos de partida,* Tenth Edition, the textbook you are using in your Spanish class. Each chapter of this supplement is based on the corresponding chapter of the textbook so that you may practice and review on your own what you are learning in class. The Workbook/ Laboratory Manual activities are integrated within each section of every chapter, allowing you to practice the vocabulary and grammar points through reading, writing, listening, and speaking. In addition, most direction lines of the Workbook/Laboratory Manual will start in English and will gradually be replaced by Spanish by **Capítulo 5.** An exception has been made for the Listening Passage direction lines, which will remain in English throughout due to their complex nature.

Throughout the audio portion of this edition, you will have the opportunity to hear a variety of accents from the Hispanic world. The rate of speech will start out slower than native speed in the earlier chapters and will gradually increase to a moderate pace. In the audio activities that feature different characters, you will hear Spanish as it is spoken naturally by native speakers in the form of interviews and conversations.

Here are some features of the Workbook/Laboratory Manual that you will want to keep in mind as you work with it.

- To get the most out of the Workbook/Laboratory Manual, you should complete its sections after your instructor covers the corresponding material in class. Listen to the audio as often as you need to in order to complete the activities successfully, and pay close attention to the pronunciation and the intonation of the native speakers.
- In most sections of the Workbook/Laboratory Manual, the first exercises are generally mechanical or more controlled in nature. As you do these exercises, you should focus primarily on providing the correct forms: the right form of a new verb tense, the correct adjective ending, the exact spelling of new vocabulary, and so on. The activities that follow will require more thought and comprehension. Here's a tip: As you write your answers to all activities, read aloud what you are writing. Doing so will help you to remember the new vocabulary and structures.
- The Audio Program, which contains the listening activities from the Workbook/Laboratory Manual, is available as streaming audio at www.mhhe.com/puntos10. You will need the Workbook/Laboratory Manual when you listen to the Audio Program, since the activities are based on visual and/or written cues. Audio activities in the Workbook/Laboratory Manual are easily identified by this headphones icon .
- Each chapter of the Workbook/Laboratory Manual concludes with a section called **Puntos personales.** Answers for most of the activities in this section are not provided, given their personalized nature. In this final section, you will have the opportunity to express your own opinions and answer personalized questions, both orally and in writing. A recurring feature of **Puntos personales** is the Guided Composition, which includes questions and/or vocabulary to help you organize your thoughts and write a composition that is more connected. Another repeating feature is **Mi diario.** Its purpose is to encourage you to write freely in Spanish about your own opinions and experiences, using the vocabulary and structures you are currently studying, without worrying about making errors. Your instructor will read your diary or journal entries and react to them, but he or she will not grade them. Because you will be writing these **Mi diario** entries for the entire year, it is a good idea to buy a separate notebook in which to write them. By the end of the year, you will find that you are writing more and with greater ease in Spanish, and your journal will have a wonderful record of the progress you have made in your study of Spanish.
- An Answer Key for written activities is provided in the Appendix, at the back of the Workbook/ Laboratory Manual. In general, answers to audio activities are on the Audio Program immediately after each item or at the end of a series of items. When not given on the Audio Program, answers to audio activities can be found in the Answer Key. Activities marked with this symbol (❖) are activities for which no answers are provided in the Answer Key, largely due to the fact that they are

personalized in nature. Most activities marked with this symbol (❖) appear in the **Puntos personales** section. Here's a tip: Check your answers for each activity before proceeding to the next one. This is particularly important in activities that contain more than one **paso** (step), as in many cases, successful completion of the second **paso** is dependent on having the correct answers to the first.

We sincerely hope that beginning Spanish will be a satisfying experience for you!

Alice A. Arana
Oswaldo Arana
María Francisca Sabló-Yates
Amy Uribe

ABOUT THE AUTHORS

Alice A. Arana is Associate Professor of Spanish, Emeritus, at Fullerton College. She received her M.A.T. from Yale University and her Certificate of Spanish Studies from the University of Madrid. Professor Arana has also taught Spanish at the elementary and high school levels and has taught methodology at several NDEA summer institutes. She is coauthor of several McGraw-Hill supplementary materials, including the previous editions of the Workbook to accompany *Puntos de partida,* both volumes of the Workbook/ Laboratory Manual to accompany *Apúntate: Español introductorio* (2010), seven editions of the Workbook/ Laboratory Manual to accompany *¿Qué tal? An Introductory Course,* and the first and second editions of the Workbook/Laboratory Manual for *Puntos en breve.* She is also coauthor of the first edition of *A-LM Spanish,* of *Reading for Meaning–Spanish,* and of several elementary school guides for the teaching of Spanish. In 1992, Professor Arana was named Staff Member of Distinction at Fullerton College and was subsequently chosen as the 1993 nominee from Fullerton College for Teacher of the Year. In 1994, she served as Academic Senate President.

Oswaldo Arana is Professor of Spanish, Emeritus, at California State University, Fullerton, where he taught Spanish American culture and literature. A native of Peru, he received his Ph.D. in Spanish from the University of Colorado. Professor Arana has taught at the University of Colorado, the University of Florida (Gainesville), and at several NDEA summer institutes. He is coauthor of several McGraw-Hill supplementary materials, including the previous editions of the Workbook to accompany *Puntos de partida,* both volumes of the Workbook/Laboratory Manual to accompany *Apúntate: Español introductorio* (2010), seven editions of the Workbook/Laboratory Manual to accompany *¿Qué tal? An Introductory Course,* and the first and second editions of the Workbook/Laboratory Manual for *Puntos en breve.* In addition, Dr. Arana served as a language consultant for the first edition of *A-LM Spanish,* and is coauthor of *Reading for Meaning–Spanish,* and of several articles on Spanish American narrative prose.

María Francisca Sabló-Yates holds a B.A. and an M.A. from the University of Washington (Seattle). A native of Panama, she has taught at the University of Washington and Central Michigan University (Mt. Pleasant, Michigan), and is currently an Associate Professor of Spanish at Delta College (University Center, Michigan). She is the author and coauthor of several McGraw-Hill supplementary materials, including previous editions of the *Puntos de partida* Laboratory Manual, both volumes of the Workbook/Laboratory Manual to accompany *Apúntate: Español introductorio* (2010), the first through seventh editions of the Workbook/Laboratory Manual to accompany *¿Qué tal? An Introductory Course,* and the first and second editions of the *Puntos en breve* Laboratory Manual.

Amy Uribe has taught Spanish for eight years at Lone Star College CyFair in Houston, Texas. There she served as Department Chair for Foreign Languages and Chair of the system-wide Foreign Language Curriculum Team. She earned her B.A. in Spanish from St. Norbert College in DePere, Wisconsin, and her M.A. in Curriculum and Instruction from the University of Northern Iowa in Cedar Falls. Amy has experience designing, evaluating and teaching online, hybrid and face-to-face courses. She is a regular presenter in McGraw-Hill's annual professional development series and works as a digital faculty consultant, training instructors on McGraw-Hill products and software programs. Amy has studied and traveled in Spain, Guatemala, Mexico, and throughout South America.

Capítulo 1

Ante todo

PRIMERA° PARTE

First

Saludos y expresiones de cortesía*

A. ¿Formal o informal? Mark each of the following questions as **F** (formal) or **I** (informal).

1. _____ ¿Cómo te llamas?   4. _____ ¿Cómo está?

2. _____ ¿Y tú?   5. _____ ¿Qué tal?

3. _____ ¿Y usted?   6. _____ ¿De dónde eres?

 B. Diálogos. In the following dialogues, you will practice greeting others appropriately in Spanish. First, you will hear the dialogue in its entirety. Next, you will listen to a sentence of dialogue at a time and repeat it. Then, after each dialogue, you will hear a statement. Circle **C** for **cierto** (*true*) or **F** for **falso** (*false*), based on the information in each dialogue.

1.
JOSÉ:	Hola, Carmen.
CARMEN:	¿Qué tal, José? ¿Cómo estás?
JOSÉ:	Muy bien. ¿Y tú?
CARMEN:	Regular. Nos vemos mañana, ¿eh?
JOSÉ:	Bien. Hasta mañana.

Respuesta (*Answer*): **C   F**

2.
ELISA VELASCO:	Buenas tardes, señor Gómez.
MARTÍN GÓMEZ:	Muy buenas, señora Velasco. ¿Cómo está?
ELISA VELASCO:	Bien, gracias. ¿Y usted?
MARTÍN GÓMEZ:	Muy bien, gracias. Hasta luego.
ELISA VELASCO:	Adiós.

Respuesta: **C   F**

3.
LUPE:	Buenos días, profesor.
MARTÍN GÓMEZ:	Buenos días. ¿Cómo se llama usted, señorita?
LUPE:	Me llamo Lupe Carrasco.
MARTÍN GÓMEZ:	Mucho gusto, Lupe.
LUPE:	Igualmente.

Respuesta: **C   F**

_____

*Answers to written activities appear in the Appendix. Some listening activities have recorded answers; when correct answers are *not* presented in the audio recording, check your work in the Appendix.

4. MIGUEL RENÉ: Hola. Me llamo Miguel René. ¿Y tú? ¿Cómo te llamas?

    KARINA: Me llamo Karina. Mucho gusto.

    MIGUEL RENÉ: Encantado, Karina. Y, ¿de dónde eres?

    KARINA: Yo soy de Venezuela. ¿Y tú?

    MIGUEL RENÉ: Yo soy de México.

Respuesta: **C F**

C. Situaciones

Paso 1. You will hear a series of questions or statements. Circle the letter of the best response or reaction to each.

1. a. Me llamo Ricardo Barrios.   **b.** Bien, gracias.
2. a. Encantada, Eduardo.   **b.** Muchas gracias, Eduardo.
3. a. Regular. ¿Y tú?   **b.** Mucho gusto, señorita Paz.
4. a. Con permiso, señor.   **b.** No hay de qué.
5. a. De nada, señora Colón.   **b.** Buenas noches, señora Colón.
6. a. Soy de Guatemala.   **b.** ¿Y tú?

Paso 2. Now, listen to the questions and statements again and read the correct answers in the pauses provided. Repeat the correct answer after you hear it.

    MODELO: *(you hear)* **1.** Hola. ¿Cómo te llamas?

        (you say) Me llamo Ricardo Barrios.

    (you hear and repeat) Me llamo Ricardo Barrios.

2. ... 3. ... 4. ... 5. ... 6. ...

D. Hola, Carmen. On your way to class, you meet Carmen, a student from Spain, and exchange greetings with her. Complete the brief dialogue.

    USTED: Hola, Carmen, ¿_____?[1]

    CARMEN: Bien, gracias. ¿_____?[2]

    USTED: Regular.

    CARMEN: Adiós, _____[3] mañana.

    USTED: Adiós, Carmen. _____.[4]

E. Diálogo. Complete the following dialogue between you and your new Spanish instructor. Be sure to use your own name and that of your instructor in the appropriate blanks.

    USTED: _____[1] noches, profesor(a) _____ *(instructor's name)*.

    ¿Cómo _____[2]?

    PROFESOR(A): Bien, _____.[3] ¿Cómo _____[4] usted?

    USTED: _____[5] _____ *(your name)*.

    PROFESOR(A): Mucho _____.[6]

    USTED: _____.[7]

F. Unos amigos hispanos

 Paso 1. Listen to the following conversation between Rubén and Karina. Read the conversation silently as you listen to the speakers.

RUBÉN: Hola, María.
KARINA: ¿María? Me llamo Karina. ¿Y tú? ¿Cómo te llamas?
RUBÉN: Me llamo Rubén.
KARINA: Mucho gusto.
RUBÉN: ¿Cómo estás, Karina?
KARINA: Muy bien, gracias. ¿Y tú?
RUBÉN: Bien.
KARINA: ¿De dónde eres?
RUBÉN: Soy de Pamplona, España. ¿Y tú? ¿De dónde eres?
KARINA: Yo soy de Venezuela.

 Paso 2. Now a portion of the conversation, starting with Rubén's third line, will be read with pauses for repetition. Repeat, imitating the speaker.

Paso 3. Now imagine that a student is asking you these questions and answer them appropriately.

1. ¿Cómo te llamas? _____

2. ¿Cómo estás? _____

3. ¿De dónde eres? _____

G. Situaciones. What would you say in the following situations?

1. _____   2. _____   3. _____

Now give at least one appropriate response to your answer to item 1.

4. _____

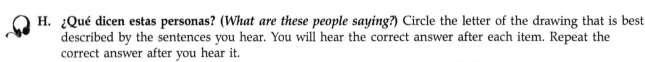

H. ¿Qué dicen estas personas? (*What are these people saying?*) Circle the letter of the drawing that is best described by the sentences you hear. You will hear the correct answer after each item. Repeat the correct answer after you hear it.

1. a.

 b.

2. a.

 b.

3. a.

 b.

Pronunciación: Las vocales: *a, e, i, o, u*

A. Las vocales. Compare the pronunciation of the following words in both English and Spanish. Listen for the schwa, the *uh* sound in English, and notice its absence in Spanish.

English:	*banana*	Spanish:	**banana**
	capital		**capital**

Now, listen to and repeat the following words, imitating the speaker. Be careful to avoid the English schwa. Remember to pronounce each vowel with a short and tense sound.

1.	**a**	hasta	tal	nada	mañana	natural
2.	**e**	me	qué	Pérez	usted	rebelde
3.	**i**	sí	señorita	permiso	imposible	tímido
4.	**o**	yo	con	cómo	noches	profesor
5.	**u**	tú	uno	mucho	Perú	Lupe

B. ¡A escuchar y escribir! (*Let's listen and write!*)

Paso 1. You will hear a series of words that are probably unfamiliar to you. Listen carefully, concentrating on the vowel sounds, and write in the missing vowels.

1. r_____d_____ll_____

2. M_____r_____b_____l

3. _____n_____l_____t_____r_____l

4. s_____lv_____v_____d_____s

5. _____lv_____d_____d_____z_____

Note: Check your answers to **Paso 1** in the Appendix before beginning **Paso 2**.

Paso 2. Now, when you hear the number, read each word from **Paso 1**. Then listen to and repeat the correct pronunciation, imitating the speaker.

Paso 3. Imagine that you work as a hotel receptionist in Miami. Listen to how some Hispanic guests spell out their last names for you. Write down the names as you hear them.

1. _____   3. _____

2. _____   4. _____

El alfabeto español

A. El alfabeto español. You will hear the names of the letters of the Spanish alphabet, along with a list of place names spelled with the corresponding letters. Listen and repeat, imitating the speaker. Notice that most Spanish consonants are pronounced differently than in English. In future chapters, you will have the opportunity to practice the pronunciation of these letters individually.

a	a	la Argentina	**ñ**	eñe	España
b	be	Bolivia	**o**	o	Oviedo
c	ce	Cáceres	**p**	pe	Panamá
d	de	Durango	**q**	cu	Quito
e	e	el Ecuador	**r**	ere	Monterrey
f	efe	Florida	**s**	ese	San Juan
g	ge	Guatemala	**t**	te	Toledo
h	hache	Honduras	**u**	u	el Uruguay
i	i	Ibiza	**v**	uve	Venezuela
j	jota	Jalisco	**w**	doble uve	Washington
k	ca	Kansas	**x**	equis	Extremadura
l	ele	Lima	**y**	ye	el Paraguay
m	eme	México	**z**	ceta (zeta)	Zaragoza
n	ene	Nicaragua			

B. Repeticiones. Repeat the following words, phrases, and sentences, imitating the speaker. Pay attention to the difference in pronunciation between Spanish and English.

c/ch	Colón	Cecilia	Muchas gracias.	Buenas noches.
g/gu	Ortega	gusto	Miguel	guitarra
h	la Habana	Héctor	hotel	historia
j/g	Jamaica	Jiménez	Geraldo	Gilda
l/ll	Lupe	Manolo	Sevilla	me llamo
y	Yolanda	yate	Paraguay	y
r/rr	Mario	arte	Roberto	carro
ñ	Begoña	Toño	señorita	Hasta mañana.

C. Preguntas sobre (*Questions about*) el alfabeto español. Answer the following questions about the Spanish alphabet.

1. _____ What is the one letter in the Spanish alphabet that is not found in the English alphabet?

2. _____ What letter in the Spanish alphabet is never pronounced?

3. _____ Sounds like the Spanish **b**.

4. _____ Sounds like the *y* in the word *yes*.

5. _____ When within a word, the letter that sounds like the *tt* in the English word *butter*. When at the beginning of a word, it is trilled.

D. ¿Cómo se escribe? (*How do you write . . . ?*) Write only the Spanish name of the underlined letter.

1. Se escribe <u>J</u>osé con _____.

2. Se escribe Oli<u>v</u>ia con _____.

3. Se escribe e<u>x</u>perto con _____.

4. Se escribe <u>Y</u>aneli con _____.

5. Se escribe Pére<u>z</u> con _____.

6. Se escribe <u>H</u>olanda con _____.

Nota comunicativa: Los cognados

A. Pronunciación. First, look at the following adjectives that are similar in English and Spanish. These adjectives can be used in Spanish to describe a man or a woman. Then when you hear each number, read the following pairs of words aloud, placing stress on the italicized syllable. After you read each pair of words, you will hear the correct pronunciation in English and Spanish. Note how the stress shifts in most of the Spanish words. Repeat the word in Spanish, imitating the speaker.

	ENGLISH	SPANISH			ENGLISH	SPANISH
1.	*no*rmal	nor-*mal*	8.	*te*rrible	te-*rri*-ble
2.	e*mo*tional	e-mo-cio-*nal*	9.	res*pon*sible	res-pon-*sa*-ble
3.	*el*egant	e-le-*gan*-te	10.	*val*iant	va-*lien*-te
4.	*cru*el	cru-*el*	11.	*ho*rrible	ho-*rri*-ble
5.	pessi*mis*tic	pe-si-*mis*-ta	12.	im*por*tant	im-por-*tan*-te
6.	opti*mis*tic	op-ti-*mis*-ta	13.	in*tel*ligent	in-te-li-*gen*-te
7.	im*pa*tient	im-pa-*cien*-te	14.	re*bel*lious	re-*bel*-de

B. Los cognados

❖ **Paso 1.** Scan the following selection, then underline all the cognates and other words that look familiar to you.

Un producto natural, protector de la salud

El aceite de oliva, especialmente el aceite de oliva virgen, es un producto que cada día gana mayor aceptación en la preparación de las comidas. Contiene mucha vitamina E, un antioxidante por excelencia. Además, el aceite de oliva virgen no contiene colesterol. En efecto, su uso reduce la concentración de colesterol en la sangre. Por lo tanto, es preferible a las grasas de origen animal, que son malas para el sistema cardiovascular.

Paso 2. Based on your understanding of the article, check the box for either **cierto (C)** (*true*) or **falso (F)** (*false*). ¡OJO! The sentences will help you understand the meaning of the paragraph.

		C	F
1.	Virgin olive oil is gaining more acceptance in the preparation of meals.	☐	☐
2.	One of the benefits of this oil is that it contains a lot of vitamin C.	☐	☐
3.	Olive oil contains as much cholesterol as animal fats.	☐	☐
4.	Animal fats are unhealthy because they are bad for the heart.	☐	☐
5.	The use of olive oil instead of animal fats reduces the amount of cholesterol in our blood.	☐	☐
6.	Olive oil is beneficial for the cardiovascular system.	☐	☐

¿Cómo es usted? (Part 1)

A. **¿Cualidades positivas o negativas?**

Paso 1. Indique si cada (each) adjetivo es **P** (positivo) o **N** (negativo).

1. _____ arrogante   5. _____ optimista

2. _____ impaciente   6. _____ paciente

3. _____ inteligente   7. _____ pesimista

4. _____ irresponsable   8. _____ responsable

❖ **Paso 2.** Now complete these sentences with adjectives from **Paso 1** to describe what you are and are not like.

Yo soy _____, _____ y _____.

Yo no soy _____, _____ o _____.

B. **Descripción.** In this activity, you will practice *gisting*–that is, getting the main idea, an important skill in language learning. Although some of the vocabulary you hear will not be familiar to you, concentrate on the words that you *do* know. Listen once, then choose the statement that best describes the passage.

1. ☐ This person is describing her country and the sports that are played there.
2. ☐ This person is describing herself, her studies, and her outside interests.

C. **Encuesta (Survey)**

❖ **Paso 1.** You will hear a series of questions. For each question, check an answer that is true for you. No answers will be given.

1. ☐ Sí, soy independiente.   3. ☐ Sí, soy eficiente.
   ☐ No, no soy independiente.   ☐ No, no soy eficiente.
2. ☐ Sí, soy sentimental.   4. ☐ Sí, soy flexible.
   ☐ No, no soy sentimental.   ☐ No, no soy flexible.

Paso 2. Now you will hear each question again. Respond by saying the answer that you checked in **Paso 1.** Then you will hear a possible answer. Repeat the answer you hear.

MODELO: (you hear)   **1.** ¿Es usted independiente?

(you say)   Sí, soy independiente.

(you hear and repeat)   Sí, soy independiente.

2. ...   3. ...   4. ...

D. **Preguntas. (Questions.)** Ask the following people about their personalities, using **¿Eres... ?** or **¿Es usted... ?**, as appropriate. Then listen to and repeat the correct question. When you hear the answer to your question, circle either **Sí** or **No**, based on the answer.

MODELO: (you see)   **1.** Marisol / tolerante   Sí   No

(you hear)   Uno.

(you say)   Marisol, ¿eres tolerante?

(you hear and repeat)   Marisol, ¿eres tolerante?

(you hear)   Sí, soy tolerante.

(you circle Sí))   No

2. Ramón / optimista   Sí   No
3. Señora Alba / flexible   Sí   No
4. Señor Castán / cruel   Sí   No
5. Anita / inteligente   Sí   No

¿Cómo son? (*What are they like?*) You will hear five sentences. Listen carefully and write the missing words.

1. El hotel es _____.

2. El estudiante es muy _____.

3. El _____ no es difícil (*difficult*).

4. El museo es muy _____.

5. Íñigo no es _____.

¡Aquí se habla español!

A. El mapa. Complete the following statements based on the following map of the Spanish-speaking world.

1. The two countries in South America that do not have a coast are

   _____ and _____.

2. The Spanish-speaking country east of Colombia is _____.

3. The Spanish-speaking country that lies just south of Mexico is _____.

4. The country just west of Argentina is _____.

5. The country in Africa where Spanish is spoken is _____.

B. **¿Cierto o falso?** Indicate if the following statements are **C** for **cierto** (*true*) or **F** for **falso** (*false*), based on information from the **¡Aquí se habla español!** reading and map on pages 11–12 of the textbook.

    1. Spanish is spoken by about 450 million people, making it the second most widely spoken language in the world.   C   F

    2. There are more than 40 million people in the United States who speak Spanish.   C   F

    3. Spanish and French are the official languages of Puerto Rico.   C   F

    4. An abbreviation in Spanish for the United States of America is EEUU.   C   F

    5. Spanish is second only to Chinese in terms of the number of people studying it.   C   F

    6. The only difference between the Spanish of Spain and the Spanish of Mexico is the pronunciation.   C   F

SEGUNDA° PARTE

Second

Los números del 0 al 30; *Hay*

A. **Cantidades.** (*Quantities.*) Write out the numbers indicated in parentheses. Remember that the number **uno** changes to **un** before a masculine noun and to **una** before a feminine noun.

    1. (1) _____ clase (*f.*)

    2. (4) _____ dólares

    3. (7) _____ días

    4. (13) _____ personas

    5. (11) _____ señoras

    6. (1) _____ estudiante (*m.*)

    7. (20) _____ señoras

    8. (23) _____ personas

    9. (26) _____ clases

    10. (21) _____ señores (*m.*)

    11. (21) _____ profesoras (*f.*)

    12. (30) _____ estudiantes

B. **Problemas de matemáticas.** Complete each equation, then write out the missing numbers in each statement.

    1. $14 + \underline{\hspace{1cm}} = 22$ Catorce y _____ son veintidós.

    2. $15 - 4 = \underline{\hspace{1cm}}$ Quince menos cuatro son _____.

    3. $2 + 3 = \underline{\hspace{1cm}}$ Dos y tres son _____.

    4. $8 + \underline{\hspace{1cm}} = 14$ Ocho y _____ son catorce.

    5. $13 + \underline{\hspace{1cm}} = 20$ Trece y _____ son veinte.

    6. $15 + 7 = \underline{\hspace{1cm}}$ Quince y siete son _____.

    7. $\underline{\hspace{1cm}} - 3 = 27$ _____ menos tres son veintisiete.

C. **¿Cuánto es?** (*How much is it?*)

Paso 1. In this activity, you will hear the price in **pesos** (the unit of currency in many Hispanic countries) of three different brands of items you want to purchase. Repeat the price of the least expensive brand, and then write it in the blank using numerals. Then listen to and repeat the correct answer.

1. el café: _____ pesos
2. el diccionario: _____ pesos
3. la banana: _____ pesos
4. el chocolate: _____ pesos
5. el papel (*paper*): _____ pesos

Note: Check your answers to **Paso 1** in the Appendix before beginning **Paso 2.**

Paso 2. Now you will hear questions about the prices listed in **Paso 1.** Answer using the prices you wrote in the blanks, then repeat the correct answer after you hear it.

MODELO: (*you hear*)   **1.**   ¿Cuánto es el café?
                  (*you say*)   Es ocho pesos.
        (*you hear and repeat*)   Es ocho pesos.

2. ...   3. ...   4. ...   5. ...

D. **¿Qué hay en el salón de clase?** (*What is there in the classroom?*)

Paso 1. You will hear a series of questions based on the following drawing. Write out the numbers in the blanks.

1. Hay _____ personas.
2. Hay _____ estudiantes.
3. No, no hay _____ profesor.
4. No, hay _____ profesora.

Note: Check your answers to **Paso 1** in the Appendix before beginning **Paso 2.**

Paso 2. Now you will hear the questions from **Paso 1** again. Answer using the numbers you wrote in the blank, then listen to and repeat the correct answer.

MODELO: (*you hear*)   **1.**   ¿Cuántas (*How many*) personas hay en el salón de clase?
                  (*you say*)   Hay tres personas.
        (*you hear and repeat*)   Hay tres personas.

2. ...   3. ...   4. ...

E. Problemas de matemáticas

Paso 1. Solve the following math problems using numerals.

a. $2 + 18 =$ _____

b. $15 - 2 =$ _____

c. $30 -$ _____ $= 12$

d. $14 + 3 + 2 =$ _____

e. _____ $+ 4 = 10$

f. $21 + 3 + 0 =$ _____

g. _____ $- 8 = 14$

h. $11 + 5 =$ _____

Note: Check your answers to **Paso 1** in the Appendix before beginning **Paso 2.**

Paso 2. When you hear the corresponding letter, read the math problem from **Paso 1** aloud. Then listen to and repeat the correct answer.

MODELO:　　　　　　(*you hear*)　a.

　　　　　　　　　(*you say*)　Dos y dieciocho son veinte.

　　　　(*you hear and repeat*)　Dos y dieciocho son veinte.

b. ...　**c.** ...　**d.** ...　**e.** ...　**f.** ...　**g.** ...　**h.** ...

Los gustos y preferencias (Part 1)

A.　¿Le gusta o no? Complete these short phrases.

1.	**a.**	I like to ski.	_____ **gusta esquiar.**
	b.	I don't like to ski.	**No** _____ **gusta esquiar.**
2.	**a.**	Do you (*familiar*) like coffee?	**¿**_____ **gusta el café?**
	b.	You (*formal*) don't like coffee?	**¿No** _____ **gusta el café?**
3.	**a.**	Do you (*familiar*) like soccer?	**¿**_____ **gusta el fútbol?**
	b.	Do you (*formal*) like soccer?	**¿(A usted)** _____ **gusta el fútbol?**

B.　Los gustos y preferencias. Imagine that you are asking your instructor and several classmates whether they like the following items and activities. Complete the brief dialogues by writing the correct **gustar** expression.

1. —Profesor(a), ¿_____ la música *jazz*?

　　—No, no _____ (la música *jazz*).

2. —Profesor(a), ¿_____ esquiar?

　　—Sí, _____ (esquiar).

3. —Miguel, ¿_____ el chocolate?

　　—Sí, _____ (el chocolate).

4. —Carolina, ¿_____ jugar al tenis?

　　—No, no _____ (jugar al tenis).

C. *Listening Passage:** **La música que (*that*) me gusta**

> In the Listening Passage section of the Workbook / Laboratory Manual, you will hear authentic passages from Hispanics about a variety of subjects, including their school experiences, food preferences, and hobbies. As you listen, try not to be distracted by unfamiliar vocabulary. Concentrate instead on what you *do* know and understand.

In addition to the types of music that most young people listen to in this country, Hispanic students also listen to music that is typical of their own country or region. Have you heard of **la salsa, el merengue,** or **la cumbia?** These are all types of music from different regions of Latin America. You will hear a passage, which also appears here, in which a student talks about the music she likes.

First, listen to the **Vocabulario útil** (*Useful vocabulary*). Next, listen to the passage to get a general idea of the content. Then go back and listen again for details. You will then hear a series of statements. Circle **C (cierto)** if the statement is true or **F (falso)** if the statement is false.

Vocabulario útil (*Useful vocabulary*)

pues	well	**en la actualidad**	currently
mucho	a lot	**el conjunto**	musical group
también	also	**además de**	in addition to

Here is the passage. Teresa is speaking.

¡Hola! ¿Te gusta la música? Pues, ¡a mí me gusta todo tipo de música! Me gustan mucho la música pop y la música rock en español. También me gusta el flamenco moderno. En la actualidad, mi cantante favorito es Tommy Torres, y mi conjunto favorito es Chambao. Tommy Torres es de Puerto Rico, y Chambao es un conjunto de España. Además de la música latina moderna, también me gustan los ritmos tradicionales como el merengue y la cumbia. ¡Me gusta la música latina mucho!

1. C F   **2.** C F   **3.** C F   **4.** C F

D. **¿Qué le gusta a usted? (*What do you like?*)**

❖ **Paso 1.** You will hear a series of questions. For each question, check an answer that is true for you. No answers will be given.

1. ☐ Sí, me gusta.	☐ No, no me gusta.	
2. ☐ Sí, ¡creo que (*I think that*) es fantástica!	☐ No, no me gusta.	
3. ☐ Sí, me gusta.	☐ No, no me gusta.	
4. ☐ Sí, me gusta.	☐ No, no me gusta.	

Paso 2. Now, listen to the questions again. Respond by saying the answer that you checked in **Paso 1.** Then you will hear a possible answer. Repeat the answer you hear.

Paso 3. Imagine that you are to interview Professor Morales about his likes and dislikes. Use the visual cues and **¿Le gusta... ?** to help you form your questions. Then listen to and repeat the correct question. When you hear professor Morales's answer to your question, circle either **Sí** or **No**, based on the answer he gives.

MODELO:	(*you see*)	**1.** la universidad	Sí	No
	(*you hear*)	Uno.		
	(*you say*)	¿Le gusta la universidad?		
(*you hear and repeat*)		¿Le gusta la universidad?		
	(*you hear*)	Sí, me gusta mucho.		
	(*you circle* **Sí**)	**1.** la universidad	(Sí)	No

2.	la música	Sí	No	**4.**	beber café	Sí	No
3.	el chocolate	Sí	No	**5.**	comer pizza	Sí	No

*The text for the Listening Passage sections will appear in the *Workbook / Laboratory Manual* through **Capítulo 2.**

¿Qué hora es?

A. Son las... Match the following statements with the clock faces shown.

1. _____ Son las cuatro y diez.

2. _____ Son las diez y cuarto.

3. _____ Es la una menos veinte.

4. _____ Son las siete en punto.

5. _____ Son las dos y media.

6. _____ Son las ocho y veinticinco.

a.

b.

c.

d.

e.

f.

B. ¿Qué hora es? Write out the times indicated in full sentences. Use **de la mañana, de la tarde,** or **de la noche,** as required.

1. It's 12:20 A.M. _____

2. It's 1:05 P.M. _____

3. It's 7:30 P.M. _____

4. It's 11:00 A.M. sharp. _____

5. It's 9:45 P.M. _____

C. ¿Qué hora es?

Paso 1. You will hear a series of times. Circle the letter of the clock that indicates the time you hear.

MODELO: *(you hear)* Son las doce menos veinte de la noche. → *(you circle the letter* **a***)*

(a.)

b.

1. a.

   b.

2. a.

   b.

3. a.

   b.

Paso 2. Now when you hear a number, tell the time that you see on the corresponding clock. You will hear a possible answer. Repeat the answer you hear.

MODELO:	(you see)	**1.**
	(you hear)	Uno.
	(you say)	Son las tres y media (y treinta) de la tarde.
	(you hear and repeat)	Son las tres y media (y treinta) de la tarde.

2.    **3.**    **4.**

D. ¿A qué hora es... ? You will hear a series of questions about Marisol's schedule. First, pause and look at the schedule, then listen to and answer the questions based on her schedule. Next, you will hear a possible answer. Repeat the answer you hear.

MODELO:	(you hear)	¿A qué hora es la clase de español?
	(you say)	Es a las ocho y media de la mañana.
	(you hear and repeat)	Es a las ocho y media de la mañana.

Horario escolar[a]
Nombre:[b] Marisol Abad
Dirección:[c] Calle Alfaro, 16
Teléfono: 72-45-86

8:30   Español
9:40   Ciencias
11:00   Matemáticas
12:25   Inglés
2:15   Arte

1. ...   **2.** ...   **3.** ...   **4.** ...

---

[a]Horario... *Class Schedule*   [b]*Name*   [c]*Address*

Póngase... *Test yourself*

A. Saludos y expresiones de cortesía. Complete las siguientes (*following*) frases en español.

1. *To a friend:* _____, Sara. ¿Qué tal?

2. Complete the greetings with the correct form of **bueno**.

   _____ días. _____ tardes. _____ noches.

3. To ask a classmate her name, you say: ¿Cómo _____?

4. The responses to **muchas gracias** are:

   _____

   _____

B. ¿Cómo es usted? Escriba (*Write*) la forma apropiada de **ser**.

1. yo _____   2. tú _____   3. usted, él, ella _____

C. Los gustos y preferencias. Complete las oraciones (*sentences*) con la palabra o palabras apropiadas para expresar los gustos.

MARTA: ¿Te _____[1] el chocolate?
ISABEL: No, no _____.[2]

ESTUDIANTE: ¿A usted _____[3] gusta la música clásica?
PROFESOR: Sí, me _____.[4]

D. La hora

1. To ask what time it is, you say: ¿_____?

2. To answer, use:

   _____ la una (y cuarto, y media).

   _____ las dos (tres, etcétera).

PRUEBA CORTA°

Prueba... Short Quiz

A. Conversaciones. Empareje (*Match*) la situación con la expresión apropiada.

How do you. . .

1. ask your instructor what his or her name is? _____
2. ask the student next to you what his or her name is? _____
3. ask a classmate where he/she is from? _____
4. ask your instructor where he/she is from? _____
5. ask your instructor if he or she likes history? _____
6. ask a classmate if he or she likes history? _____
7. respond when someone gives you a gift? _____
8. respond when you meet someone for the first time? _____

a. ¿De dónde eres?
b. ¿De dónde es usted?
c. Mucho gusto.
d. ¿Le gusta la historia?
e. ¿Cómo se llama usted?
f. Muchas gracias.
g. ¿Te gusta la historia?
h. ¿Cómo te llamas?

B. Hablando (*Speaking*) de las clases. You will hear a conversation between two students, Geraldo and Delia. Listen carefully. Try not to be distracted by unfamiliar vocabulary; concentrate instead on what you do know. Then you will hear a series of statements. Circle **C (cierto)** if the statement is true or **F (falso)** if the statement is false.

1. C F   2. C F   3. C F   4. C F   5. C F

◆ PUNTOS PERSONALES

A. Diálogo. You meet another student who asks you the following questions. Write your answers in Spanish.

Vocabulario útil

mi   my

ESTUDIANTE: ¿Eres estudiante?

USTED: _____

ESTUDIANTE: ¿Cómo te llamas?

USTED: _____

ESTUDIANTE: ¿De dónde eres?

USTED: _____

ESTUDIANTE: ¿Cómo se llama tu (*your*) profesor(a) de español?

USTED: _____

(Continúa.)

ESTUDIANTE:	¿Cómo es él/ella? ¿paciente? ¿inteligente? ¿interesante?
USTED:	_____
ESTUDIANTE:	¿Te gusta la clase?
USTED:	_____
ESTUDIANTE:	¿Sabes (Do you know) qué hora es?
USTED:	Sí, _____
ESTUDIANTE:	¡Uf! Con permiso. ¡Es tarde (late)! Hasta luego.
USTED:	_____

B. Los gustos y preferencias

Paso 1. You will hear a series of questions. You should be able to guess the meaning of the activities based on context. Answer based on your own experience.

MODELO: (you see)   _____ jugar al tenis.

          (you hear)   ¿Te gusta jugar al tenis?

          (you write)   Sí, me gusta jugar al tenis.

          or   No, no me gusta jugar al tenis.

1. _____ jugar al golf.

2. _____ estudiar historia.

3. _____ tocar el piano.

4. _____ comer ensalada.

Paso 2. Now, you will hear the questions again. Answer aloud, based on what you wrote in **Paso 1.**

C. Guided Composition

On a separate sheet of paper, write a brief dialogue between you and your professor in which:

* You greet your professor appropriately (it's 1:00 P.M.) and ask how he/she is.
* He/She responds and asks you what your name is.
* You reply. You say you like the class.
* Your professor thanks you and says that it is nice to meet you.
* You reply.

D. Un diálogo en clase

Paso 1. You are going to hear a dialogue between two students, Juan Carlos Alarcón and Eduardo Robledo, who meet in a university class. First, listen to the **Vocabulario útil**. Then listen to the conversation. As you listen, mark a check beside the sentences that you hear in the conversation.

Vocabulario útil

oye	hey
¿tomas también?	are you also taking?
también tomo	I'm also taking

1. ☐ ¿Es la clase de economía?
2. ☐ No, es la clase de sociología.
3. ☐ ¿Qué tal?
4. ☐ Son las once y cinco.
5. ☐ ¿A qué hora es la clase de sociología?
6. ☐ ¿Cómo te llamas?
7. ☐ Me llamo Eduardo Robledo.
8. ☐ ¿Qué hora es?
9. ☐ Es a la una y cuarto.
10. ☐ Es a la una y media.

❖ **Paso 2.** Now you will participate in a similar conversation with Raquel, a classmate. Listen to Raquel's questions and answer them aloud with your personal information.

RAQUEL: ...

USTED: Es a la(s) _____.

RAQUEL: ...

USTED: Me llamo _____. ¿Y tú?

RAQUEL: ...

USTED: _____.

RAQUEL: ...

USTED: Son las _____.

RAQUEL: ...

USTED: _____.

E. **Mi diario (*My diary*).** In this repeating section, you will write brief diary entries in Spanish. The purpose of this section is to encourage you to write freely in Spanish about your own opinions and experiences using the vocabulary and structures you are currently studying but without worrying about making errors. It is a good idea to have a separate notebook for these **diario** entries.

For this diary entry, you will write about yourself. Include at least the following information in your first entry.

- First, write today's date in numerals. Note that in Spanish the day comes first, then the month, and finally the year. Thus, 9/10/12 is October 9, 2012.
- Now greet your diary as you would a friend and introduce yourself.
- Write down what time it is. (Write out the hour.)
- Describe your personality, using adjectives such as: arrogante, cruel, elegante, importante, inteligente, interesante, optimista, paciente, pesimista, responsible, sentimental, terrible, tolerante, and other adjectives you might know.
- List two things you like (or like to do) and two things you do *not* like (or do not like to do).

F. **Intercambios.** Listen to the following questions and answer them in writing.

1. _____

2. _____

3. _____

4. _____

5. _____

Capítulo 2

En la universidad

VOCABULARIO   Preparación

En el salón de clase*

A. Identificaciones. Identify the person, place, or objects shown in each drawing.

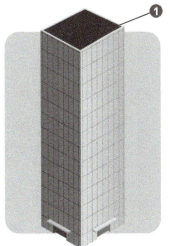

1. _____   2. _____   5. _____
3. _____   6. _____
4. _____   7. _____
8. _____

(Continúa.)

---

*Answers to written activities appear in the Appendix. Some listening activities have recorded answers; when correct answers are *not* presented in the audio recording, check your work in the Appendix.

9. _____	14. _____	19. _____
10. _____	15. _____	20. _____
11. _____	16. _____	21. _____
12. _____	17. _____	22. _____
13. _____	18. _____	23. _____

B. **¡Busque al intruso!** (*Look for the intruder!*)

Paso 1. Circle the item that does *not* belong in each series of words. *Hint:* Think about the category to which each word may belong.

Categorías posibles: un lugar   un objeto   una persona

MODELO: el bolígrafo / el estudiante / el profesor / el hombre

1. la consejera / la profesora / la calculadora / la compañera de clase

2. la residencia / la librería / la biblioteca / la mochila

3. el papel / el lápiz / el hombre / el bolígrafo

4. el diccionario / el libro / el cuaderno / el salón de clase

5. la bibliotecaria / la cafetería / el edificio / la oficina

Paso 2. Now determine the category to which each **intruso** belongs by organizing the **intruso** words into the categories **persona, lugar** or **objeto**.

PERSONA	LUGAR	OBJETO
_____	_____	_____
_____	_____	_____

C. **Descripción: El cuarto de Ignacio.** You will hear Ignacio describe his room. First, listen to the **Vocabulario útil** and look at the drawings. Then listen to the passage. As you listen, circle the number of the drawing that best matches his description.

Vocabulario útil

la vista	view
dejo	I leave
la cama	bed

1.  **2.**

 D. **¿Qué necesita Luisa? (*What does Luisa need?*)** Luisa is making a list of things that she will need for her classes this semester. First, listen to the list of items. Then listen carefully to her list. Mark the items that she needs with a check and write (in digits) how many of each item she needs. **¡OJO!** Not all items on the list will be mentioned. *Hint:* If a noun ends in **-s,** it is plural.

COSAS	SÍ	¿CUÁNTOS O CUÁNTAS?
bolígrafo(s)		
calculadora(s)		
cuaderno(s)		
diccionario(s)		
lápiz (lápices)		
libro(s) de texto		
mochila(s)		
papel (papeles)		
pizarrón blanco (pizarrones blancos)		

E. **¿Qué es?** Identify the following items when you hear the corresponding number. Begin each sentence with **Es el...** or **Es la...** . Then listen to and repeat the correct answer.

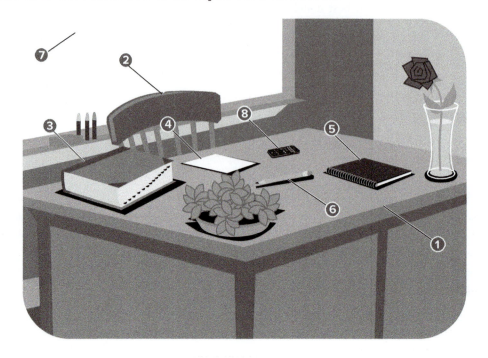

1. ...   **2.** ...   **3.** ...   **4.** ...   **5.** ...   **6.** ...   **7.** ...   **8.** ...

Las materias

A. **Las materias.** What classes would you take if you were majoring in the following areas? Choose your classes from the list.

Álgebra
Antropología
Astronomía
Biología 2
Cálculo 1
Economía
Física

Francés 304
Gramática alemana
La novela moderna
Química orgánica
Sicología del adolescente
Sociología urbana
Trigonometría

1. Lenguas y literatura

    a. _____

    b. _____

    c. _____

2. Matemáticas y administración de empresas

    a. _____

    b. _____

    c. _____

    d. _____

3. Ciencias sociales

    a. _____

    b. _____

    c. _____

4. Ciencias naturales

    a. _____

    b. _____

    c. _____

    d. _____

B. Asociaciones. Match the class subjects **(las materias)** with the people and topics **(las personas y temas)** associated with that field.

1. _____ Nietzche, Sócrates, Platón (*Plato*)

2. _____ Diego Rivera, Vincent van Gogh

3. _____ J.K. Rowling, Miguel de Cervantes

4. _____ el oxígeno, el hidrógeno

5. _____ francés, inglés, español

6. _____ el cálculo, la geometría

   a. el arte
   b. la filosofía
   c. las lenguas
   d. la literatura
   e. las matemáticas
   f. la química

 C. Cursos y materias

Paso 1. You will hear two students, Rubén and Tané, answer the question, **¿Cuántos cursos tomas?** (*How many courses are you taking?*) First, listen to the **Vocabulario útil** and the list of subjects (**materias**). Then as you listen to their answers, mark a check on the following chart to indicate that the person is studying a particular subject. **¡OJO!** Rubén and Tané will not mention all of the subjects listed in the chart.

Vocabulario útil

este año	this year
la informática	**la computación**

MATERIAS	RUBÉN	TANÉ
Biología		
Computación/Informática		
Historia del teatro		
Historia universal		
Inglés		
Literatura		
Sicología		

Note: Check your answers to **Paso 1** in the Appendix before beginning **Paso 2**.

Paso 2. Now you will hear questions about what Rubén and Tané are studying. Answer the questions aloud, based on your answers to **Paso 1**. Then listen to the correct answer and repeat it, imitating the speaker.

Vocabulario útil

¿Cuántos?	How many?
toma	takes, is taking

1. ... **2.** ... **3.** ... **4.** ...

Nota comunicativa: Las palabras interrogativas

A. Preguntas. (*Questions.*) Complete las preguntas con la palabra interrogativa más lógica. Use las palabras de la lista.

Palabras interrogativas

¿A qué hora?	¿Cuándo?	¿Dónde?
¿Cómo?	¿Cuánto?	¿Qué?
¿Cuál?	¿Cuántos?	¿Quién?

1. ¿_____ es este (*this*) diccionario? ¿Treinta dólares?

2. ¿_____ es la clase de historia? ¿A la una o a las dos?

3. Buenos días, Sr. Vargas. ¿ _____ está usted hoy?

4. ¿_____ es la capital de la Argentina? ¿Buenos Aires o Lima?

5. ¿_____ estudias (*do you study*), en casa (*at home*) o en la biblioteca?

6. —¿_____es usted?

    —Soy María Castro, profesora de filosofía.

7. ¿_____ es el examen, hoy o mañana?

8. ¿_____ es esto? ¿Una trompeta o un saxofón?

B. El Cine Bolívar. Your friend asks you some questions about a movie (**una película**) at the Cine Bolívar. Use an appropriate interrogative phrase to complete each of his questions.

AMIGO: ¿_____[1] se llama la película?

USTED: *Avengers: Era de Ultrón*

AMIGO: ¿_____[2] es el actor principal?

USTED: Robert Downey Jr.

AMIGO: ¿_____[3] tipo (*type*) de película es?

USTED: Es de aventuras.

AMIGO: ¿_____[4] es la entrada (*admission*)?

USTED: Siete pesos.

AMIGO: ¿_____[5] está el cine?

USTED: Está en la Avenida Bolívar.

AMIGO: ¿_____[6] es la película?

USTED: A las siete de la tarde.

AMIGO: ¿_____[7] hora es ahora?

USTED: Son las cinco y cuarto en punto.

C. Preguntas y respuestas. (*Questions and answers*.) Imagine that your friend Marisa has just made some statements that you didn't quite understand. Listen to the statements and circle the letter of the interrogative word or phrase you would use to obtain information about what she said.

1.	a. ¿A qué hora?	b. ¿Cómo es?	4.	a. ¿Cuántos?	b. ¿Cuándo?
2.	a. ¿Quién?	b. ¿Dónde?	5.	a. ¿Qué es?	b. ¿Cómo es?
3.	a. ¿Cuál?	b. ¿Dónde está?	6.	a. ¿Cómo está?	b. ¿Qué es?

PRONUNCIACIÓN   Diphthongs and Linking

A. Repaso: Las vocales. Repeat the following words, imitating the speaker. Pay close attention to the pronunciation of the indicated vowels.

WEAK VOWELS

i, y	Pili	silla	soy	y
u	gusto	lugar	uno	mujer

STRONG VOWELS

a	calculadora	Ana	banana	lápiz
e	trece	papeles	clase	general
o	profesor	hombre	Lola	bolígrafo

B. Los diptongos. Remember that diphthongs are formed by two successive weak vowels (**i** or **y, u**) or by a combination of a weak vowel and a strong vowel (**a, e, o**). The two vowels are pronounced as a single syllable. Repeat the following words, imitating the speaker. Pay close attention to the pronunciation of the indicated diphthongs.

1.	ia	media	gracias	8.	uo	cuota	arduo
2.	ie	bien	siete	9.	ai	aire	hay
3.	io	Julio	edificio	10.	ei	veinte	treinta
4.	iu	ciudad (*city*)	viuda (*widow*)	11.	oi, oy	soy	estoy
5.	ua	cuaderno	Managua	12.	au	auto	pausa
6.	ue	buenos	nueve	13.	eu	deuda (*debt*)	Ceuta
7.	ui	muy	fui (*I was / I went*)				

C. Más sobre (*about*) los diptongos

Paso 1. Remember that diphthongs can occur within a word or between words, causing the words to be "linked" and pronounced as one long word. Repeat the following phrases and sentences, imitating the speaker. Pay close attention to how the words are linked.

1.	oi/ia	Armando‿y‿Alicia	las letras o‿y‿hache
2.	ei/ie	el tigre‿y‿el chimpancé	Vicente‿y‿Elena
3.	oi/ie, ai/io	Soy‿extrovertida‿y‿optimista.	
4.	ai/iu	Elena‿y‿Humberto necesitan una mochila‿y‿unos libros.	

Paso 2. Remember that linking occurs naturally between many word boundaries in Spanish. When you hear the number, read the corresponding sentence. Try to say each without pause, as if it were one long word. Then listen to and repeat the correct pronunciation.

1. ¿Es usted eficiente?
2. ¿Dónde hay un escritorio?
3. Tomás y Alicia están en la oficina.
4. Están en la Argentina y en el Uruguay.
5. No hay estudiantes en el edificio a estas horas (*at this hour*).

GRAMÁTICA

1. Naming People, Places, Things, and Ideas (Part 1) • Singular Nouns: Gender and Articles

A. **¿*El* o *la*?** Escriba (*Write*) el artículo definido apropiado: **el** o **la**.

1. _____ tarde
2. _____ libertad
3. _____ nación
4. _____ profesor
5. _____ día
6. _____ mujer
7. _____ clase
8. _____ hombre

B. **¿*Un* o *una*?** Escriba el artículo indefinido apropiado: **un** o **una**.

1. _____ diccionario
2. _____ universidad
3. _____ lápiz
4. _____ dependienta
5. _____ día
6. _____ mochila
7. _____ mesa
8. _____ programa.

C. **¿Qué es?** Dé (*Give*) la categoría de las siguientes (*following*) palabras, según (*according to*) el modelo.

MODELO: hotel → El hotel es un edificio.

Categorías: edificio, materia, objeto, persona

1. bibliotecaria _____
2. lápiz _____
3. puerta _____
4. administración de empresas _____
5. alemán _____
6. compañero _____
7. librería _____
8. teléfono celular _____
9. biblioteca _____

D. **¿Qué hay en estos (*these*) lugares?**

Paso 1. For each drawing, write the names of the items (**objetos y personas**) that you see and where you see them (**lugares**).

OBJETOS Y PERSONAS

un diccionario   **un profesor**
un estudiante   **una silla**

LUGARES

la biblioteca   **el escritorio**
el cuarto   **el salón de clase**

1.

2.

3.

4.

Note: Check your answers to **Paso 1** in the Appendix before beginning **Paso 2.**

Paso 2. After you hear the corresponding number, identify the items in each drawing, based on your answers to **Paso 1.** Begin each sentence with **Hay un...** or **Hay una...** .

MODELO: (*you hear*) Uno.

                (*you see*) un diccionario el escritorio

                (*you say*) Hay un diccionario en el escritorio.

    (*you hear and repeat*) Hay un diccionario en el escritorio.

2. ...   3. ...   4. ...

2. Naming People, Places, Things, and Ideas (Part 2) • Nouns and Articles: Plural Forms

A. Singular → plural. Escriba (*Write*) la forma plural.

1. la amiga _____

2. el bolígrafo _____

3. la clase _____

(Continúa.)

4. un profesor _____

5. el lápiz _____

6. una extranjera _____

7. la universidad _____

8. un programa _____

B. **Plural → singular.** Escriba la forma singular.

1. los edificios _____

2. las fiestas _____

3. unos clientes _____

4. unos lápices _____

5. los papeles _____

6. los lugares _____

7. unos problemas _____

8. unas mujeres _____

C. **El salón de clase de la profesora Gómez.** ¿Qué hay en el salón de clase de la profesora Gómez? Use el artículo indefinido.

MODELO: Hay una mesa.

1. _____   **4.** _____

2. _____   **5.** _____

3. _____

D. ¿Qué necesita Lupe? You will hear part of a conversation between two students, Lupe and Diego. Your goal in listening is *only* to determine whether Lupe mentions each item that she needs to buy in the singular or plural form. Try not to be distracted by unfamiliar vocabulary and structures. First, listen to the **Vocabulario útil,** then listen to the conversation. As you listen, indicate the form Lupe uses when mentioning each item.

Vocabulario útil

las plumas = los bolígrafos

		SINGULAR	PLURAL
1.	cuaderno	☐	☐
2.	lápiz	☐	☐
3.	pluma	☐	☐
4.	diccionario	☐	☐

 E. Cambios. You will hear a series of articles and nouns. Give the plural forms of the first four items and the singular forms of the next four. Then listen to and repeat the correct answers.

SINGULAR → PLURAL   PLURAL → SINGULAR

1. ... **2.** ... **3.** ... **4.** ...   **5.** ... **6.** ... **7.** ... **8.** ...

 F. Los errores de Inés. You will hear some statements that your friend Inés makes about the following drawing. Correct her statements, then listen to and repeat the correct answers.

MODELO:	*(you hear)*	Hay dos libros en el escritorio de la profesora.
	(you say)	No. Hay un libro en el escritorio de la profesora.
	(you hear and repeat)	No. Hay un libro en el escritorio de la profesora.

1. ... **2.** ... **3.** ... **4.** ... **5.** ...

3. Expressing Actions • Subject Pronouns (Part 1); Present Tense of -ar Verbs; Negation

A. **Los pronombres personales.** What subject pronouns would you use to speak *about* the following persons?

1. your female friends _____

2. your brother _____

3. yourself _____

4. your friends Eva and Jesús _____

5. your male relatives _____

6. you and your sister _____

B. **Más sobre (*about*) los pronombres.** What subject pronouns would you use to speak *to* the following persons?

1. your cousin Roberto _____

2. your friends (*m.*) _____   _____
                   (*in Spain*)   (*in Latin America*)

3. your instructors _____

4. the store clerk _____

5. your friend _____
           (*in Spain and Latin America*)

C. **¿De quién habla?** You will hear a series of sentences. Listen carefully and circle the letter that corresponds to a possible *subject* of each sentence.

1.	**a.** yo	**b.** ella		4.	**a.** Alberto	**b.** Alberto y tú
2.	**a.** él	**b.** tú		5.	**a.** Uds.	**b.** nosotras
3.	**a.** Ana y yo	**b.** los estudiantes				

D. **De (*By*) día y de noche**

Paso 1. Describe what the following people are doing, using the verbs given. Not all of the verbs will be used.

1.

En la discoteca

Verbos: bailar, cantar, hablar, tocar, tomar

Jorge y yo estamos (*are*) al lado del (*next to the*) bar.

Nosotros _____ y _____

bebidas (*drinks*). Ana y Raúl _____ en la

pista de baile (*dance floor*). Dos hombres

_____ la guitarra en el escenario (*stage*).

2.

En la libería

Verbos: buscar, necesitar, pagar, trabajar, escuchar

Yo _____ comprar un libro de texto de sicología.

Yo _____ el libro en la librería. Un dependiente

_____ allí (*there*), y me ayuda a (*helps me*) buscar

el libro. Encontramos (*We find*) el libro. Yo _____

cien dólares por el libro.

3.

En la clase

Verbos: desear, enseñar, estudiar, practicar, regresar

La profesora Cantellini _____ italiano. Los estu-

diantes _____ la pronunciación y el vocabulario

en clase. Después de (*After*) clase,

los estudiantes _____ en la biblioteca con sus

compañeros y la profesora _____ a su (*her*)

oficina.

Paso 2. Based on the images and the descriptions from **Paso 1,** correct the following statements, making them all negative. Use subject pronouns in your answers.

MODELO: Yo busco una mochila en la librería. → Yo no busco una mochila en librería.

1. Yo canto en la discoteca.

_____

2. Jorge y yo bailamos en la discoteca.

_____

3. El dependiente trabaja en la discoteca.

_____

4. La profesora Cantellini enseña francés.

_____

5. Los estudiantes escuchan música.

_____

E. ¿Quién... ? Answer each of the following questions aloud, using the oral and written cues. Then listen to and repeat the correct answer.

> MODELO: (*you hear*)   ¿Quién canta bien?
> (*you see and hear*)   Juan y Patricio
> (*you say*)   Juan y Patricio cantan bien.
> (*you hear and repeat*)   Juan y Patricio cantan bien.

1. **a.** nosotras   **b.** ellos   **c.** la profesora   **d.** los estudiantes
2. **a.** Nati y Alberto   **b.** Alicia   **c.** ellas   **d.** nosotros

F. Mis compañeros y yo. Answer each question about yourself and others aloud, using the oral and written cues. Then listen to and repeat the correct answer.

> MODELO: (*you hear*)   ¿Quién paga la matrícula?
> (*you see*)   yo / la matrícula →
> (*you say*)   Yo pago la matrícula.
> (*you hear and repeat*)   Yo pago la matrícula.

1. Ana y yo / a casa
2. Chela y Roberto / libros
3. el profesor / matemáticas
4. tú / mucho
5. Ud. / español

Nota comunicativa: El verbo *estar*

A. ¿Dónde están todos (*everyone*) ahora? Write complete sentences about where you and your classmates are, using the words provided in the order given. **¡OJO!** Provide the necessary words to complete the sentence. Follow the model.

> MODELO: Ud. / cafetería → Ud. está en la cafetería.

1. Raúl y Carmen / salón de clase

   _____

2. yo / biblioteca

   _____

3. tú / clase de biología

   _____

4. Uds. / residencia

   _____

B. ¿Dónde están?

Paso 1. First, pause and look at each of the drawings. When you hear the question, say where the people are. You will hear a possible answer. Repeat the answer you hear.

MODELO:	(you hear)	¿Dónde está Alicia?
	(you say)	Está en el salón de clase.
	(you hear and repeat)	Está en el salón de clase.

1.

2.

3.

4.

(Continúa.)

Paso 2. Now complete each sentence with a verb in the present tense to explain what the people are doing in each location. Follow the model.

MODELO: Alicia escucha en el salón de clase.

1. Héctor y Juan _____

2. Julio y Juana _____

3. María _____

4. (Nosotros) _____

4. Getting Information (Part 1) • Asking Yes/No Questions

A. **De compras** (*Shopping*). Martín necesita comprar unos libros. Conteste (*Answer*) las preguntas según el dibujo (*according to the drawing*). Use oraciones completas.

1. ¿Dónde compra libros Martín? _____

2. ¿Hay libros en italiano en la librería? _____

3. ¿Qué otros objetos hay? _____

    _____

4. ¿Cuántos libros compra Martín? _____

5. ¿Qué lengua hablan la dependienta y Martín? _____

6. ¿Cuánto paga Martín por los libros? _____

B. **¿Es una pregunta?** You will hear a series of statements and questions. First, listen carefully, paying close attention to intonation. Then decide whether what you heard was a statement or a question and circle the letter of the correct answer.

1. **a.** statement   **b.** question
2. **a.** statement   **b.** question
3. **a.** statement   **b.** question
4. **a.** statement   **b.** question
5. **a.** statement   **b.** question

C. Entrevista con la profesora Villegas. Imagine that you are interviewing Professor Villegas for your school newspaper. Using the written cues, ask her questions using the **Ud.** form of the verbs. Then listen to and repeat the question. When you hear Professor Villegas' answer to your question, circle either **Sí** or **No,** based on her answer. *Hint:* Remember that subject pronouns are not used as frequently in Spanish as they are in English, so use the subject pronoun **Ud.** in your first question only.

MODELO: *(you see and hear)*   **1.** enseñar inglés   Sí   No

               (you say)   ¿Enseña Ud. inglés?

      (you hear and repeat)   ¿Enseña Ud. inglés?

           (you hear)   No, enseño español.

       (you circle **No***)*   Sí   (No)

2. enseñar cuatro clases	Sí No	**5.** comprar libros en la librería	Sí No
3. trabajar por la noche	Sí No	**6.** bailar en casa	Sí No
4. hablar con los estudiantes	Sí No		

D. Una entrevista. In this activity you will hear an interview with Carlos Rivera, a university professor. The first time you hear the interview, in **Paso 1,** you will hear only his answers. In **Paso 2,** you will play the role of the interviewer.

Paso 1. You are going to hear Professor Rivera respond to three questions. First, listen to the **Vocabulario útil** and pause to read the questions that he has been asked. Then as you listen to his answers, match them with the questions that they correspond to. That is, when you hear his first response, write the number 1 next to the question that it answers, and so on.

Vocabulario útil

preferida   favorite   **porque**   because

_____ **a.** ¿Cuántas clases enseña Ud.?

_____ **b.** ¿Cuál es su clase preferida?

_____ **c.** ¿Cómo se llama Ud. y de dónde es?

Paso 2. Now you will play the role of the interviewer. Ask each question, and then listen to and repeat the question you hear. Begin by asking the question corresponding to number one in **Paso 1.**

ENTREVISTADORA: [...]

     PROFESOR: Me llamo Carlos Rivera. Y soy de San Antonio, Tejas, pero ahora vivo en Los Ángeles. Estoy de visita aquí en México. Y soy profesor de literatura.

ENTREVISTADORA: [...]

     PROFESOR: Este semestre enseño tres clases. Una clase de literatura contemporánea de los Estados Unidos, una clase de literatura chicana y una clase de composición.

ENTREVISTADORA: [...]

     PROFESOR: Mi clase preferida es la de literatura chicana, porque me identifico personalmente con ella.

Un poco de todo°

A. La profesora López. Complete the following description of a favorite teacher. Write the correct form of the verbs in parentheses, as suggested by context. When the subject pronoun is given with the verb in parentheses, don't include it in the sentence. When two possibilities are given in parentheses, write the correct word.

Nosotros _____ [1] (ser) veintidós estudiantes en _____ [2] (el / la) clase de

_____ [3] (el / la) profesora López. Ella _____ [4] (enseñar) Español 101 y nosotros

_____ [5] (necesitar) hablar solo en español en clase. _____ [6] (*Nosotros:* Escuchar)

y _____ [7] (practicar) mucho en clase. A veces[a] la profesora trae[b] la guitarra y nosotros

_____ [8] (cantar) canciones folclóricas en español con ella. _____ [9] (*Ella: Regresar*)

a su[c] oficina _____ [10] (en / a) _____ [11] (los / las) nueve y media para hablar con

_____ [12] (el / los) estudiantes que _____ [13] (necesitar) ayuda.[d] La profesora López

es muy popular en _____ [14] (el / la) universidad.

[a]*A... Sometimes* [b]*brings* [c]*her* [d]*help*

B. *Listening Passage:** Hablando (*Speaking*) de universidades y cursos

❖ **Antes de escuchar.** You are going to hear a passage about some of the differences between Hispanic and U.S. universities and the courses they offer. Before you listen to the passage, do the following activities.

Paso 1. The passage contains information about Julia Carrasco's studies. What information do you think she will give you?

☐ her major   ☐ which courses she is taking

☐ which professors she likes best   ☐ the name of the university she attends

Paso 2. The passage also contains some general information about Hispanic universities. Check the specific information that you might expect to hear in the passage.

☐ how the academic year is divided (that is, into semesters, quarters, or another division)

☐ the number of courses or credits that students are required to take

☐ the length of the academic year

☐ how much professors are paid

☐ how soon students need to declare their major

☐ whether or not foreign students attend Hispanic universities

Listening Passage. Now you will hear the following passage about Hispanic universities. In this passage, Julia Carrasco talks about her major and some of the differences between Hispanic and U.S. universities. First, listen to the **Vocabulario útil.** Then listen to the passage as you read along.

---

*This is the last Listening Passage section to include a transcript of the spoken text in the Workbook / Laboratory Manual.

Vocabulario útil

la ciudad	city	el curso	course
el mundo	world	además	in addition
por lo general	in general	aprobar	to pass (*a course*)
el año	year		

Hola. Me llamo Julia Carrasco y soy estudiante en la Universidad Nacional Autónoma de México en la Ciudad de México. Mi carrera es ciencias políticas. La carrera es la especialización académica, como *major* o concentración.

En el mundo hispano las universidades son muy diferentes de las de los Estados Unidos. Por lo general, no hay semestres. El año académico es de nueve meses. Los estudiantes toman de cuatro a siete cursos en un año. Además, los estudiantes no esperan dos años para declarar su carrera o especialización.

Yo tomo muchos cursos en relación con las ciencias políticas. ¿Cuáles? Pues, tomo cursos de historia, filosofía, economía y estadística. También tomo inglés. Estudio mucho porque, como en todas las universidades, es necesario estudiar mucho en las universidades de México para aprobar los cursos.

En general, me gusta la vida universitaria. En la Ciudad de México hay muchos estudiantes extranjeros, y muchos son de los Estados Unidos, como mi amiga Heather, que es de Carolina del Norte. Nosotras practicamos el español y el inglés mucho. ¿Con quién practicas tú el español?

Después de escuchar. Listen to the passage again. Then complete the following sentences with words from the list. Not all of the words will be used.

el alemán	ciencias naturales	especialización	el inglés
carrera	ciencias políticas	extranjeros	semestres

1. Para expresar el concepto de *major* en español, es correcto usar las palabras

    _____ y _____

2. Según (*According to*) Julia, por lo general no hay _____ en el año académico hispano.

3. Julia toma cursos en relación con las _____

4. Julia también toma una lengua extranjera: _____

5. En la Ciudad de México, hay muchos estudiantes _____

C. El primer (*first*) día de clase

Paso 1. You will hear a conversation between two students, Juan Carlos and Eduardo, who meet in a university class. Juan Carlos speaks first. After they introduce themselves, they will talk about another class they have together. Eduardo notices a music CD that Juan Carlos has with him, and they will start to talk about music. First, listen to the **Vocabulario útil** and read the sentences. Then, listen to the conversation and indicate to whom the following sentences refer.

Vocabulario útil

oye	hey, listen	allí	there
esa	that	¡Qué bacán!	How great!
este	this		

	JUAN CARLOS	EDUARDO	LOS DOS (*BOTH*).
1. Su apellido (*His last name*) es Robledo.	☐	☐	☐
2. Su apellido es Alarcón.	☐	☐	☐
3. Estudia sociología.	☐	☐	☐
4. Le gusta el *jazz*.	☐	☐	☐
5. Trabaja en el Café Azul.	☐	☐	☐

(*Continúa.*)

Note: Check your answers to **Paso 1** in the Appendix befote starting **Paso 2**.

Paso 2. Listen to the conversation again and pay attention to the questions. As you listen to the conversation, complete the following questions that you hear in the conversation.

1. ¿Es la clase de _____?

2. ¿_____ tal?

3. ¿Qué _____ es?

4. Oye, ¿_____ también la clase de _____ con el profesor Ramón?

5. ¿A _____ _____ es la clase de _____?

6. ¿Es a la una o a _____ _____ y _____?

7. ¡Qué bacán! ¿_____ _____ hora?

8. Oye, ¿_____ hora _____?

Paso 3. Now, listen to and repeat some lines of dialogue from the conversation.

CULTURA

A. Mapa. En el siguiente (*following*) mapa de los Estados Unidos, identifique estas (*these*) seis ciudades (*cities*) con nombres españoles.

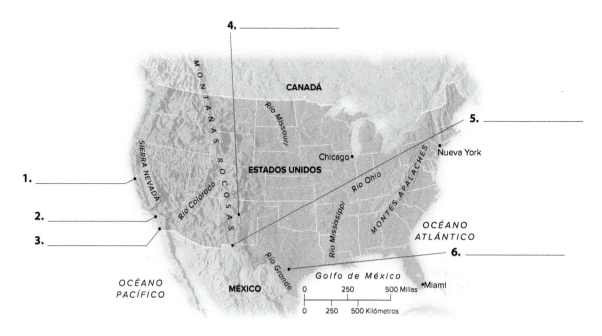

B. Comprensión. Complete las siguientes oraciones (*following sentences*) con palabras de la lista. Esta actividad se basa en información de las lecturas **Algo sobre...** (p. 29 y 50), **Nota cultural** (p. 30) y **Lectura cultural** (p. 54) del libro de texto o del eBook.

América Latina   conferencias   España   latinos

prestigiosas   preuniversitaria   universitaria

1. En el mundo hispano, la palabra **colegio** se refiere a (*refers to*) la educación _____.

2. La Universidad de Salamanca, fundada (*founded*) en 1218, es la universidad más antigua (*oldest*) de _____.

3. Muchas universidades en los Estados Unidos tienen departamentos de estudios _____

4. Las organizaciones latinas en muchas universidades estadounidenses coordinan (*coordinate*) eventos sociales y académicos como bailes y _____.

5. Las universidades nacionales en los países hispanos son gratuitas o muy económicas, y con frecuencia muy _____.

PÓNGASE A PRUEBA

A. Gender and Articles. Escriba (*Write*) el artículo apropiado.

DEFINITE ARTICLES (*THE*)
    SINGULAR   PLURAL

INDEFINITE ARTICLES (*A, AN, SOME*)
    SINGULAR   PLURAL

1. *m.* _____ _____

2. *f.* _____ _____

3. *m.* _____ _____

4. *f.* _____ _____

B. Present Tense of -*ar* Verbs. Escriba la forma apropiada del verbo **buscar**.

1. yo _____

2. tú _____

3. Ud., él, ella _____

4. nosotros/as _____

5. Uds., ellos, ellas _____

C. Negation. Rewrite the sentences to make them negative.

1. Yo deseo tomar café.

   _____

2. Hablamos alemán en la clase.

   _____

3. Marta baila el tango.

   _____

D. El verbo *estar*. Escriba la forma plural de los pronombres y verbos que faltan (*that are missing*).

SINGULAR   PLURAL

yo estoy   _____   _____ ¹

tú estás   vosotros/vosotras   estáis

Ud. está   Uds.   _____ ²

él está   _____   _____ ³

ella está   _____   _____ ⁴

E. Las palabras interrogativas. Write the appropriate interrogative word. Be sure to write accent marks and question marks.

1. Where? _____   4. Who? (*singular*) _____
2. How? _____   5. What? _____
3. When? _____   6. Why? _____

PRUEBA CORTA

A. Los artículos definidos. Escriba (*Write*) el artículo definido.

1. _____ papel   4. _____ libro de texto   7. _____ lápices
2. _____ mochila   5. _____ nación   8. _____ programas
3. _____ universidad   6. _____ días

B. Los artículos indefinidos. Escriba el artículo indefinido.

1. _____ librería   4. _____ problema   7. _____ mujer
2. _____ señores   5. _____ clase   8. _____ horas
3. _____ hombres   6. _____ tardes   9. _____ mensaje

C. Los verbos. Complete las oraciones con la forma apropiada de los verbos de la lista. Use todos (*all*) los verbos.

enseñar   escuchar   estudiar   hablar   mandar   necesitar   regresar   tocar

1. Los estudiantes _____ para sus (*their*) exámenes en la biblioteca.
2. Yo _____ música todos los días (*every day*) en mi (*my*) iPod.
3. En la clase de español (nosotros) no _____ en inglés, solo en español.
4. ¡Alberto es fantástico! _____ el piano como (*like*) un profesional.
5. La profesora García _____ ciencias naturales.
6. (Yo) _____ comprar un diccionario bueno.

7. ¿A qué hora _____ el consejero a su (*his*) oficina?

8. Celia _____ un mensaje.

D. Cosas de todos los días

Paso 1. Practice talking about your university, using the written cues. When you hear the corresponding number, form sentences using the words provided in the order given, making any necessary changes or additions. Then listen to and repeat the correct answer.

MODELO: (*you see*)   **1.** profesores / llegar / temprano
                    (*you hear*) Uno.
                    (*you say*) Los profesores llegan temprano.
    (*you hear and repeat*) Los profesores llegan temprano.

2. mi (*my*) amiga y yo / estudiar / biblioteca
3. (nosotros) / escuchar / a los profesores
4. (yo) / practicar / español / por la tarde
5. (yo) / mirar / televisión / por la noche
6. mis (*my*) amigos y yo / bailar / discoteca

Paso 2. Now you will hear a series of questions. Answer based on the sentences from **Paso 1.** Then listen to the correct answer.

1. ...   2. ...   3. ...   4. ...   5. ...   6. ...

❖ PUNTOS PERSONALES

A. **¿Qué estudias? (*What are you studying?*)** Write about the courses you need to study, like to study, and do not like to study by combining phrases from the two columns.

Necesito estudiar...
Me gusta estudiar...
No me gusta estudiar...
Deseo estudiar...

administración de empresas, alemán, arte, biología, cálculo, ciencias políticas, economía, español, filosofía, francés, literatura, matemáticas, música, química, sicología

MODELO: Necesito estudiar francés.

1. _____

2. _____

3. _____

B. **Una cuestión de gustos.** Indicate how you feel about the following places or things. Remember to use the definite article (**el** or **la**).

MODELO: café → (No) Me gusta el café.

1. clase de literatura   _____

2. consejera   _____

3. música salsa   _____

4. Disneylandia   _____

(Continúa.)

5. limonada _____

6. comida (*food*) mexicana _____

7. profesor de física _____

8. programa *American Idol* _____

C. Preguntas. Conteste (*Answer*) con información verdadera (*truthful*). Use pronombres para reemplazar (*replace*) los sujetos.

MODELO: ¿Escuchan o bailan Uds. en clase? → Nosotros escuchamos en clase.

1. ¿Estudia Ud. en la biblioteca o en casa?

_____

2. ¿Practican Uds. español o francés?

_____

3. ¿Escuchan o mandan Uds. mensajes en clase?

_____

4. ¿Toma Ud. Coca-Cola o agua (*water*)?

_____

5. Y sus (*your*) amigos, ¿toman Coca-Cola o agua?

_____

D. Un día normal

Paso 1. You will hear a series of sentences that describe a typical day in Armando's life. Listen carefully and circle the letter of the drawing that best matches each sentence. First, pause and look at the drawings.

1. a.    b.

2. a.    b.

3.   a.

b.

Paso 2. Now you will hear a series of questions about what you do on a typical day. Pause after each question and write information that is true for you.

1.   Por la mañana, _____

2.   Por la tarde, _____

3.   Por la noche, _____

E.   Guided Composition

Paso 1. You and a friend have just met Daniel, a new student at the university. He wants to know about your Spanish class and instructor. Answer his questions in complete sentences.

DANIEL: ¿Estudian Uds. español?

    UD.:   _____

DANIEL: ¿Dónde practican Uds. español?

    UD.:   _____

DANIEL: ¿Cuántos estudiantes hay en la clase?

    UD.:   _____

DANIEL: ¿Hablan Uds. español en la clase?

    UD.:   _____

DANIEL: ¿Quién enseña la clase?

    UD.:   _____

DANIEL: ¿Él/Ella manda emails a los estudiantes?

    UD.:   _____

Paso 2. Now based on the above dialogue, write a short paragraph describing your Spanish class and your instructor.

_____

_____

_____

_____

_____

_____

F. **Mi diario.** For this diary entry, you will write about yourself. Write the date first. (Remember that in Spanish, the day comes first, then the month: 5/10/12 = el 5 de octubre de 2016 [dos mil dieciséis].)

Write in complete sentences, limiting yourself to vocabulary you have learned so far. (Do *not* use a dictionary!)

Include the following information in this entry.

- your name and where you are from
- how you would describe yourself as a student (**Como estudiante, soy...**) (Review the cognates in **Capítulo 1** if you need to do so.)
- the courses you are taking this term (**este semestre/trimestre**) and at what time they are given
- the school materials and equipment that you have (**tengo...**) and those you need
- what you like to do (**me gusta...**) at different times of the day (**por la mañana, por la tarde, por la noche**)

 G. **Intercambios.** First, listen to the **Vocabulario útil.** Then, listen to the questions and answer them in writing.

Vocabulario útil

su	your
mi	my

1. _____

_____

2. _____

_____

3. _____

_____

4. _____

_____

Capítulo 3
La familia

VOCABULARIO — Preparación

La familia y los parientes

A. Identificaciones. Identifique a los parientes de Enrique.

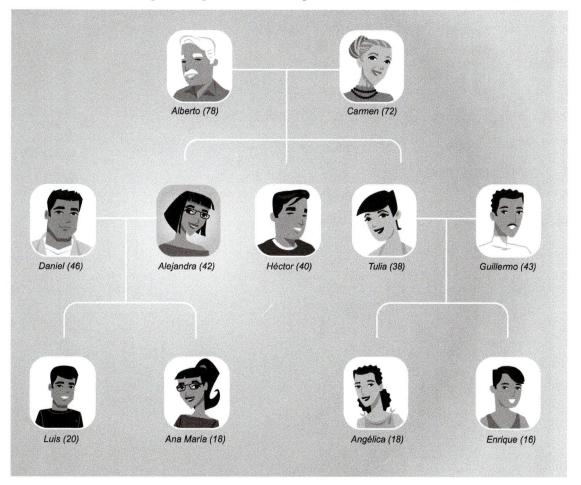

Alberto (78) — Carmen (72)

Daniel (46) — Alejandra (42) — Héctor (40) — Tulia (38) — Guillermo (43)

Luis (20) — Ana María (18) — Angélica (18) — Enrique (16)

(Continúa.)

MODELO: Guillermo es el padre de Enrique.

1. Tulia

   _____

2. Héctor

   _____

3. Alberto y Carmen

   _____

4. Angélica

   _____

5. Luis

   _____

6. Ana María

   _____

7. Daniel y Alejandra

   _____

B. **¿Qué son?** Complete las oraciones (*sentences*) lógicamente. Use cada (*each*) palabra solo una vez (*once*).
    Algunas (*Some*) palabras no se van a usar (*will not be used*).

abuela	hermana	mascota	padres	sobrino
abuelos	hermano	nieta	parientes	tía

    1. El hijo de mi (*my*) hermano es mi _____.

    2. La madre de mi primo es mi _____.

    3. Los padres de mi madre son mis (*my*) _____.

    4. La madre de mi madre es mi _____.

    5. Yo soy la _____ de mis abuelos.

    6. Hay muchos _____ en mi familia. Tengo seis tíos y veintiún primos.

    7. El perro o gato de una familia es su (*their*) _____.

C. Familias

Paso 1. Una entrevistadora (*interviewer*) habla con Karina y Rubén sobre (*about*) los miembros de sus (*their*) respectivas familias. Primero (*First*), escuche el **Vocabulario útil**. Luego (*Then*) escuche las respuestas (*answers*) de Karina y Rubén. Indique **C** (cierto), **F** (falso) o **ND** (no lo dice [*he/she does not say*]), según (*according to*) sus respuestas.

Vocabulario útil

grande   large
bastantes   a fairly large number

1.	Karina no tiene (*does not have*) hermanos.	C	F	ND
2.	Karina no tiene primos.	C	F	ND
3.	Karina no tiene papá.	C	F	ND
4.	Rubén tiene una familia pequeña.	C	F	ND
5.	Rubén tiene abuelos.	C	F	ND
6.	Rubén tiene diez tíos.	C	F	ND
7.	Rubén no tiene sobrinos.	C	F	ND

Paso 2. Ahora imagine que Ud. es Karina. Conteste (*Answer*) las siguientes preguntas (*questions*) como si fuera (*as if you were*) ella. Luego (*Then*) escuche la respuesta (*answer*) correcta y repítala (*repeat it*).

ENTREVISTADORA: ¿Cómo es su familia?
KARINA: ...
ENTREVISTADORA: ¿Cuántos hermanos tiene?
KARINA: ...

D. Definiciones.

Definiciones. You will hear some definitions having to do with family relationships. First, listen to the list of words that will be defined. Second, listen carefully and write the number of the definition next to the word defined. Then listen to and repeat the answer and definition.

MODELO: (*you hear*)   **1.** Es el hermano de mi (*my*) padre.
      (*you write*)   __1__ mi tío
(*you hear and repeat*)   Mi tío es el hermano de mi padre.

_____ mi abuelo   _____ mi hermano   _____ mi tía

_____ mi abuela   _____ mi prima   ___**1**___ mi tío

E. **La familia Muñoz**

Paso 1. You will hear a brief description of Sara Muñoz's family. First, pause and look at the following family tree. Then listen carefully and complete the family tree according to the description.

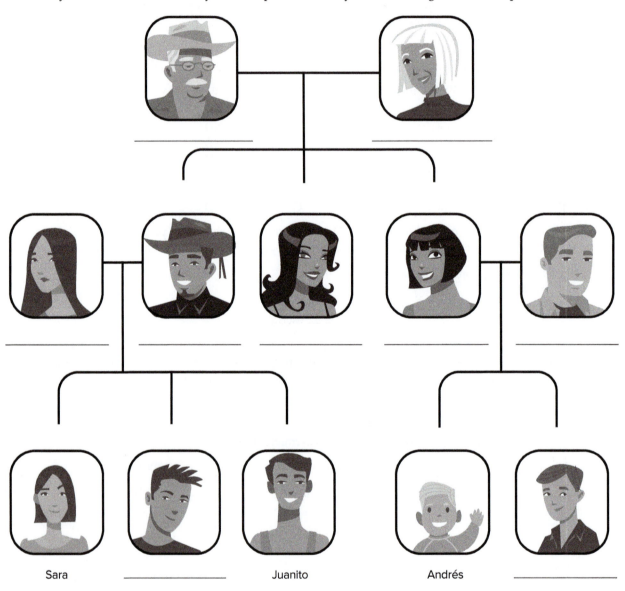

Sara   _____   Juanito   Andrés   _____

Note: Check your answers to **Paso 1** in the Appendix before beginning **Paso 2.**

Paso 2. Now you will hear the names of some of the people in the family tree in **Paso 1.** When you hear each name, say the relationship of that person to Sara. Then listen to and repeat the correct answer.

MODELO: (*you hear*)   Roberto

(*you say*)   Roberto es el abuelo de Sara.

(*you hear and repeat*)   Roberto es el abuelo de Sara.

1. ...   **2.** ....   **3.** ...   **4.** ...   **5.** ....   **6.** ...

Nota cultural: Los apellidos hispanos

1. _____ Miguel Martín Soto married Carmen Arias Bravo. Thus, their daughter Emilia's legal name is . . .

   a. Emilia Soto Bravo   **c.** Emilia Martín Arias
   b. Emilia Martín Bravo   **d.** Emilia Soto Arias

2. _____ Ángela Rebolleda Castillo married César Aragón Saavedra. Their son Francisco's name is . . .

   a. Francisco Castillo Saavedra   **c.** Francisco Saavedra Castillo
   b. Francisco Aragón Rebolleda   **d.** Francisco Rebolleda Saavedra

Los números del 31 al 100

A. El inventario. Write out the number of textbooks and other items that are in the library. Remember that **uno** becomes **un** before a masculine noun and **una** before a feminine noun.

1. 100 _____ libros de texto

2. 31 _____ computadoras

3. 57 _____ enciclopedias

4. 91 _____ diccionarios

5. 76 _____ escritorios

❖ Nota comunicativa: ¿Cuántos años tienen? (*How old are they?*)

Answer the questions to tell how old your friends and family are. Write out the numbers. For relatives you don't have, simply write **No tengo**.

MODELO: ¿Cuántos años tiene su (*your*) abuela?

Tiene ochenta y dos años. / No tengo.

1. ¿Cuántos años tiene su mejor (*best*) amigo/a? _____

2. ¿Cuántos años tiene su abuelo? _____

3. ¿Cuántos años tiene su madre? _____

4. ¿Cuántos años tiene su hermano/a mayor (*older*)? _____

5. ¿Cuántos años tiene su hermano/a menor (*younger*)? _____

B. Más inventario

Paso 1. Imagine que Ud. trabaja en una librería. Primero (*First*), escuche la lista de palabras. Luego (*Then*) escuche el número de los varios objetos que hay y escriba (*write*) el número correspondiente en dígitos. **¡OJO!** Las palabras no están en orden.

a. _____ mochilas   **d.** _____ novelas

b. _____ lápices   **e.** _____ calculadoras

c. _____ cuadernos   **f.** _____ libros de español

Nota: Verifique sus respuestas (*answers*) al **Paso 1** en el Apéndice antes de empezar (*before beginning*) el **Paso 2.**

(Continúa.)

Paso 2. Ahora va a oír (*you will hear*) una serie de preguntas (*a series of questions*) sobre (*about*) el inventario. Use la información del **Paso 1** para contestarlas (*to answer them*). Escuche la respuesta (*answer*) correcta y repítala (*repeat it*).

MODELO:

(Ud. oye [*you hear*]) ¿Cuántas calculadoras hay?

(Ud. ve [*you see*]) 31 calculadoras

(Ud. dice [*you say*]) Hay treinta y una calculadoras.

(Ud. oye y repite [*you hear and repeat*]) Hay treinta y una calculadoras.

1. ... **2.** ... **3.** ... **4.** ... **5.** ...

C. **Sumas y restas (*Additions and subtractions*)**

Paso 1. Escriba en forma de dígitos las respuestas (*answers*) a los siguientes problemas de matemáticas.

a. $50 - 10 = $ _____

b. $65 - 30 = $ _____

c. $80 + 20 = $ _____

d. $10 + 20 + 48 = $ _____

e. $100 - 8 = $ _____

f. $14 + 72 = $ _____

Nota: Verifique sus respuestas al **Paso 1** en el Apéndice antes de empezar (*before beginning*) el **Paso 2.**

Paso 2. When you hear the corresponding letter, read the math problem from **Paso 1** aloud and give the answer. To express *plus*, use **y**; to express *minus*, use **menos**; to express *are*, use **son**. Then listen to and repeat the correct answer.

Los adjetivos

A. **Descripciones.** Describe the drawings using adjectives from the following list. Some adjectives will be repeated.

grande   joven   moreno   nuevo   pequeño   perezoso   trabajador   viejo

1. 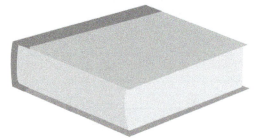   **2.**

1. El libro es _____ y _____.

2. El libro es _____ y _____.

3.

4.

3. El hombre es _____ y _____.

4. El hombre es _____ , _____ y _____.

 **B.** **¿Cuál es?** Va a oír (*You are going to hear*) una serie de descripciones. Escoja (*Choose*) la letra de la cosa o persona que se describe.

1. **a.**  **b.**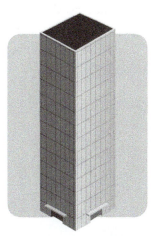

2. **a.** **b.**

(Continúa.)

3. **a.**  **b.**

4. **a.**  **b.**

C. **¿Cómo son Ricardo y Felipe?** Ricardo es el opuesto de (*the opposite of*) Tomás, y Felipe es el opuesto de Alberto. ¿Cómo son Ricardo y Felipe?

1. Tomás es alto, guapo, tonto y perezoso, pero Ricardo es _____, _____,

   _____ y _____.

2. Alberto es gordo, joven, antipático y rubio, pero Felipe es _____, _____,

   _____ y _____.

D. Anuncios personales. Lea (*Read*) los anuncios y corrija (*correct*) los comentarios falsos. Siga el modelo.

Profesor, 48 años,
rubio, guapo.
Me gusta el ciclismo,
la música clásica.
Tel: 2-95-33-51, Luis

Ejecutivo, Banco Internacional,
32 años, graduado en MIT,
listo, delgado. Aficiones:
basquetbol, viajar, bailar, ciencia
ficción. Tel: 9-13-66-42, Carlos

Secretaria ejecutiva bilingüe,
alta, morena, 28 años.
Me gusta la playa, el *camping*,
la comida francesa.
Tel: 7-14-21-77, Diana

MODELO: Luis es moreno y guapo. → No, Luis es rubio y guapo.

1. Diana es joven y rubia. No, Diana es _____.

2. Luis tiene cincuenta y ocho años. No, Luis _____.

3. Carlos es tonto y gordo. No, Carlos es _____.

4. A Luis le gusta la música rock. No, a Luis _____.

5. El teléfono de Diana es el siete, cuarenta, veintiuno, setenta y siete. No, el teléfono es _____.

_____.

E. Descripciones: ¿Cómo son?

Paso 1. Va a (*You are going to*) escuchar una serie de oraciones (*a series of sentences*) sobre (*about*) cuatro hombres. Primero (*First*), mire el dibujo (*drawing*). Luego indique si las oraciones son ciertas (**C**) o falsas (**F**), según el dibujo.

1. C   F   **2.** C   F   **3.** C   F   **4.** C   F

Paso 2. Ahora va a escuchar una serie de preguntas (*questions*) sobre el dibujo. Conteste (*Answer*), basándose en el dibujo. Luego escuche la respuesta correcta y repítala.

1. ...   **2.** ...   **3.** ...   **4.** ...

PRONUNCIACIÓN

Stress and Written Accent Marks (Part 1)

 A. Repeticiones. Repeat the following words, imitating the speaker. The underlined syllable receives the stress in pronunciation.

1. **Las palabras llanas** have the spoken stress on the second-to-the-last syllable. When these words end in a vowel, **-n,** or **-s,** they do not require a written accent mark.

   sin-<u>ce</u>-ra   in-te-re-<u>san</u>-te   <u>bus</u>-can   a-fri-<u>ca</u>-no   <u>com</u>-pras

2. **Las palabras agudas** have the spoken stress on the last syllable. When these words end in a consonant other than **-n** or **-s**, they do not require a written accent mark.

   pa-<u>pel</u>   li-be-<u>ral</u>   li-ber-<u>tad</u>   can-<u>tar</u>   se-<u>ñor</u>

B. Más repeticiones. Repeat the following words, imitating the speaker. The words have been divided into syllables for you. Pay close attention to which syllable receives the spoken stress.

1. **Más palabras llanas**

li-bro	si-lla	cla-se	bai-lan	Ca-ro-li-na
con-se-je-ra	cien-cias	o-ri-gen	com-pu-ta-do-ra	es-cu-cha-mos

2. **Más palabras agudas**

tra-ba-ja-dor	mu-jer	fa-vor	ac-tor	co-lor
po-pu-lar	ac-ti-tud	ge-ne-ral	sen-ti-men-tal	u-ni-ver-si-dad

C. ¿Llanas o agudas? You will hear the following words. Listen carefully and circle the syllable that receives the spoken stress. Then indicate if the word is **llana (L)** or **aguda (A)**.

1. con-trol _____
2. e-le-fan-te _____
3. mo-nu-men-tal _____
4. com-pa-ñe-ra _____
5. bue-nos _____
6. us-ted _____

D. El acento

Paso 1. Underline the stressed vowel in each of the following words.

1. doc-tor
2. mu-jer
3. mo-chi-la
4. ac-tor
5. per-mi-so
6. po-si-ble
7. lo-cal
8. pro-fe-so-res
9. u-ni-ver-si-dad
10. Car-men
11. I-sa-bel
12. bi-blio-te-ca
13. us-ted
14. li-ber-tad
15. o-ri-gen
16. a-ni-mal

Note: Check your answers to **Paso 1** in the Appendix before beginning **Paso 2**.

Paso 2. When you hear the corresponding number, say the word using the correct stress. Then listen to and repeat the correct answer.

GRAMÁTICA

5. Describing Adjectives: Gender, Number, and Position

A. ¿Cómo son? Empareje (*Match*) cada (*each*) adjetivo con el nombre correspondiente, según su forma.

alta	guapo	pobres
bajos	inteligentes	rubios
bonita	jóvenes	simpático
delgado	listo	trabajadora
gordos	moreno	tonta

1. María es _____

2. Javier es _____

3. Los Sres. (*Mr. and Mrs.*) Cruz son _____

B. Hablando (*Speaking*) de la familia

Paso 1. Graciela is describing her family. Listen to her description and write the correct form of the adjectives that apply to each member of her family. **¡OJO!** Not all of the adjectives will be used, and not all adjectives in the description appear in the chart.

	ACTIVO	MORENO	BAJO	ALTO	JOVEN
SU (*HER*) PADRE					
SU TÍO					
SU HERMANA					
LOS ABUELOS					
SUS (*HER*) PRIMOS					

Note: Check your answers to **Paso 1** in the Appendix before beginning **Paso 2**.

Paso 2. Now you will hear a series of questions. Answer, using information in the chart. Then listen to the correct answer and repeat it.

1. ...   **2.** ...   **3.** ...   **4.** ...   **5.** ...

C. Descripciones de los miembros de la familia

Paso 1. Escuche unas descripciones que dan (*give*) Karina y Rubén. Escuche solo para captar (*to grasp*) la idea principal. Luego (*Then*) indique la idea más apropiada.

1. ☐ Hablan de sus parientes y amigos.   **2.** ☐ Hablan de sus padres y hermanos.

Paso 2. Ahora va a (*you're going to*) escuchar las respuestas de Karina y Rubén otra vez (*again*). Primero (*First*), escuche el **Vocabulario útil**. Luego escuche las respuestas y complete las oraciones con la forma apropiada de los adjetivos que usan para describir a sus (*their*) parientes.

Vocabulario útil

bajito/a	short (*affectionate term*)
mediano/a	neither fat nor thin
flaco/a	delgado/a

alto	delgado	mediano	pequeño
bajo	joven	moreno	rubio

1. El padre de Karina es alto y _____.

2. La madre de Karina es bajita y _____.

3. Las hermanas de Karina son muy _____.

4. La madre de Rubén es _____ y bajita.

5. El hermano de Rubén es _____ y más alto que él.

6. La hermana de Rubén es pequeña y _____.

D. Más descripciones. You are going to describe a series of images. First, listen to a list of adjectives that you will use to describe the images. Then describe the image aloud, using an appropriate adjective from the list in its correct form. Use each adjective only once. Finally, listen to the correct answer and repeat it.

bajo   moreno   pequeño   perezoso   viejo

MODELO: (*you hear*) Uno.

(*you see*) **1.** el perro
(*you say*) El perro es pequeño.
(*you hear and repeat*) El perro es pequeño.

2.

Miguel

3.

Mónica

4.

el libro

5.

Ana

E. Personas, objetos y lugares internacionales. Complete con el adjetivo de nacionalidad apropiado.

1. Berlín es una ciudad _____.

2. San José es la capital _____.

3. Marta y Mario son de Buenos Aires; son _____.

4. Londres (*London*) es la capital _____.

5. Guadalajara es una ciudad _____.

6. Marta y Roberto son de Bogotá; son _____.

7. París y Marsella son dos ciudades _____.

8. Vladimir Putin es de Rusia; es _____.

9. Bagdad es la capital _____.

10. El sushi es un ejemplo de la comida (*food, cuisine*) _____.

F. **¿De dónde son y qué idioma hablan?** Imagine that your friend Carmen is asking you about some of the exchange students on campus. First, listen to the list of countries and nationalities. Next, listen to Carmen's questions. Answer according to the model, giving the nationality of the persons she mentions and the language they might speak. Then listen to and repeat the correct answer. **¡OJO!** Remember that nationalities are adjectives: as for all adjectives, you need to make them agree with the noun they modify.

Países y nacionalidades

Alemania: alemán	**Inglaterra: inglés**
España: español	**Italia: italiano**
Francia: francés	**Portugal: portugués**

> MODELO: (you hear)   ¿Bruna es de Portugal?
>
>   (you say)   Sí, (ella) es portuguesa y habla portugués.
>
> (you hear and repeat)   Sí, (ella) es portuguesa y habla portugués.

1. Jonathan   **2.** Gina y Sofía   **3.** Marta   **4.** Jacques y Pierre   **5.** Heidi

G. **En busca de... (In search of . . .)** Describe what you or your friends are looking for by inserting the adjectives given in parentheses in their proper position in these sentences. Be sure that the adjectives agree with the nouns they modify.

> MODELO: Ana busca coche. (italiano, otro) →
>
>   Ana busca otro coche italiano.

1. Buscamos motocicleta. (alemán, otro) _____

2. Paco busca bolígrafos. (francés, otro) _____

3. Busco al escritor (*writer*) Mario Vargas Llosa. (grande).

_____

4. Jorge busca perros. (pequeño, dos) _____

6. Expressing *to be* • Present Tense of *ser,* Summary of Uses (Part 2)

¿Recuerda Ud.?

Las formas del verbo *ser.* Complete la tabla con la forma correcta del verbo **ser.**

1. yo _____   **4.** nosotros/as _____

2. tú _____   **5.** Uds., ellos, ellas _____

3. Ud., él, ella _____

A. Identificaciones. Match each sentence with the statement that best identifies the people described.

_____ **1.** Miguel trabaja en un hospital.

_____ **2.** Dolores y Olga trabajan en una biblioteca.

_____ **3.** Tú estudias mucho.

_____ **4.** La señora Martínez tiene muchos nietos.

_____ **5.** Enseño español.

_____ **6.** Tocamos la guitarra.

a. Eres estudiante.

b. Es abuela.

c. Es médico.

d. Somos músicos (*musicians*).

e. Son bibliotecarias.

f. Soy profesora.

B. Estudiantes mexicanos. Muchos estudiantes en la universidad son de México. Imagine que Ud. es uno/a de ellos.

1. Yo _____ de Puebla.

2. Miguel y David _____ de la Ciudad de México.

3. Ana _____ de Oaxaca.

4. Uds. _____ de Monterrey.

5. Tú _____ de Guadalajara.

6. Todos nosotros _____ mexicanos.

C. **Regalos.** Imagine that you are giving presents to the following people. Justify each gift choice by using one of these phrases. Add other details if you wish.

es estudiante de lenguas   necesitan comprar una computadora nueva
es gordo/a
le gusta escribir (*he/she likes to write*)   tienen (*they have*) cuatro niños

> MODELO: diccionario bilingüe / Alberto →
> El diccionario bilingüe es para Alberto. Es estudiante de lenguas.

1. programa de *Weight Watchers* / mi tía _____

_____

2. casa grande / los Sres. (*Mr. and Mrs.*) Walker _____

_____

3. dinero / mis padres _____

_____

4. bolígrafos / mi hermana Ana _____

_____

D. **¿De dónde son?** Practice saying where people are from, using the written and oral cues. First, listen to the list of countries. Next, you will be told the nationalities of each of the people. Write what country they are from, then listen to and repeat the correct answer. Check your written answers in the Appendix.

Países

Chile	Cuba
Colombia	España
Costa Rica	

> MODELO: (*you see*) Mi amigo Arístides _____.
> (*you hear*) Mi amigo Arístides es colombiano.
> (*you write*) Mi amigo Arístides es de Colombia.
> (*you say*) Mi amigo Arístides es de Colombia.
> (*you hear and repeat*) Mi amigo Arístides es de Colombia.

1. Mi amigo Lorenzo _____.

2. Sus (*His*) abuelos _____.

3. Mi amiga Mariela _____.

4. Tú _____.

E. **¿De quién son estos objetos?** Escriba la pregunta (*question*) que hace (*you ask*) para saber (*find out*) de quién son los siguientes objetos. Luego escriba la respuesta (*answer*), según (*according to*) el modelo.

> MODELO: el Sr. Ortega
> —¿De quién es el cuaderno?
> —Es del Sr. Ortega.

1.

la profesora

—¿————————————————?

—————————————————

2.

Cecilia

—¿————————————————?

—————————————————

3.

Sr. Alonso

—¿————————————————?

—————————————————

4.

la familia Olivera

—¿————————————————?

—————————————————

F. **¿De quién son estas cosas?** Imagine that your friend wants to know to whom certain items belong. Listen to her questions and answer them, using the written cues. Then listen to and repeat the correct answer. **¡OJO!** Don't forget that **de** + **el** form the contraction **del.**

MODELO: (*you hear*) ¿De quién es el escritorio?

(*you see*) el cliente

(*you say*) Es del cliente.

(*you hear and repeat*) Es del cliente.

1. el estudiante **2.** la profesora **3.** las consejeras **4.** el Sr. Costas

G. **¿Para quién son los regalos?** Imagine that you need to give gifts to several of your friends and relatives, and money is no object! First, listen to the list of gifts you have decided to give them. Next, you will hear the name and a brief description of each person. Select appropriate gifts for them from the list, and use the phrases **para ella, para él,** and **para ellos,** as in the model. Then listen to and repeat the correct answer.

Los regalos

la calculadora   los libros de filosofía
el coche nuevo   las novelas románticas
el iPod

MODELO: (*you hear*) Tu (*Your*) hermano Juan es estudiante universitario.

(*you say*) Los libros de filosofía son para él.

(*you hear and repeat*) Los libros de filosofía son para él.

1. ... **2.** ... **3.** ... **4.** ...

7. Expressing Possession • Unstressed Possessive Adjectives (Part 1)

¿Recuerda Ud.?

El uso de la preposición *de* + sustantivo para expresar posesión. ¿Cómo se dice en español?

MODELO: It's Raúl's family. → Es la familia de Raúl.

1. She's Isabel's sister. _____

2. They're Mario's relatives. _____

3. They're Marta's grandparents. _____

A. **¿De quién son estas cosas y estos parientes?**

Paso 1. Complete con la forma apropiada del adjetivo posesivo.

1. —¿El cuaderno es del Sr. Ortega?   —Sí, es _____ cuaderno.

2. —¿Los libros son de la profesora?   —Sí, son _____ libros.

3. —¿La mochila es de Cecilia?   —Sí, es _____ mochila.

4. —¿Los bolígrafos son del Sr. Alonso?   —Sí, son _____ bolígrafos.

5. —¿La casa es de los Sres. (*Mr. and Mrs.*) Olivera?   —Sí, es _____ casa.

Paso 2. Exprese en español.

1. my family _____

2. her relatives _____

3. my grandparents _____

4. our parents _____

5. their brother _____

B. **Hablando (*Speaking*) de la familia.** Conteste (*Answer*) en forma afirmativa. Use adjetivos posesivos.

MODELO: ¿Son ellos los hijos de tu hermana? → Sí, son sus hijos.

1. ¿Es ella la suegra (*mother-in-law*) de Tomás? _____

2. ¿Es Carlos el hermano de Uds.? _____

3. ¿Son ellos los padres de tu novia? _____

4. ¿Son Uds. los primos de Marta? _____

5. ¿Es Carmen la sobrina de tu mamá? _____

6. ¿Eres el nieto / la nieta de los señores? _____

C. ¿Cómo es la familia de Vicente? When you hear the corresponding number and family member, say what Vicente's family is like. Use the written cues and the correct form of the possessive adjective **su.** Then listen to and repeat the correct answer. **¡OJO!** Be sure to use the correct form of the verb **ser.**

> MODELO: (*you see*)   **1.** bajos
>   (*you hear*)   **1.** tíos
>   (*you say*)   Sus tíos son bajos.
>   (*you hear and repeat*)   Sus tíos son bajos.

  2. simpáticas
  3. altos
  4. delgada
  5. mayores (*older*)
  6. bonita

 D. ¿Cómo es su universidad? When you hear the corresponding number and noun, describe your university to an exchange student who has recently arrived. Use the written cues, the appropriate form of **nuestro,** and the verb **ser.** Then listen to and repeat the correct answer.

> MODELO: (*you see*)   **1.** vieja
>   (*you hear*)   **1.** universidad
>   (*you say*)   Nuestra universidad es vieja.
>   (*you hear and repeat*)   Nuestra universidad es vieja.

  2. buenos   **5.** amables
  3. pequeñas   **6.** buenos
  4. grande

E. ¿Tu o su?

Paso 1. Mire (*Look at*) las fotos e indique si debe usar el posesivo **tu** o **su** para hablar con cada persona. Escriba **tu** o **su** debajo de (*under*) las fotos.

         la Sra. Dolores Suárez   Tané

1. _____   **2.** _____

Nota: Verifique sus respuestas (*answers*) al **Paso 1** en el Apéndice antes de empezar (*before beginning*) el **Paso 2.**

(Continúa.)

Paso 2. Ahora va a (*you are going to*) escuchar dos entrevistas breves (*brief interviews*) con la Sra. Dolores Suárez y Tané, las personas de las fotos del **Paso 1.** Para cada uno de los siguientes adjetivos, escriba la inicial de la persona que lo usa (*who uses it*) en su respuesta (*answer*): **D** (la Sra. Dolores Suárez) o **T** (Tané). Si ambas (*both*) usan el adjetivo, escriba las dos iniciales.

Mi familia es...

_____ numerosa

_____ pequeña

_____ bonita

_____ unida (*close*)

¿Recuerda Ud.?

Verbos que terminan con -*ar*. ¿Qué terminaciones se emparejan (*match*) con los siguientes sujetos?

	-o	**-as**	**-a**	**-amos**	**-an**

1. nosotros _____

2. yo _____

3. tú _____

4. Uds., ellos, ellas _____

5. Ud., él, ella _____

---

8. Expressing Actions • Present Tense of *-er* and *-ir* Verbs; Subject Pronouns (Part 2)

A. En el centro estudiantil (*student union*). Use la forma apropiada de los verbos de la lista para describir las acciones de los estudiantes.

beber   comer   escribir   estudiar   leer

1. Luis _____ mucho.

2. Gloria _____ francés.

3. José y Ramón _____ Coca-Cola.

4. Inés _____ una carta.

5. Carlos _____ un periódico.

B. Una carta de Ramón. Ramón y Pepe son dos hermanos mexicanos. Ahora viven en California. Complete el comienzo (*beginning*) de una carta que escribe Ramón a su familia en Morelia, México.

Queridos[a] padres:

Pepe y yo _____[1] (vivir) bien aquí en California, en la casa de una señora muy

simpática. Yo _____[2] (asistir) a clases cinco días a la[b] semana. Mis clases son

difíciles,[c] pero los profesores son buenos. En la clase de inglés _____,[3]

_____[4] y _____[5] (*nosotros:* hablar, leer, escribir) mucho. Todos los

días _____[6] (*nosotros:* aprender) algo nuevo. Sin embargo,[d] hay estudiantes que

nunca _____[7] (abrir) los libros para estudiar.

   Pepe y yo _____[8] (comer) en la cafetería estudiantil por la mañana. Por la noche

_____[9] (*nosotros:* deber) regresar a casa porque la señora nos[e] _____[10]

(preparar) la comida. ¡Es muy amable!

[a]*Dear* [b]*a... per* [c]*difficult* [d]*Sin... However* [e]*for us*

C. Las actividades de Micaela

Paso 1. Escuche una breve narración en la cual (*which*) Micaela habla de sus actividades.

Paso 2. Ahora, escuche la narración de Micaela otra vez (*again*). Mientras escucha la narración, complete las siguientes oraciones con los verbos que dice (*says*) Micaela. ¡OJO! Los verbos van a estar (*are going to be*) en la forma de **yo**.

1. _____ en una residencia estudiantil en el *campus*.

2. _____ a clases de lunes a viernes.

3. Los fines de semana (*On the weekends*) _____ pizza en un restaurante con mis amigos en nuestro restaurante favorito.

4. Los fines de semana, también _____ estudiar para mis clases.

5. Por lo general, _____ mucho y _____ buenas notas.

6. Creo que mi clase de física es muy difícil (*difficult*) y a veces, no _____ todo (*everything*) bien.

D. Un sábado típico de la familia Robles. Describe what happens on a typical Saturday in the Robles household, using the written and oral cues. Then listen to and repeat the correct answer. **¡OJO!** Remember that subject pronouns are used less frequently in Spanish than they are in English.

MODELO: (*you hear*)   nosotros

                 (*you see*)   estar en casa

                 (*you say*)   Estamos en casa.

     (*you hear and repeat*)   Estamos en casa.

1. leer el periódico
2. escribir mensajes de texto
3. asistir a un partido (*game*) de fútbol
4. abrir una carta de mi prima
5. comer a las seis

E. ¿Qué hacen (*are they doing*)?

Paso 1. You will hear a series of statements. First, listen to the **Vocabulario útil** and look at the drawings. Then listen to the statements and write the number of the statement next to the drawing that matches the activity mentioned.

Vocabulario útil

la tarta de cumpleaños   birthday cake

a. _____

Nina

b. _____

tú

c. _____

Aurelia

d. _____

Ricardo   yo

e. _____

f. _____

Laura · Mario · Rogelio · Paulina

Paso 2. When you hear the corresponding letter, say what the people in the drawings from **Paso 1** are doing. Then listen to and repeat the correct answer.

a. ... **b.** ... **c.** ... **d.** ... **e.** ... **f.** ...

F. **¿Qué hacen (*are doing*) estas personas? Ud.** va a (*are going to*) escuchar unas oraciones sobre (*about*) los siguientes dibujos (*drawings*). Indique si cada oración es cierta (**C**) o falsa (**F**). Luego escuche la respuesta correcta y repítala (*repeat it*).

Nuria · Marta

MODELO: (Ud. oye [*You hear*])   Nuria y Marta estudian en la biblioteca.
(Ud. selecciona F [*You select* F])   C   Ⓕ
(Ud. oye y repite [*You hear and repeat*])   Es falso. Nuria y Marta beben café.

1.    C   F

María

2.    C   F

Briana · Petra

(*Continúa.*)

3. Cristóbal   Isabel   C   F

4. Miguel   C   F

5. Marco   Juan   C   F

Un poco de todo

A. Una familia chilena en México. Complete the description of the Rangel family with the correct forms of the words in parentheses. When two possibilities are given in parentheses, select the correct word.

En _____¹ (mi / mis) familia _____² (*nosotros:* ser) cinco personas. Todos

_____³ (somos / estamos) chilenos, pero ahora _____⁴ (vivir) en Guadalajara,

_____⁵ (un / una) ciudad mexicana grande y _____⁶ (bonito / bonita).

_____⁷ (Mi / Mis) padre _____⁸ (trabajar) para el Banco Internacional. Vamos

aᵃ vivir aquí dos años más.ᵇ Mi hermano Carlos y yo _____⁹ (asistir) a la escuela

secundaria. Él _____¹⁰ (tener) dieciséis años, y yo _____¹¹ (tener) quince.

Mi abuela Gabriela _____¹² (vivir) con nosotros. Ella tiene _____¹³ (67) años;

es _____¹⁴ (baja / corta), un poco gorda y muy _____¹⁵ (simpático / simpática). Le gusta

caminar y verᶜ todo. Mi madre Ángela es muy bonita y _____¹⁶ (trabajador / trabajadora).

_____¹⁷ (Somos / Estamos) de acuerdo en queᵈ es fabuloso vivir en este país. Pero,

también _____¹⁸ (*nosotros:* extrañarᵉ) a _____¹⁹ (nuestro / nuestros) amigos

_____²⁰ (chileno / chilenos).

ᵃVamos... *We're going to* ᵇ*more* ᶜ*to see* ᵈ*that* ᵉ*to miss*

B. *Listening Passage:* **La familia hispana tradicional**

❖ **Antes de escuchar.** You are going to hear a passage about the traditional Hispanic family. Before you listen to the passage, do the following activities.

Paso 1. Read the following statements about Hispanic families and circle **C** (**cierto**) if you think the statement might be true or **F** (**falso**) if you think it might be false. As you read the statements, try to infer what information you will hear in the passage, as well as the specific information for which you will need to listen.

1. **C** **F** En las familias hispanas a veces vive más de (*more than*) una generación en una sola (*only one*) casa.
2. **C** **F** En general, los abuelos no participan activamente en el cuidado (*care*) de sus nietos.
3. **C** **F** Por lo general, las personas viejas viven en asilos (*nursing homes*) y no con sus familias.
4. **C** **F** Muchos abuelos ayudan en el cuidado (*help with the care*) de sus nietos.
5. **C** **F** Tradicionalmente, los hijos y los nietos cuidan de (*take care of*) sus padres o de sus abuelos cuando estos (*the latter*) están viejos o enfermos.

Paso 2. The passage contains information about Hispanic families in general and about Julia's family in particular. Indicate the statements that you *think* apply to the Hispanic family in general.

☐ The Hispanic family is typically smaller than the average American or Canadian family.

☐ Many Hispanic families are extended families; that is, more than one generation lives in the same household.

☐ The elderly and the sick are often sent to nursing homes.

☐ Grandparents are important in the daily lives of families.

☐ Many newlyweds live with the parents of one member of the couple until they can become independent.

Listening Passage. Now you will hear the passage. First, listen to the **Vocabulario útil**, then listen to the passage.

Vocabulario útil

conservan	they keep	**murió**	he died
se ayudan	they help each other	**ayudó**	helped
el cuidado	care	**la cuidamos**	we take care of her
enfermas	sick		

Después de escuchar

Paso 1. Here are the true/false statements from **Paso 1** of **Antes de escuchar** again. Circle **C** (**cierto**) if the statement is true or **F** (**falso**) if it is false, based on the information in the passage. Correct the statements that are false and check your answers in the Appendix. Were any of your answers different than the ones you gave before you listened to the passage?

1. C   F   En las familias hispanas a veces vive más de una generación en una sola casa.

   _____

2. C   F   En general, los abuelos no participan activamente en el cuidado de sus nietos.

   _____

3. C   F   Por lo general, las personas viejas viven en asilos y no con sus familias.

   _____

4. C   F   Muchos abuelos ayudan en el cuidado de sus nietos.

   _____

5. C   F   Tradicionalmente, los hijos y los nietos cuidan de sus padres o de sus abuelos cuando estos están viejos o enfermos.

   _____

Paso 2. Now go back and listen to the passage again. Then complete each sentence with the correct word from the list. Check your answers in the Appendix.

esposos   grandes   materna   viejos

1.   La madre de mi madre es mi abuela _____.

2.   Tradicionalmente, muchas familias hispanas son _____.

3.   Si (*If*) los nuevos _____ no tienen (*have*) dinero, viven con los padres de uno de ellos.

4.   En las familias hispanas, es tradicional cuidar de (*to take care of*) los parientes enfermos o

_____.

C.   ¿Cómo es tu familia?

Paso 1. Ud. va a (*are going to*) escuchar una conversación entre (*between*) unos compañeros de la universidad. Tané pregunta (*asks*) a Karina y Rubén sobre (*about*) sus familias. Primero (*First*), escuche el **Vocabulario útil.** Luego (*Then*) escuche la conversación e (*and*) indique si las oraciones son ciertas (**C**) o falsas (**F**).

Karina

Rubén

Tané

Vocabulario útil

¿no extrañan...?	don't you miss. . . ?
no puedo ir	I can't go
tengo unas ganas locas de ver	I'm really dying to see
sobre todo	especially

1.   Karina no extraña a su familia.   C   F
2.   Rubén visita a su familia con frecuencia.   C   F
3.   Rubén desea ver (*see*) sobre todo a sus hermanos.   C   F

Paso 2. Ahora Ud. va a participar en una conversación similar entre Manuel y Gema. Primero, deje de escuchar (*stop listening*) y lea la lista de las respuestas (*answers*) de Gema y también el fragmento de la conversación que contiene las preguntas (*that contains the questions*) de Manuel. Luego (*Next*) escriba la respuesta más lógica a cada pregunta. Verifique sus respuestas en el Apéndice antes de escuchar la conversación. Luego escuche cada pregunta de Manuel y contéstela (*answer it*) en voz alta (*aloud*) con la respuesta de Gema. Escuche la respuesta correcta y repítala (*repeat it*).

Las respuestas de Gema

Miguel tiene 20 años y es muy alto.
Sí, mucho.
Tengo dos hermanos, Miguel y Mateo.
Tiene 17 años y es muy simpático.

MANUEL: Ahora que vives en la universidad, ¿extrañas a tu familia?

GEMA: _____¹

MANUEL: Yo también. Tengo unas ganas locas de ver a toda mi familia. Oye, ¿cuántos hermanos tienes?

GEMA: _____²

MANUEL: Ah, yo tengo un hermano y una hermana. ¿Y cómo es tu hermano Miguel?

GEMA: _____³

MANUEL: ¿Y Mateo? ¿Cómo es?

GEMA: _____⁴

CULTURA

A. Mapa. En el siguiente mapa, identifique: la Ciudad de México, Monterrey, Oaxaca, Guadalajara y Puebla.

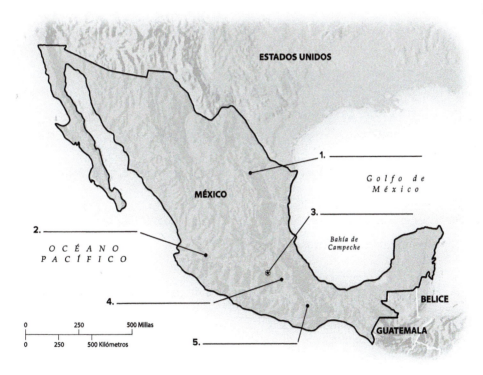

B. Comprensión. Indique la mejor (*best*) respuesta para completar cada oración (*each sentence*). Esta actividad se basa en información de las lecturas **Algo Sobre**... (p. 72, 85 y 89) y **Lectura cultural** (p. 92) del libro de texto o del eBook.

1. **Americano** es el término que se usa para referirse a las personas de _____.

   a. los Estados Unidos   **b.** todo el continente

2. El tamal consiste en masa de _____ con otros ingredientes, envuelta (*wrapped*) y cocida (*cooked*) en hojas de maíz u otras plantas.

   a. maíz   **b.** plátanos

3. Frida Kahlo pinta autorretratos (*self-portraits*) que incluyen elementos de la cultura _____.

   a. mexicana   **b.** colombiana

4. Las familias mexicanas, por tradición, _____ muy unidas.

   a. son   **b.** no son

5. En México, el 18.5% de los hogares familiares es _____.

   a. tradicional   **b.** monoparental

6. Las ruinas _____ de Chichén Itzá cerca de Cozumel son un símbolo arqueológico importante de México.

   a. mayas   **b.** zapotecas

PÓNGASE A PRUEBA

A. Adjectives: Gender, Number, and Position. Complete con la información apropiada.

1. Escriba la forma correcta del adjetivo **guapo**.

   a. hermana _____   **b.** primos _____

2. Escriba la forma plural de los adjetivos.

   a. grande _____   **b.** sentimental _____

3. Complete la tabla con la forma correcta de los adjetivos de nacionalidad.

	DE MÉXICO	DE FRANCIA	DE ESPAÑA
FEMININE SINGULAR	*mexicana*		
MASCULINE SINGULAR			
FEMININE PLURAL			*españolas*
MASCULINE PLURAL		*franceses*	

B. Present Tense of *ser*. Match each of the following statements with the particular use of **ser**.

1. _____ Lola es de Puerto Rico.

2. _____ La carta es para mi madre.

3. _____ Los papeles son del profesor.

4. _____ Alicia es mi prima.

a. With **para**, to tell for whom or what something is intended.

b. With **de**, to express possession.

c. With **de**, to express origin.

d. To identify people and things.

C. Possessive Adjectives (*Unstressed*). Express the following possessive adjectives and nouns in Spanish.

1. my brother _____

2. her uncle _____

3. our grandparents _____

4. their house _____

D. Present Tense of *-er* and *-ir* Verbs. Complete la tabla con la forma correcta de los verbos.

LEER	ESCRIBIR
yo _____	tú _____
él _____	ella _____
nosotros _____	Uds. _____

PRUEBA CORTA

A. Las nacionalidades. Complete the following sentences with the adjective of nationality that corresponds to the country in parentheses.

MODELO: Marta es *mexicana*. (México)

1. Paolo es un estudiante _____. (Italia)

2. París es una ciudad _____. (Francia)

3. El Volkswagen es un coche _____. (Alemania)

4. Diane y Margaret son dos mujeres _____. (Inglaterra)

B. El verbo *ser*. Escriba la forma apropiada del verbo **ser**.

1. La mochila no _____ nueva.

2. Yo _____ de los Estados Unidos.

3. Guanajuato y Mérida _____ dos ciudades viejas y fascinantes.

4. ¿Tú _____ de México?

5. Él y yo _____ de California.

C. Los adjetivos posesivos. Complete el párrafo con los adjetivos posesivos apropiados.

La madre de _____¹ (*my*) sobrino Mauricio se llama Cecilia. Ella es

_____² (*my*) cuñada.ᵃ _____³ (*My*) hermanos Enrique y Luis

todavíaᵇ viven con _____⁴ (*our*) padres. El padre de Cecilia se llama Marco;

_____⁵ (*her*) madre se llama Elena. Elena y Marco son italianos, pero viven en

México. Ellos piensanᶜ que _____⁶ (*our*) cultura es muy interesante. Todos

_____⁷ (*their*) nietos son mexicanos. ¿De dónde es _____⁸

(*your* [*informal*]) familia?

ᵃ*sister-in-law* ᵇ*still* ᶜ*think*

D. Los verbos -er e (*and*) -ir. Complete las oraciones con la forma correcta del verbo apropiado de la lista. **¡OJO!** No se repiten los verbos.

asistir   beber   comprender   escuchar   estudiar   hablar   leer   recibir   vender

1. Nosotros no _____ mucho cuando la profesora _____ rápidamente (*quickly*).

2. ¿(*Tú*) _____ música mientras (*while*) (**tú**) _____ para tus exámenes?

3. Mi padre nunca _____ libros de ciencia ficción.

4. ¿Siempre _____ Uds. los libros al final (*at the end*) del semestre?

5. Mi hermana siempre _____ muchos regalos y tarjetas (*cards*) el Día de San Valentín.

6. Yo no _____ café por la noche.

7. Nosotros _____ a esta clase todos los días.

E. La familia de doña Isabel. You will hear a passage about the family of doña Isabel. Read the passage along with the speaker and circle the numbers you hear.

¡La familia de doña Isabel es muy grande y extendida! Ella tiene **30 / 20** nietos en total, y **16 / 26** bisnietos (*great-grandchildren*). Doña Isabel tiene **89 / 99** años. Su hijo mayor (*oldest*), Diego, tiene **67 / 77** años. Su hija menor (*youngest*), Alida, tiene **64 / 54**. Doña Isabel tiene **10 / 6** hijos en total. El próximo (*next*) año, todos sus hijos, nietos y bisnietos celebran los **100 / 50** años de edad (*of age*) de doña Isabel.

F. Cosas de todos los días. When you hear the corresponding number, form sentences using the words provided in the order given, making any necessary changes or additions. If the subject is in parentheses, don't use it. Then listen to and repeat the correct answer.

> MODELO:　　　　(*you see*) **1.** mi familia: ser / muy grande
> 　　　　　　　　(*you hear*) Uno.
> 　　　　　　　　(*you say*) Mi familia es muy grande.
> 　　(*you hear and repeat*) Mi familia es muy grande.

2. (nosotros): vivir / en una ciudad / pequeño
3. nuestra casa: ser / bonito
4. mis padres: ser / muy simpático
5. (nosotros): siempre comer / juntos (*together*)
6. mis hermanos: asistir / a un concierto esta tarde
7. Pero (yo): deber estudiar / para mis clases.

PUNTOS PERSONALES

A. **¿Qué opina Ud.?** Conteste (*Answer*) con todos los adjetivos apropiados.

   1. Los estudiantes de esta clase son _____.

   2. Mi profesor(a) de _____ es _____.

   3. Mi mejor (*best*) amigo/a es _____.

   4. Y yo soy _____.

B. **¿De dónde son?** Complete las oraciones para indicar el estado o el país de donde son las siguientes personas. Use la forma apropiada del verbo **ser**.

   1. Yo _____.

   2. Mi mejor (*best*) amigo/a _____.

   3. Mi profesor(a) de español _____.

   4. Muchos estudiantes en mi clase _____.

C. **Más opiniones.** Conteste (*Answer*) con su opinión personal.

   1. ¿Es importante estudiar lenguas extranjeras? _____

   _____

   2. ¿Es práctico estudiar matemáticas? _____

   _____

   3. ¿Es difícil (*difficult*) hablar español en clase? _____

   _____

D. **Ud. y sus amigos.** Express what you and your friends do or do not do, using **nosotros** verb forms. Write complete sentences by using an adverbial phrase and a verb from the lists below in each sentence. Be sure to limit yourself to writing only those things you have learned how to say in Spanish.

   MODELO: A veces comemos en casa. Casi nunca comemos en la cafetería.

   ADVERBIOS   a veces
   nunca   con frecuencia
   casi nunca
   todos los días

   VERBOS   escribir
   aprender a   estudiar
   asistir (a)   leer
   beber   practicar
   deber   trabajar

(Continúa.)

1. _____

2. _____

3. _____

4. _____

5. _____

E. **¿Con qué frecuencia?**

Paso 1. Primero (*First*), indique con qué frecuencia hace (*you do*) las siguientes acciones.

	CON FRECUENCIA	A VECES
1. Escribo e-mails.	☐	☐
2. Asisto a un concierto.	☐	☐
3. Leo el periódico.	☐	☐
4. Como en un restaurante.	☐	☐
5. Bebo café.	☐	☐
6. Vendo cosas (*things*) en eBay.	☐	☐

Paso 2. Ahora, conteste (*answer*) las preguntas que oye con la información que completó (*you completed*) en el **Paso 1.**

MODELO: (Ud. ve [*see*]) **1.** Escribo e-mails. / con frecuencia ☑

(Ud. oye [*hear*]) Uno. ¿Con qué frecuencia escribe e-mails?

(Ud. dice [*say*]) Escribo e-mails con frecuencia.

2. ...   **3.** ...   **4.** ...   **5.** ...   **6.** ...

F. **Guided Composition**

Paso 1. Conteste las siguientes preguntas sobre su familia con oraciones completas.

1. ¿Cuántas personas hay en su familia?

   _____

2. ¿De dónde son sus padres?

   _____

3. ¿Dónde trabaja su padre ahora? ¿Y su madre?

   _____

4. ¿Qué estudia(n) sus hermano(s)? ¿Cuántos años tiene(n)? ¿Cómo es/son?

   _____

   _____

5. ¿Cómo es la casa de su familia?

   _____

   _____

Paso 2. Now write a descriptive paragraph about your family by combining your answers from **Paso 1** and using connecting words such as **y, pero, por eso, porque, también,** and **aunque** (*although*).

_____

_____

_____

_____

_____

_____

_____

G. Mi diario. For this diary entry, you will write a description of your favorite relative. Be sure to include the following information.

- name and relationship to you
- age: **tiene** (**más o menos** [*less*]) _____ **años**
- where he/she is from
- what he/she does for a living
- appearance
- personality

Use all the adjectives you can! For a better description, refer to the **En resumen: Vocabulario** of your textbook as well as to lists of additional adjectives within the textbook (such as the list for **Conversación B** on page 71).

_____

_____

_____

_____

H. Intercambios. Escuche las siguientes preguntas y contéstelas por escrito (*answer them in writing*).

1. _____

_____

2. _____

_____

3. _____

_____

4. _____

_____

Capítulo 4

De compras

VOCABULARIO Preparación

De compras: La ropa

A. La ropa. Identifique la ropa que llevan estas personas. Use el artículo indefinido.

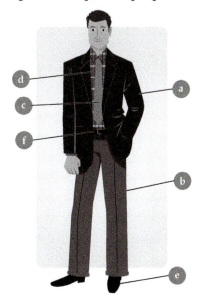

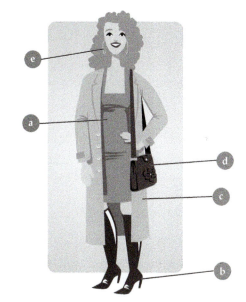

1. a. _____

   b. _____

   c. _____

   d. _____

   e. _____

   f. _____

2. a. _____

   b. _____

   c. _____

   d. _____

   e. _____

B. **De compras en la Ciudad de Guatemala.** Imagine that you are visiting the capital of Guatemala and you ask a friend where and how to shop. Complete your friend's answer with the appropriate items from the list provided.

almacén	fijos	rebajas	venden de todo
centro	gangas	regatear	
de última moda	mercado	tiendas	

En el _____[1] comercial de la calle Colón, hay un _____[2] grande donde

_____[3] Allí (*There*) los precios son _____[4] y caros, pero la ropa es

_____[5] Ahora, en las _____[6] del centro, hay muchas _____.[7]

O puedes ir (*you can go*) al _____[8] Allí los precios no son fijos y es posible

_____[9] También puedes encontrar (*find*) muchas _____[10] de artículos típicos.

C. **¿Qué opina Ud.?** Complete los comentarios con el español de las palabras entre paréntesis y estas palabras: **algodón, cuero, lana, seda.**

1. La ropa interior de _____ es más fresca que[a] la de nilón.

2. Las _____ (*ties*) de _____ son elegantes y bonitas.

3. Los _____ (*sweaters*) y las _____ (*skirts*) de _____

son caros y abrigados.[b]

4. Las botas altas de _____ están de moda.

[a]más... *cooler than*   [b]*warm*

D. **Preguntas.** Imagine that you are talking with a friend, trying to confirm some information. Change the following statements into questions with tag phrases.

MODELO: Nunca usas botas. → Nunca usas botas, ¿verdad?

1. Necesitas una sudadera nueva. _____

2. Buscas una camisa de seda. _____

3. Tus sandalias son cómodas. _____

4. No necesito llevar corbata. _____

5. Esta chaqueta es perfecta. _____

E. **Identificaciones.** Identifique la ropa en el dibujo cuando oiga (*you hear*) el número correspondiente. Empiece (*Begin*) cada (*each*) una de sus oraciones con **Es un... , Es una...** o **Son...** Luego escuche la respuesta correcta y repítala.

1.   **2.**   **3.**   **4.**

5. 6. 7.

8. 9.

F. La ropa que me gusta

❖ **Paso 1.** Antes de escuchar (*Before listening to*) la entrevista (*interview*) de Karina en el **Paso 2,** indique si las siguientes oraciones son ciertas (**C**) o falsas (**F**) para Ud.

	C	F
1. Me gusta ir de compras (*to go shopping*).	☐	☐
2. Me gusta ir de compras a los centros comerciales.	☐	☐
3. Para ir a clase, con frecuencia llevo *jeans* y camisetas.	☐	☐
4. Para mí, estar a la moda (*to be trendy*) es importante.	☐	☐

Paso 2. En esta entrevista, Karina contesta (*answers*) varias preguntas sobre las compras. Primero (*First*), escuche el **Vocabulario útil** y lea (*read*) las preguntas. Luego mientras (*while*) escucha las cuatro respuestas de Karina, empáréjelas (*match them*) con las preguntas correspondientes a continuación. La primera respuesta de Karina es número 1, su segunda respuesta es número 2, etcétera.

Vocabulario útil

me encanta	**me gusta mucho**
voy	I go
de marca	name-brand (*adj.*)
según lo que quiera	according to what you want
franelitas	cute little T-shirts
la apariencia hay que cuidarla	one has to take care of one's appearance

_____ ¿Es importante estar a la moda y por qué?

_____ Normalmente, ¿qué ropa llevas a la universidad y por qué?

___1___ ¿Te gusta ir de compras y por qué?

_____ Cuando vas (*you go*) de compras, ¿adónde vas?

Nota: Verifique sus respuestas del **Paso 2** en el Apéndice antes de empezar (*before beginning*) el **Paso 3.**

(Continúa.)

Paso 3. Ahora Ud. va a hacer el papel de la entrevistadora (*play the part of the interviewer*) en la entrevista completa. Primero, haga (*ask*) en voz alta (*aloud*) cada (*each*) una de las cuatro preguntas para completar la entrevista. Luego escuche la pregunta correcta y repítala (*repeat it*).

(*ENTREVISTADORA*):	...
KARINA:	Me encanta ir de compras porque me gusta tener muchas cosas nuevas.
(*ENTREVISTADORA*):	...
KARINA:	Cuando voy de compras, voy a centros comerciales o a tiendas de marca, según lo que quiera comprar.
(*ENTREVISTADORA*):	...
KARINA:	Hmmm, para ir a la universidad llevo *jeans* o franelitas, así estoy cómoda y a la moda.
(*ENTREVISTADORA*):	...
KARINA:	Sí, es muy importante para mí estar a la moda porque la apariencia hay que cuidarla.

Los colores: ¿De qué color es?

A. **¿De qué color es?** Complete las oraciones con la forma apropiada de los colores de la lista. Todos los colores se dan (*are given*) en la forma masculina singular. Haga (*Make*) los cambios necesarios. Algunos colores se usan más de una vez (*more than once*).

amarillo	azul	color café	morado	rosado
anaranjado	blanco	gris	rojo	verde

1. Las plantas son _____.

2. La bandera (*flag*) guatemalteca tiene tres bandas (*stripes*) verticales: una banda _____,
   (*blue*)
   una _____ y una _____.
         (*white*)   (*blue*)

3. La bandera de los Estados Unidos es _____, _____ y _____.

4. La naranja (*orange*) es _____ y el limón es _____.

5. El color _____ es una combinación de blanco y negro.

6. El color _____ es una combinación de rojo y azul.

7. El color tradicional para las bebés (*baby girls*) es _____.

8. Generalmente la tierra (*dirt*) es de _____.

B. **Hablando de la moda**

Paso 1. Listen to the description of the clothing that a group of classmates are wearing to a popular nightclub tonight night. As you listen, check the clothing worn by each person. **¡OJO!** The clothes are not listed in the order in which you will hear them.

	TENIS	CALCETINES	CAMISA	PANTALONES	CINTURÓN	CAMISETA	CORBATA
Luis							
Ana							
Juan							

Paso 2. Now listen again. As you listen, write the colors mentioned for each article of clothing, making sure that the colors you write agree with the gender and number of the articles of clothing described. **¡OJO!** The clothes are not listed in order.

ARTÍCULOS	COLOR(ES)
calcetines	
camisa	
camiseta	
cinturón	
corbata	
pantalones	
tenis	

Note: Check your answers to **Pasos 1** and **2** in the Appendix before beginning **Paso 3.**

Paso 3. Now, answer the questions you hear using the information in the charts in **Pasos 1** and **2.** You will hear a possible answer. Repeat the answer you hear.

MODELO: (Ud. oye)   ¿Quiénes llevan tenis?

           (Ud. dice)   Ana y Juan llevan tenis.

   (Ud. oye y repite)   Ana y Juan llevan tenis.

1. ...   **2.** ...   **3.** ...   **4.** ...   **5.** ...

Los números a partir del 100

A. Los números. Write the following numbers using Arabic numerals (digits).

1. ciento once _____

2. cuatrocientos setenta y seis _____

3. quince mil setecientos catorce _____

4. setecientos mil quinientos _____

5. mil novecientos sesenta y cinco _____

6. un millón trece _____

B. ¿Cuánto cuesta? Complete each price with the correct word for the missing numbers.

1. 28.510 dólares: veintiocho mil _____ diez dólares

2. 14.625 dólares: catorce _____ seiscientos _____ dólares

3. 7.354 quetzales: _____ mil _____ cincuenta y cuatro quetzales

4. 3.782 quetzales: tres mil _____ _____ y dos quetzales

5. 1.843 lempiras: mil _____ cuarenta y _____ lempiras

6. 920 lempiras: _____ veinte lempiras

C. El inventario del Almacén Robles

Paso 1. Imagine that you and a coworker are doing a partial inventory for a department store. First, listen to the list of items being inventoried. Next, listen to what your coworker says is in the inventory, and write the quantity, in numerals, next to the correct items. **¡OJO!** The items are not listed in sequence.

ARTÍCULOS	NÚMERO (CANTIDAD)
pares de medias	
camisas blancas	
suéteres rojos	
pares de zapatos	
blusas azules	
faldas negras	

Nota: Verifique sus respuestas del **Paso 1** en el Apéndice antes de empezar (*before beginning*) el **Paso 2.**

Paso 2. Ahora va a oír (*you are going to hear*) una serie de preguntas sobre la ropa del **Paso 1.** Conteste usando la información de la tabla.

MODELO: (Ud. oye [*you hear*]) ¿Cuántas blusas azules hay?

(Ud. ve [*you see*]) 111 →

(Ud. dice [*you say*]) Hay ciento once blusas azules.

(Ud. oye y repite) Hay ciento once blusas azules.

1. ... **2.** ... **3.** ... **4.** ... **5.** ...

PRONUNCIACIÓN — Stress and Written Accent Marks (Part 2)

A. Sílabas acentuadas. Remember that in Spanish, a written accent mark is required when a word does not follow the two basic rules:

1. a word that ends in a vowel, **-n**, or **–s** is stressed on the next-to-last syllable
2. a word that ends in a consonant is stressed on the last syllable

1. The following words end in a vowel, **-n,** or **-s.** However, native speakers of Spanish do not pronounce these words according to the first basic rule. Repeat the following words, imitating the speaker.

ac-**ción**	ca-pi-**tán**	sim-**pá**-ti-ca	be-**bé**
fran-**cés**	qui-**zás**	me-**nú**	te-**lé**-fo-no

2. These words break the second basic rule because they end in a consonant other than **-n** or **-s** and are not stressed on the last syllable. Repeat the following words, imitating the speaker.

fá-cil	**már**-tir	**Cá**-diz
a-**zú**-car	**Pé**-rez	**Gó**-mez

B. Más sílabas acentuadas. Here are other instances in which a Spanish word requires a written accent.

    1. All words that are stressed on the third-to-last syllable must have a written accent mark on the stressed syllable, regardless of which letter they end in. These are called **palabras esdrújulas.** Repeat the following words, imitating the speaker.

        sá-ba-do   **fór**-mu-la   **prác**-ti-cas   di-**fí**-ci-les   ar-**tí**-cu-lo   **Lá**-za-ro

    2. Remember that when two consecutive vowels do not form a diphthong, the vowel that receives the spoken stress will have a written accent mark. This is very common in words ending in **-ía.** Compare the pronunciation of these pairs of words. Repeat each word, imitating the speaker.

        in-fan-cia, de-cí-a   cien-cias, guí-a
        his-to-ria, ge-o-lo-gí-a   a-gua, grú-a

    3. Remember that some one-syllable words have accents to distinguish them from other words that sound like them but have different meanings. This accent is called a diacritical accent, and it has no effect on the pronunciation of the word. Repeat each word, imitating the speaker.

        él (*he*) / el (*the*)   tú (*you*) / tu (*your*)
        sí (*yes*) / si (*if*)   mí (*me*) / mi (*my*)

    4. Remember that interrogative and exclamatory words require a written accent on the stressed vowel. Repeat each sentence, imitating the speaker.

        ¿Qué estudias?   ¿Cómo te llamas?
        ¿Quién es tu profesora?   ¡Qué bueno! (*How great!*)
        ¿Dónde está Venezuela?

C. Palabras divididas. The following words have been divided into syllables for you. Read them when you hear the corresponding number. Then you will hear each word pronounced in Spanish. Repeat each word, imitating the speaker. **¡OJO!** Some of the words will be unfamiliar to you. This should not be a problem because you have pronunciation rules to guide you.

    1. nor-mal   **4.** a-na-to-mí-a   **7.** ter-mó-me-tro
    2. prác-ti-co   **5.** cu-le-bra   **8.** co-li-brí
    3. á-ni-mo   **6.** con-ver-ti-bles   **9.** con-di-cio-nal

D. ¿Acento escrito (*written*) o no? You will hear the following words. Listen carefully and write in a written accent where required. **¡OJO!** Some of the words will be unfamiliar to you. This should not be a problem because you have the rules and the speaker's pronunciation to guide you.

    1. metrica   **4.** Rosalia   **7.** jóvenes
    2. distribuidor   **5.** actitud   **8.** magico
    3. anoche   **6.** sabiduría   **9.** esquema

E. Las vocales acentuadas

Paso 1. Underline the stressed vowel in each of the following words.

1. doctor	**6.** permiso	**11.** universidad	**16.** López
2. mujer	**7.** posible	**12.** Bárbara	**17.** Ramírez
3. mochila	**8.** Tomás	**13.** lápices	**18.** biblioteca
4. inglés	**9.** general	**14.** Carmen	**19.** sicología
5. actor	**10.** profesores	**15.** Isabel	**20.** usted

Paso 2. The following words are stressed on the underlined syllables. If a written accent is required, add it above the stressed vowel.

    1. ex-<u>a</u>-men   **4.** bo-<u>li</u>-gra-fo   **7.** <u>Pe</u>-rez
    2. lu-<u>gar</u>   **5.** <u>jo</u>-ven   **8.** e-di-<u>fi</u>-cio
    3. ma-<u>tri</u>-cu-la   **6.** sen-ti-men-<u>tal</u>   **9.** a-le-<u>man</u>

Paso 3. Cuando oiga (*you hear*) el número correspondiente, lea en voz alta (*read aloud*) las siguientes oraciones. Luego escuche la pronunciación y repita la oración.

1. El señor Pérez no es alemán.
2. Hay dos edificios nuevos en este lugar.
3. Nicolás y Ángela son jóvenes y simpáticos.
4. La profesora Rodríguez enseña filosofía.
5. Hay ciento dieciséis lápices en el almacén.

9. Pointing out People and Things • Demonstrative Adjectives (Part 2) and Pronouns

¿Recuerda Ud.?

Formas de este. Escriba la forma apropiada: **este, esta, estos, estas.**

1. _____ (*This*) color está de moda este año.

2. _____ (*These*) colores son feos.

3. Me gusta _____ (*this*) camisa blanca.

4. No me gustan _____ (*these*) camisas grises.

A. Las formas. Complete the following chart with the appropriate demonstrative adjectives.

		SINGULAR	PLURAL
1.	a.	_____ (*this*) zapato (aquí)	_____ (*these*) zapatos (aquí)
	b.	_____ (*this*) sandalia (aquí)	_____ (*these*) sandalias (aquí)
2.	a.	_____ (*that*) zapato (allí)	_____ (*those*) zapatos (allí)
	b.	_____ (*that*) sandalia (allí)	_____ (*those*) sandalias (allí)
3.	a.	_____ (*that*) zapato (allá)	_____ (*those*) zapatos (allá)
	b.	_____ (*that*) sandalia (allá)	_____ (*those*) sandalias (allá)

B. **¿*Este, ese* o *aquel*?** Complete las oraciones con la forma apropiada de **este, ese** o **aquel.** También escriba las prendas (*items*) de ropa que lleva cada (*each*) persona.

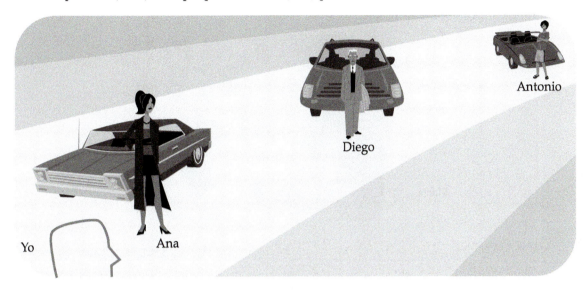

_____[1] coche es de Ana. Ella lleva una _____[2] corta y un _____[3] largo.

_____[4] coche grande es de Diego. Diego lleva un _____[5] gris y un impermeable

en el brazo (*arm*). _____[6] coche fantástico y nuevo es de Antonio. Como siempre, él lleva

_____[7] y una _____.[8]

C. **¿De quién son?** You and a friend are trying to figure out to whom the following items belong. Answer your friend's questions affirmatively, with the appropriate demonstrative adjective.

Note: **Aquí** (*Here*), **allí** (*there*), and **allá** (*over there*), like **este, ese,** and **aquel,** respectively, suggest closeness to, or distance from, the speaker.

MODELO: Aquí hay unos zapatos negros. ¿Son de Pablo? →
            Sí, estos zapatos negros son de Pablo.

1. Aquí hay una chaqueta de rayas. ¿Es de Miguel?

_____

2. Allí veo unos calcetines. ¿Son de Daniel?

_____

3. Allá veo unos impermeables. ¿Son de Margarita?

_____

4. Aquí hay unas chanclas. ¿Son de Ceci?

_____

5. Allá hay un reloj de oro. ¿Es de Pablo?

_____

6. Allí veo unos papeles. ¿Son de David?

_____

D. Los precios de la ropa

Paso 1. María va de compras en esta tienda. Mire el dibujo y complete las oraciones con el adjetivo demostrativo apropiado.

MARÍA: _____¹ suéter negro aquí me gusta mucho. ¿Cuánto es?

VENDEDORA (*Salesperson*): Treinta dólares.

MARÍA: ¿Y _____² faldas largas allá? ¿Cuánto cuestan?

VENDEDORA: Setenta dólares.

MARÍA: Me gustan mucho _____³ blusas allí. ¿Están de rebaja (*on sale*)?

VENDEDORA: No, lo siento (*I'm sorry*). El precio normal es cincuenta dólares.

MARÍA: Muchas gracias.

Nota: Verifique sus respuestas al **Paso 1** en el Apéndice antes de empezar (*before beginning*) el **Paso 2.**

Paso 2. Escuche la conversación y repita las líneas de María.

E. Aquí, allí y allá. Ud. y su amiga están en un almacén. Va a oír (*Your will hear*) una serie de oraciones y preguntas que le hace su amiga (*that your friend asks you*). Conteste las preguntas usando el adjetivo demostrativo apropiado, según los adverbios que oye (*that you hear*): **aquí, allí** y **allá.** Luego escuche la respuesta correcta y repítala (*repeat it*).

MODELO: (Ud. oye) Uno. *Aquí* hay unas sandalias verdes. ¿Te gustan?

(Ud. ve) **1.** Sí

(Ud. dice) Sí, me gustan *estas* sandalias.

(Ud. oye y repite) Sí, me gustan *estas* sandalias.

1. Sí   **3.** No   **5.** Sí
2. Sí   **4.** No   **6.** No

10. Expressing Actions and States • *Tener, venir, preferir, poder, and querer;* Some Idioms with *tener*

¿Recuerda Ud.?

Tener. Complete las formas de **tener.**

1. tú t_____ nes   **2.** yo t_____ ngo   **3.** Ud. t_____ ne

A. **Las formas.** Complete la tabla con la forma apropiada de los verbos.

	yo	tú	Ud., él, ella	nosotros	Uds., ellos, ellas
tener	tengo			tenemos	
venir		vienes			vienen
preferir		prefieres	prefiere		
poder	puedo	puedes			
querer			quiere	queremos	

B. **Diálogo.** Complete the following dialogue between you and a friend to make plans to go to a movie.

—¿_____[1] (*Tú*: Querer) ir al cine[a] esta noche?

—Hoy no_____[2] (*yo*: poder) porque _____[3] (tener) que estudiar para un

examen de sicología. ¿_____[4] (*Nosotros*: Poder) ir mañana? _____[5] (*Yo*: Creer)

que Javier y Marta _____[6] (querer) ir también.

—Está bien. Entonces[b] _____[7] (*yo*: venir) por Uds. mañana a las siete y media. No

_____[8] (*yo*: querer) llegar tarde; _____[9] (preferir) llegar un poco temprano.

[a]ir... *to go to the movies* [b]*Then*

C. **Quiero aprender español, pero...** A new student in Spanish class writes about her obstacles in learning the language. Complete the sentences using idioms with **tener.**

Me llamo María Montaño. _____[1] 18 años y tengo _____[2] de aprender español

porque quiero hablar con mis abuelos y otros parientes que viven en México. Desgraciadamente,[a]

en clase tengo _____[3] de hablar. El profesor cree que debo practicar más en el laboratorio.

Él tiene _____,[4] pero no tengo mucho tiempo libre.[b] Trabajo muchas horas y cuando

quiero estudiar, tengo _____[5] y a veces me quedo dormida.[c]

[a]*Unfortunately* [b]*free* [c]me... *I fall asleep*

D. **¿Qué hacen estas personas?**

Paso 1. Escriba la forma apropiada del verbo en los espacios en blanco.

1. querer → Nosotros no _____ estudiar ahora.

2. poder → Yo _____ bailar bien.

3. preferir → ¿ _____ tú esta camiseta o esa?

4. venir → Uds. _____ a mi fiesta, ¿no?

5. tener → Ella _____ muchos parientes.

Nota: Verifique sus respuestas al **Paso 1** en el Apéndice antes de empezar (*before beginning*) el **Paso 2.**

(Continúa.)

Paso 2. Cuando oiga (*you hear*) el número correspondiente, lea en voz alta (*read aloud*) la oración completa del **Paso 1.** Luego escuche la respuesta correcta y repítala (*repeat it*).

E. Cambios (*Changes*). Cambie (*Change*) las siguientes oraciones del singular al plural. Luego escuche la respuesta correcta y repítala.

MODELO: (Ud. ve y oye)   Vengo a las siete. →

    (Ud. dice)   Venimos a las siete.

    (Ud. oye y repite)   Venimos a las siete.

1. Quiero mandar un texto.
2. Tengo mucha ropa.
3. ¡No puedo cantar!
4. Prefiero esos pantalones.
5. No vengo a clase mañana.

F. Situaciones y reacciones

Paso 1. You will hear a series of partial conversations. Listen carefully and circle the letter of the reaction or response that best completes each conversation.

1. **a.** Ay, ¡tú siempre tienes prisa!   **b.** Tienes razón, ¿verdad?
2. **a.** ¿Por qué tienes sueño?   **b.** Sí, tienes razón, pero tienes que estudiar más.
3. **a.** ¿Tienes que comer en un restaurante?   **b.** ¿Tienes ganas de ir a un restaurante?
4. **a.** ¿Cuántos años tienes?   **b.** La verdad es que tienes miedo, ¿no?
5. **a.** No, no tengo ganas de comprar ropa.   **b.** ¿Cuántos años tiene la niña ahora?

Paso 2. Now, you will hear each partial conversation again. After each one, read the correct reaction or response aloud. Then listen to and repeat the correct reaction or response, imitating the speaker.

1. ...   2. ...   3. ...   4. ...   5. ...

G. Un mensaje telefónico importante

Paso 1. Escuche el mensaje telefónico que deja (*leaves*) Luis Carlos para su hermana Cecilia.

Paso 2. Ahora haga oraciones completas con información del mensaje y las frases de la lista. ¡No se olvide de (*Don't forget*) conjugar los verbos!

no poder esperar más   tener cosas elegantes
poder ir a un centro comercial   tener el coche
querer ir de compras al centro   tener un aniversario

1. Los padres de Luis Carlos y Cecilia _____.

2. Los hermanos _____ o al centro.

3. Luis Carlos _____.

4. Las tiendas del centro _____.

5. Cecilia _____.

6. Luis Carlos tiene prisa; (él) _____.

Nota: Verifique sus respuestas al **Paso 2** en el Apéndice antes de empezar (*before beginning*) el **Paso 3.**

Paso 3. Cuando oiga (*you hear*) el número correspondiente, lea en voz alta (*aloud*) las oraciones completas del **Paso 2.** Luego escuche la respuesta correcta y repítala.

11. Expressing Destination and Future Actions •
Ir; The Contraction *al; Ir + a + Infinitive*

A. Una fiesta familiar. Complete las oraciones con la forma apropiada del verbo **ir.**

Muchas personas van a ir a la fiesta en casa de Julio y Ana. Toda la familia de Ana _____.[1]

Los tíos y los abuelos de Julio _____[2] con los padres de Ana. Tú _____[3] también,

¿verdad? Miguel y yo _____,[4] pero yo _____[5] a llegar tarde.

B. El cumpleaños de Raúl. Using **ir + a +** an infinitive, change the verbs to indicate that the following people are *going to do* the given activities to prepare for Raúl's birthday party.

MODELO: Eduardo y Graciela buscan un regalo. →
Eduardo y Graciela van a buscar un regalo.

1. David compra las bebidas (*drinks*). _____

2. Ignacio y Pepe van con nosotros. _____

3. Por eso necesitamos tu coche. _____

4. Afortunadamente (*Fortunately*), no tengo que trabajar esa noche.

C. ¿Adónde vas? You will hear a series of statements a friend might say about what you like to do or want to do. First, listen to the list of places to do these activities. Then using the words and phrases listed below, say where you would go to do these activities. Finally, listen to and repeat the correct answer.

Lugares

el Almacén Robles	**el Club Ciclón**	**el Restaurante Gallego**
la biblioteca	**el mercado**	**la universidad**

MODELO: (Ud. ve y oye) Te gusta estudiar y aprender cosas nuevas.

(Ud. dice) Por eso voy a la universidad.

(Ud. oye y repite) Por eso voy a la universidad.

1. Te gusta regatear.
2. No tienes ganas de preparar la comida (*food*) esta noche.
3. Quieres bailar.
4. Tienes que estudiar para un examen.
5. Te gusta comprar ropa.

D. ¿Qué va a hacer Gilberto este fin de semana?

Paso 1. You will hear a brief passage in which Gilberto talks about his plans for this weekend. First, listen to the **Vocabulario útil.** Then listen to the passage. As you listen, number the following drawings so that they match the order in which Gilberto narrates his plans. Write the number in the small blank.

Vocabulario útil

cenar   to eat dinner

a. _____

_____

_____

b. _____

_____

_____

c. _____

_____

_____

d. _____

_____

_____

Paso 2. Now, in the longer blank, write a sentence that describes Gilberto's future actions. Use **ir** + **a** + *infinitive* and other words as needed.

E. ¡Rebajas hoy!

Paso 1. Escuche una conversación entre (*between*) **dos amigos,** José Miguel y Paloma. Primero, escuche el **Vocabulario útil.** Luego escuche la conversación.

Vocabulario útil

vamos al cine	to the movies
¡Qué pena!	What a shame!
ya lo sé	I (already) know
un rato	a while

Paso 2. Ahora haga oraciones completas con **ir** + **a** + *infinitivo*, según la información de la conversación y usando las frases de la lista. Puede escuchar la conversación otra vez, si quiere.

Vocabulario útil

comprar *blue jeans*   ir a la fiesta
comprar nada (*nothing*)   ir al cine
hacer (*to have*) una fiesta en su casa

1. Eduardo _____ este fin de semana.

2. Paloma no _____

3. Paloma y Gustavo _____

4. Paloma _____

5. José Miguel no _____

Nota: Verifique sus respuestas al **Paso 2** en el Apéndice antes de empezar (*before beginning*) el **Paso 3**.

Paso 3. Cuando oiga (*you hear*) el número correspondiente, lea en voz alta (*aloud*) las oraciones completas del **Paso 2**. Luego escuche la respuesta correcta y repítala (*repeat it*).

1. ...   **2.** ...   **3.** ...   **4.** ...   **5.** ...

Un poco de todo

A. **De compras en San Sebastián.** Complete el siguiente párrafo con la forma apropiada de las palabras entre paréntesis, según el contexto.

En _____ ciudad vasca[a] de San Sebastián, en el norte de España, cuando la gente[b]
        (el / la)

_____ ir de compras, tiene que _____³ a _____⁴ tiendas que
     (querer)   (ir)   (pequeño)

_____⁵ productos _____,⁶ porque en San Sebastián no permiten la
   (vender)   (especial)

construcción de _____⁷ almacenes.[c] La gente _____⁸ proteger[d] a los
                    (grande)   (preferir)

comerciantes vascos locales en vez de apoyar[e] a las grandes galerías _____⁹ como El Corte
                                                                         (español)

Inglés. Por eso, hay en _____¹⁰ ciudad muchas tiendas de ropa para niños, mujeres y
                            (este)

hombres; también hay tiendas _____¹¹ como zapaterías, librerías y papelerías. Son muy
                                (especializado)

_____¹² las tiendas que venden artículos de piel[f] como bolsos, cinturones, gorras, guantes[g]
   (popular)

y carteras. Claro, también _____¹³ pequeñas *boutiques* muy _____¹⁴ con
                              (existir)   (elegante)

productos de moda de los más _____¹⁵ nombres de la moda mundial.[h]
                                (famoso)

[a]*Basque*   [b]*people*   [c]*department stores*   [d]*to protect*   [e]*en... instead of supporting*   [f]*leather*   [g]*gloves*   [h]*moda... world fashion*

B. *Listening Passage:* **El Rastro**

❖ **Antes de escuchar** (*Before listening*). Before you listen to the passage, do the following prelistening activity. It is sometimes helpful to answer questions about yourself that are related to a passage that you will listen to or read. Answering the following questions will give you an idea of the information the passage might contain.

1. ¿Hay un mercado al aire libre (*open-air*) en la ciudad donde Ud. vive?
2. Por lo general, ¿qué venden en los mercados al aire libre?
3. ¿Cómo cree Ud. que son los precios en los mercados al aire libre?
4. ¿Le gusta a Ud. ir de compras?
5. ¿Le gusta regatear?
6. ¿Colecciona Ud. algo (*something*)? ¿Sellos (*Stamps*), monedas (*coins*), libros viejos, trenes (*trains*), muñecas (*dolls*)?

Listening Passage. Now you will hear a passage about **El Rastro**, an open-air market in Madrid, narrated by a Spaniard. First, listen to the **Vocabulario útil.** Next listen to the passage to get a general idea of the content. Then go back and listen again for specific information.

Vocabulario útil

los sellos	stamps
las monedas	coins
los domingos	on Sundays
los puestos	stalls (where salespeople display what they have for sale)

Después de escuchar. Select the letter of the phrase that best completes each sentence.

1. El Rastro es...
   a. una tienda de ropa.
   b. un centro comercial.
   c. un mercado con muchos puestos.

2. El Rastro está abierto...
   a. todo el fin de semana.
   b. los domingos por la mañana.
   c. los domingos por la tarde.

3. En el Rastro venden...
   a. solo ropa y zapatos.
   b. solo cosas para coleccionar.
   c. muchas cosas de todo tipo.

4. El Rastro está...
   a. en Madrid y es muy famoso.
   b. en España y es nuevo.
   c. en todas las ciudades de España.

C. De compras en el mercado

Paso 1. Mariela va de compras a un mercado al aire libre. Escuche el diálogo entre Mariela y la vendedora e indique solo las oraciones que escucha.

_____ Busco una chaqueta amarilla.

_____ Las chaquetas son de pura lana.

_____ Cuestan 6.000 colones.

_____ ¡El precio es una ganga!

_____ Son realmente baratas.

_____ Busco un regalo para mi mamá.

_____ Muchas gracias, muy amable.

_____ ¿Qué colores prefiere?

Paso 2. Ahora haga una pausa y conteste las siguientes preguntas por escrito (*in writing*) con oraciones completas y con información del diálogo. **Nota:** La moneda (*currency*) que se menciona es el colón de Costa Rica.

1. ¿De qué material son las chaquetas? _____

2. ¿Para (*For*) quién quiere comprar la chaqueta Mariela? _____

_____

3. En ese mercado, ¿es posible regatear? _____

4. ¿Cuánto va a pagar Mariela? _____

5. ¿Cuál es el precio original de las chaquetas? _____

Nota: Verifique sus respuestas al **Paso 2** en el Apéndice antes de empezar (*before beginning*) el **Paso 3.**

Paso 3. Cuando oiga (*you hear*) el número correspondiente, lea en voz alta (*aloud*) las preguntas del **Paso 2.** Escuche la pregunta y repítala (*repeat it*). Luego lea sus respuestas a las preguntas. Escuche la respuesta correcta y repítala.

1. ...   **2.** ...   **3.** ...   **4.** ...   **5.** ...

CULTURA

A. Mapa. Identifique los dos países y las capitales en el siguiente mapa.

B. Comprensión. Empareje (*match*) las palabras y frases con sus definiciones. Esta actividad se basa en información de las lecturas **Algo sobre...** (p. 117), **Nota cultural** (p. 104) y **Lectura cultural** (p. 124) del libro de texto o del eBook.

_____ 1. Un tipo de blusa que llevan las mujeres indígenas.

_____ 2. Ruinas mayas en Guatemala que son muy populares con los turistas. Son de la época precolombina.

_____ 3. La costumbre (*custom*) de negociar precios en los mercados.

_____ 4. El libro sagrado de los mayas que, según los mayas, contiene la historia de la creación del mundo.

_____ 5. Una materia que viene de la llama, la vicuña, la alpaca y el guanaco. Se usa para hacer suéteres, gorras, ponchos y más.

a. el huipil
b. la lana
c. el Popul Vuh
d. el regateo
e. Tikal

PÓNGASE A PRUEBA

A. Demonstrative Adjectives and Pronouns. Escriba el adjetivo demostrativo apropiado.

1. _____ (*this*) zapato

2. _____ (*these*) pantalones

3. _____ (*that*) vestido

4. _____ (*those over there*) abrigos

5. _____ (*that over there*) camiseta

6. _____ (*those*) cinturones

B. *Tener, venir, preferir, poder,* and *querer;* **Some Idioms with** *tener*

1. Complete la tabla con la forma apropiada del presente de indicativo de los verbos indicados.

	yo	Ud.	nosotros
poder			
querer			
venir			

2. Exprese en español los siguientes modismos con **tener.**

a. to be afraid (of) _____

b. to be right _____

c. to be wrong _____

d. to feel like _____

e. to have to _____

C. *Ir; Ir + a + Infinitive.* Complete each sentence with the correct form of the verb **ir.**

1. Ellos _____ de compras.

2. ¿Tú _____ a comer?

3. Julio y yo _____ al mercado.

4. Yo no _____ a _____ a la fiesta.

PRUEBA CORTA

A. Los demostrativos. Rewrite the sentences, substituting the noun provided and making all the necessary changes.

> MODELO: ¿Necesitas aquel sombrero rojo? (corbata) →
> ¿Necesitas aquella corbata roja?

1. Quiero comprar esa camisa negra. (impermeable)

   _____

2. ¿Buscas estos calcetines grises? (traje)

   _____

3. Juan va a comprar esos zapatos blancos. (chaqueta)

   _____

4. Mis padres trabajan en aquel almacén nuevo. (tienda)

   _____

B. Cinco verbos. Complete las oraciones con la forma apropiada de uno de los verbos de la lista. ¡OJO! Use todos los verbos.

poder   preferir   querer   tener   venir

1. Mis amigos y yo _____ a esta biblioteca todos los días para estudiar. Nuestras

   clases son difíciles y _____ que estudiar mucho.

2. —¿Qué (tú) _____ tomar, una Coca-Cola o un café?

   —Yo _____ un café.

3. Si Uds. _____ prisa, deben salir (*leave*) ahora.

4. En una librería, los estudiantes _____ comprar libros, cuadernos y mochilas.

C. El verbo *ir*. Rewrite each sentence, changing the simple present tense to a construction with **ir** + **a** + *infinitive* to tell what the following people are going to do.

MODELO: Estudio mucho. → Voy a estudiar mucho.

1. Roberto lleva traje y corbata.

   _____

2. Busco unas chanclas baratas.

   _____

3. Hablamos por teléfono.

   _____

4. ¿Vienes a casa esta noche?

   _____

D. Cosas de todos los días. Practice talking about the price of different items of clothing, using the written cues. When you hear the corresponding number, form sentences using the words provided in the order given, making any necessary changes. Then listen to the correct answer and repeat it. *Note:* **Cuesta** means *it costs*, **cuestan** means *they cost*.

MODELO: (Ud. ve) **1.** este / pantalones: cuestan $80

(Ud. oye) Uno.

(Ud. dice) Estos pantalones cuestan ochenta dólares.

(Ud. oye y repite) Estos pantalones cuestan ochenta dólares.

2. ese / chaqueta: cuesta $127
3. aquel / botas: cuestan $215
4. este / vestido: cuesta $149
5. aquel / traje: cuesta $578
6. ese / ropa: cuesta $1.064

E. ¿Qué van a llevar? You will hear a series of situations. First, listen to the **Vocabulario útil.** Then listen to each situation and respond aloud with what the person might wear based on the information provided and the vocabulary. Finally, listen to the correct answer and repeat it.

Vocabulario útil

un abrigo de lana	**un traje de baño**
una camiseta de algodón	**un traje y una corbata de seda**
un cinturón	**tenis**

MODELO: (Ud. oye) Los pantalones que llevo son muy grandes.

(Ud. dice) Voy a llevar un cinturón.

(Ud. oye y repite) Voy a llevar un cinturón.

1. ... 2. ... 3. ... 4. ... 5. ...

❖ PUNTOS PERSONALES

A. **Mi estilo personal.** ¿Qué ropa usa Ud. en estos lugares? Mencione los colores y el material o la tela (fabric), cuando sea (whenever it is) posible.

Vocabulario útil

la manga	sleeve
de manga corta	short-sleeved
de manga larga	long-sleeved
zapatos de tacón alto	high heels

1. En la universidad:

_____

2. En una cena (dinner) elegante:

_____

3. En la playa (beach):

_____

B. **Los planes.** Conteste las preguntas de un amigo o una amiga sobre sus planes para esta tarde, esta noche y mañana.

1. ¿Puedes ir de compras esta tarde?

_____

2. ¿Prefieres comer en casa o en la cafetería?

_____

3. ¿Qué quieres hacer esta noche?

_____

4. ¿Qué tienes que estudiar para mañana?

_____

5. ¿A qué hora vienes a la universidad mañana?

_____

C. **¿Qué van a hacer (to do) Uds.?** Imagine that you and your friends are going to the following places. Write about what you're going to do, using the **nosotros** form of the verbs.

Vocabulario útil

descansar   to rest
hacer la tarea   to do homework

MODELO: el café → En el café, vamos a charlar (*chat*).

1. la biblioteca

   _____

2. el laboratorio de lenguas

   _____

3. el restaurante

   _____

4. la fiesta

   _____

5. la casa

   _____

D. **Guided Composition**

Paso 1. Imagine que va de vacaciones a Guatemala y quiere comprar una camisa y sandalias para el viaje (*trip*). Va a un almacén para comprar la ropa. Conteste las siguientes preguntas sobre la experiencia.

1. ¿Qué quiere comprar Ud.? ¿Qué tipo (*type*) de camisa busca? _____

   _____

2. ¿A qué hora llega Ud. al almacén? _____

3. ¿Cómo son todas las camisas: caras o baratas? _____

4. ¿Qué camisa compra? ¿Cuánto cuesta? _____

   _____

5. Y, ¿cómo son las sandalias que venden? _____

6. ¿Regresa a casa contento/a o triste (*sad*) con sus compras?

   _____

Paso 2. Ahora en una hoja aparte (*on a separate sheet of paper*), use sus respuestas del **Paso 1** para escribir un párrafo sobre su experiencia en el almacén. Use las siguientes palabras para conectar mejor sus ideas: **pero, y, por eso,** y **por fin.**

E. Mi diario

Paso 1. Look in your closet and dresser drawers and take an inventory of the articles of clothing you own and the approximate number of each item. What colors are they? Now write the information in your diary.

MODELO: Tengo diez camisetas: cuatro blancas, tres negras, dos rojas y una verde.

Paso 2. Write a description of the clothing you typically wear in each of the following situations. Include the color and fabric, if possible.

MODELO: Cuando estoy en la playa (*beach*), llevo...

1. en una entrevista (*job interview*) _____

_____

2. en casa _____

_____

3. en un *picnic* en el parque _____

_____

F. Intercambios. Escuche las siguientes preguntas y contéstelas por escrito (*in writing*).

1. _____

_____

2. _____

_____

3. _____

_____

4. _____

_____

5. _____

_____

Capítulo

5

En casa

VOCABULARIO — Preparación

Los muebles, los cuartos y otras partes de la casa (Part 1)

A. Identificaciones. Identifique las partes de la casa. Use el artículo definido, según el modelo.

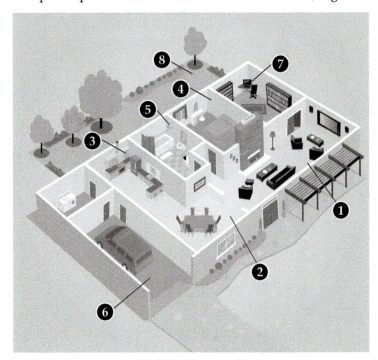

MODELO: **1.** la sala

2. _____   6. _____

3. _____   7. _____

4. _____   8. _____

5. _____

B. Los muebles. Identifique los muebles en la sala y la alcoba. Use el artículo indefinido, según el modelo.

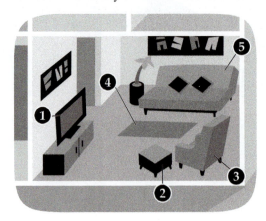

MODELO: **1.**   En la sala hay una televisión.

En la sala hay...

2. _____.

3. _____.

4. _____.

5. _____.

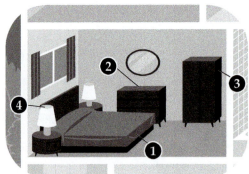

En la alcoba hay...

1. _____.

2. _____.

3. _____.

4. _____.

C. Mi casa. Escuche las descripciones y escriba la parte de la casa o el mueble apropiado para cada una. Luego escuche la respuesta correcta y repítala.

1. _____   **6.** _____

2. _____   **7.** _____

3. _____   **8.** _____

4. _____   **9.** _____

5. _____

D. Juan Carlos busca apartamento. Va a escuchar una conversación entre Juan Carlos y una agente inmobiliaria (*realtor*). Primero, escuche el **Vocabulario útil.** Luego escuche la conversación e (*and*) indique las opciones que corresponden al apartamento que desea Juan Carlos.

Vocabulario útil

cerca de	close to
el dormitorio	**la alcoba**
la ducha	shower
el lavaplatos	dishwasher

1. ☐ sala
2. ☐ tres dormitorios
3. ☐ muy grande
4. ☐ baño con bañera
5. ☐ entre 600 y 700 soles (dinero del Perú)
6. ☐ lavaplatos
7. ☐ piscina en el edificio
8. ☐ garaje

¿Qué día es hoy?

A. La semana de David. Complete las oraciones con los días de la semana apropiados, según la agenda de David.

L	M	MI	J	V	S	D
clase de física	historia del arte	clase de física	historia del arte			fiesta de cumpleaños[b] de papá en casa
portugués	laboratorio de física	portugués		portugués (examen)	12:00 partido[a] de fútbol	
	12:00 a 4:00 trabajo	1:00 dentista		fiesta de Pedro	7:00 cine con Marta	

[a]*game* [b]*birthday*

1. David tiene la clase de física los _____ y los _____, y los

   _____ tiene laboratorio.

2. Tiene la clase de portugués los _____, los _____ y los

   _____. Este _____ tiene examen.

3. Este _____ tiene un partido de fútbol.

4. El _____ hay una fiesta familiar en su casa.

5. No puede olvidar (*forget*) que el _____ tiene una cita (*appointment*) a la 1:00.

6. El _____ no puede comer al mediodía (*noon*) con sus amigos porque tiene que

   trabajar.

B. ¿Qué día es hoy? Complete las oraciones con las palabras apropiadas.

1. Hay dos días en el _____ de semana: _____ y _____.

2. El _____ es el primer (*first*) día de la semana en el calendario hispano.

3. Si hoy es martes, mañana es _____.

4. El Día de Acción de Gracias (*Thanksgiving*) es siempre el cuarto (*fourth*) _____ de noviembre.

5. Si hoy es miércoles, _____ es viernes.

6. No puedo ir de compras _____ sábado porque _____ sábados trabajo.

7. Tengo que estudiar mucho porque la _____ semana tengo tres exámenes.

C. ¿Qué día de la semana prefieren?

❖ **Paso 1.** Ud. va a escuchar a dos amigos hablar de su día favorito de la semana. Antes de escuchar, complete las oraciones con información que es verdadera (*true*) para Ud. usando el nombre de un día de la semana. Si no hace (*you don't do*) una de las actividades, seleccione la opción entre paréntesis.

1. Mi día favorito de la semana es el _____.

2. Trabajo los _____. (☐ Nunca trabajo.)

3. Practico un deporte (*sport*) los _____. (☐ Nunca practico deportes.)

4. Salgo (*I go out*) con mis amigos los _____. (☐ Nunca salgo con mis amigos.)

5. Para mí, el fin de semana comienza (*begins*) el _____.

Paso 2. Ahora va a oír (*hear*) preguntas sobre las oraciones del **Paso 1.** Contéstelas (*Answer them*) según sus respuestas escritas (*written*). Luego va a oír una respuesta posible. Repítala.

1. ...   2. ...   3. ...   4. ...   5. ...

Paso 3. Miguel René y Karina hablan de su día favorito de la semana. Primero, escuche el **Vocabulario útil** y lea las siguientes oraciones. Después de escuchar la entrevista, indique el nombre apropiado (**Miguel René** o **Karina**) por escrito (*in writing*) para cada oración. Luego escuche la respuesta correcta y repítala.

Vocabulario útil

el descanso	rest
el súper	supermarket
aprovecho	I take advantage
hago	I do
los trabajos de la escuela	homework
comenzar	to begin
descansar	to rest

1. **Miguel René / Karina** prefiere los viernes.
2. **Miguel René / Karina** prefiere el domingo.
3. **Miguel René / Karina** trabaja en un restaurante.
4. A **Miguel René / Karina** le gusta ir al cine los domingos.
5. **Miguel René / Karina** hace (*does*) trabajos de la escuela los domingos.

¿Cuándo? Las preposiciones (Part 1)

 A. ¿Qué hace Mariana hoy? Mariana va a hablar de su horario (*schedule*) de hoy. Mientras escucha a Mariana, indique la respuesta con un círculo. Luego escuche la respuesta correcta y repítala.

1. Debe llamar (*call*) a su mamá **antes de / durante / después de** la clase de historia.
2. **Antes de / Durante / Después de** la clase de historia, va a ir a la oficina del profesor de arte.
3. Tiene que llamar a Roberto **antes de / durante / después de** la reunión (*meeting*) con Camila.
4. Tiene ganas de ir al gimnasio **antes de / durante / después de** regresar a casa.

B. ¿Antes o después? ¿Cuándo hace Ud. (*do you do*) estas cosas? Haga oraciones lógicas, según el modelo.

MODELO: estudiar las lecciones / tomar el examen →
Estudio las lecciones antes de tomar el examen.

1. tener sueño / descansar

_____

2. regresar a casa / asistir a clases

_____

3. tener ganas de comer / practicar un deporte (*sport*)

_____

4. entrar en una fiesta / bailar

_____

5. lavar (*to wash*) los platos / comer

_____

PRONUNCIACIÓN   *b* and *v*

Spanish **b** and **v** are pronounced exactly the same way.

- At the beginning of a phrase, or after **m** or **n**, the letters **b** and **v** are pronounced like the English *b*, as a stop. That is, no air is allowed to escape through the lips. This sound is represented as [b].
- In all other positions, **b** and **v** are fricatives. That is, they are pronounced by allowing some air to escape through the lips. This sound is represented as [β]. There is no equivalent for this sound in English.

A. Repeticiones. Repita las siguientes palabras y frases. Fíjese en (*Pay attention to*) el sonido (*sound*) indicado.

1.	[b]	bueno	viejo	barato	baño	hombre
2.	[β]	llevar	libro	pobre	abrigo	universidad
3.	[b/β]	bueno / es bueno	bien / muy bien			
		visita / él visita	busca / Ud. busca			
		en Venezuela / de Venezuela	vamos / allí vamos			
4.	[b/β]	beber	bebida	vivir	biblioteca	vivido

B. Pronunciación. Lea las siguientes palabras y frases en voz alta. Escuche la pronunciación correcta y repítala. Luego indique por escrito los ejemplos del sonido (*sound*) [b] y los del sonido [β].

MODELO: (Ud. oye)   Uno.

            (Ud. dice)   bueno

    (Ud. oye y repite)   bueno

         (Ud. escoge)   (b)   [β]

1.	[b]	[β]	vestido	**6.**	[b]	[β]	¿verdad?	**11.**	[b]	[β]	buenos días
2.	[b]	[β]	el vestido	**7.**	[b]	[β]	nueve	**12.**	[b]	[β]	Víctor
3.	[b]	[β]	un vestido	**8.**	[b]	[β]	universidad	**13.**	[b]	[β]	bailas
4.	[b]	[β]	caverna	**9.**	[b]	[β]	también	**14.**	[b]	[β]	tú bailas
5.	[b]	[β]	hombre	**10.**	[b]	[β]	bien	**15.**	[b]	[β]	muy bien

GRAMÁTICA

12. Expressing Actions • *Hacer, oír, poner, salir, traer, ver*

A. Verbos. Complete la tabla con los verbos que faltan (*are missing*).

INFINITIVO	YO	TÚ	UD., ÉL, ELLA	NOSOTROS/AS	UDS., ELLOS, ELLAS
hacer		haces		hacemos	
oír			oye	oímos	
poner		pones	pone		
salir		sales			salen
traer			trae	traemos	
ver	ves				

B. Las actividades de Roberto. Complete las oraciones con la forma apropiada de los siguientes verbos: **hacer, oír, poner, salir, traer, ver.**

1. Los domingos (yo) _____ mi programa favorito de televisión.

2. Pablo y yo _____ con los amigos los fines de semana.

3. (Yo) _____ la televisión cuando regreso a casa.

4. (Yo) Siempre _____ el libro de texto a la clase de español.

5. A veces, mis compañeros de clase y yo no _____ bien a nuestra profesora de

   historia porque ella habla en voz baja (*a low voice*).

6. Antes del examen de español, (yo) _____ los ejercicios del cuaderno.

C. ¡Qué horror de compañera! Va a escuchar un comentario de Rocío sobre Claudia, su compañera de casa. Primero, escuche el **Vocabulario útil.** Después de escuchar, empareje las ideas de las dos columnas. Luego escuche la respuesta correcta y repítala.

Vocabulario útil

por todas partes	all over the place
a todo volumen	really loud
el novio	boyfriend

A	B
1. _____ Claudia trae...	**a.** a amigos a casa con mucha frecuencia.
2. _____ Rocío ve...	**b.** cuando oye la música de Claudia.
3. _____ Rocío no puede estudiar...	**c.** la ropa de Claudia por todas partes.
4. _____ Claudia pone...	**d.** cuando Rocío está con su novio.
5. _____ Rocío trae...	**e.** la tele a todo volumen cuando Rocío estudia.
6. _____ Claudia hace...	**f.** a su novio a casa.
7. _____ Claudia no sale de casa...	**g.** muchas fiestas en casa.

D. Soy buen compañero. Diga (*Say*) lo que Ud. hace como buen compañero (buena compañera) de casa, según el modelo. Luego escuche la respuesta correcta y repítala.

MODELO: (Ud. oye) Uno.

           (Ud. ve) **1.** poner / mi ropa en el armario

         (Ud. dice) Pongo mi ropa en el armario.

    (Ud. oye y repite) Pongo mi ropa en el armario.

2. no hacer / muchas fiestas en casa
3. no salir / sin hacer la cama
4. no poner / la tele a las once de la noche
5. no traer / a amigos a casa con frecuencia
6. no oír / música hasta muy tarde
7. no ver la televisión / cuando mis compañeros estudian

13. Expressing Actions • Present Tense of Stem-Changing Verbs (Part 2)

¿Recuerda Ud.?					
Verbos que cambian el radical. Complete la tabla con las formas que faltan (*are missing*).					
INFINITIVO	YO	TÚ	UD., ÉL, ELLA	NOSOTROS/AS	UDS., ELLOS, ELLAS
querer				*queremos*	
preferir		*prefieres*			
poder			*puede*		

A. Verbos. Cambie los verbos del singular al plural o viceversa, según los modelos.

> MODELOS: almuerzo →   almorzamos
> entendemos → entiendo

1. dormimos _____
2. vuelvo _____
3. pensamos _____
4. juego _____
5. empezamos _____
6. pido _____

B. Preferencias. ¿Qué prefieren hacer Ud. y sus amigos? Complete las oraciones con la forma apropiada de los verbos entre paréntesis.

1. **(pensar)** Isabel y Fernando _____ almorzar en casa, pero Pilar y yo

   _____ salir. ¿Qué _____ hacer tú?

2. **(volver)** Nosotras _____ en tren con Sergio, pero Felipe _____ en

   coche con Lola. ¿Cómo _____ Uds.?

3. **(pedir)** Por lo general, Tomás _____ café. Rita y Carmen _____

   Coca-Cola. Pepe y yo _____ agua mineral.

C. Un día típico de Bernardo. Describa la rutina de Bernardo con oraciones completas, según el modelo.

> MODELO: comer / casa / 6:00 A.M. → Come en casa a las seis de la mañana.

1. salir / casa / 7:15

   _____

2. su primera clase / empezar / 8:00

   _____

3. si Bernardo no / entender la lección, / hacer muchas preguntas

_____

4. con frecuencia / almorzar / cafetería

_____

5. a veces / pedir una hamburguesa y un refresco

_____

6. lunes y miércoles / jugar al tenis / con un amigo

_____

7. su madre / servir la cena (*dinner*) / 6:00

_____

8. por la noche, Bernardo / hacer la tarea / y / dormir siete horas

_____

D. **Acciones frecuentes en la vida (*life*) de Lorena.** Lorena va a hablar de las cosas que a ella le gusta hacer con frecuencia. Después de escuchar cada oración de Lorena, complete la oración correspondiente con la tercera persona singular del verbo que está en el infinitivo en la oración que oye. Luego escuche la respuesta correcta y repítala.

MODELO: (Ud. oye) Me gusta dormir la siesta con frecuencia.

(Ud. escribe) Lorena <u>duerme</u> la siesta con frecuencia.

(Ud. oye y repite) Lorena duerme la siesta con frecuencia.

1. Nunca _____ la puerta cuando estudia.

2. De lunes a viernes, _____ en la universidad.

3. A veces no _____ la clase de matemáticas.

4. Para los exámenes de matemáticas, _____ la ayuda (*help*) de su amiga Noemí.

5. Los jueves, después de ir al gimnasio, _____ a casa.

6. Los fines de semana, _____ al fútbol con unas compañeras de la universidad.

E. **Una entrevista con los Sres. Ruiz.** Hágales (*Ask*) preguntas a los Sres. Ruiz sobre lo que hacen y lo que no hacen. Repita las preguntas y las respuestas, según el modelo.

MODELO: (Ud. oye) jugar al tenis

(Ud. dice) ¿Juegan Uds. al tenis?

(Ud. oye y repite) ¿Juegan Uds. al tenis?

(Ud. oye y repite) No, no jugamos al tenis.

1. ...   **2.** ...   **3.** ...   **4.** ...   **5.** ...   **6.** ...

14. Expressing *-self/-selves* • Reflexive Pronouns (Part 1)

A. Pronombres. Escriba el pronombre reflexivo apropiado.

1. Juan _____ levanta

2. _____ levantamos

3. ellos _____ levantan

4. Ud. _____ levanta

5. _____ levantas

6. _____ levanto

7. mi hermana _____ levanta

8. Uds. _____ levantan

B. Oraciones incompletas. Complete las oraciones con la forma apropiada del pronombre reflexivo.

1. Yo _____ llamo Juan y mi hermana _____ llama Inés.

2. Nuestros padres _____ llaman Carlos y Luisa.

3. ¿Por qué _____ pones esa blusa? Está sucia (*dirty*).

4. ¿Piensan Uds. despertar_____ tarde el sábado?

5. Después de levantarnos, _____ bañamos y _____ vestimos.

6. ¿Dónde _____ diviertes más, en el teatro o en el cine?

C. La rutina de Paloma

Paso 1. Paloma va a hablar de su rutina diaria. Primero, escuche el **Vocabulario útil.** Luego escuche y ordene las acciones en la secuencia que da (*gives*) Paloma, del 1 al 7. Después de escuchar, cambie el infinitivo por escrito (*in writing*) a la tercera persona singular.

Vocabulario útil

más relajada   more relaxed

Paloma...

a. _____ vestirse   _____

b. _____ cepillarse los dientes   _____

c. _____ levantarse inmediatamente   _____

d. _____ despertarse a las 8   _____

e. ___1___ bañarse por la noche   ___se baña___

f. _____ peinarse   _____

g. _____ acostarse   _____

Nota: Verifique sus respuestas del **Paso 1** en el Apéndice antes de empezar el **Paso 2.**

Paso 2. Ahora describa la rutina diaria de Paloma, según el orden (*order*) que dio (*you gave*) en sus respuestas del **Paso 1** y el modelo. Luego escuche la respuesta correcta y repítala. ¡**OJO!** Recuerde (*Remember*) que en español se dice el sujeto con menos (*less*) frecuencia que (*than*) en inglés.

MODELO: (Ud. oye) Uno.

         (Ud. ve) **e.** __1__ bañarse por la noche <u>se baña</u>

       (Ud. dice) Se baña por la noche.

    (Ud. oye y repite) Se baña por la noche.

2. ... **3.** ... **4.** ... **5.** ... **6.** ... **7.** ...

D. Ud. y otra persona. Cambie el sujeto **yo** a **nosotros**. Luego haga todos los cambios necesarios. ¡**OJO!** En algunas oraciones hay más de un verbo.

MODELO: Me levanto a las seis. → Nos levantamos a las seis.

1. Me despierto temprano.

_____

2. Me visto después de ducharme.

_____

3. Nunca me siento para tomar el desayuno (*breakfast*).

_____

4. En la universidad, asisto a clases y me divierto.

_____

5. Después de volver a casa, hago la tarea.

_____

6. A las doce tengo sueño, me cepillo los dientes y me acuesto.

_____

7. Me duermo a las doce y media.

_____

E. **El horario de Daniel y Carlos.** Escriba dos oraciones completas para cada dibujo con los verbos a continuación. Indique también dónde ocurren las acciones. **¡OJO!** No se usan todos los verbos.

1. Daniel — Carlos

2. Carlos — Daniel

3. Daniel

4. Daniel — Carlos

Verbos

afeitarse	divertirse	levantarse	vestirse
cepillarse	dormir	quitarse	
despertarse	ducharse	sentarse	

Vocabulario útil

en un café
en el sofá

1.

_____

_____

2.

_____

_____

3.

_____

_____

4.

_____

_____

F. La rutina de los compañeros de casa

Paso 1. Diego es el nuevo compañero de casa de Antonio y Juan. En la conversación que Ud. va a escuchar, Diego y Antonio hablan de la rutina de la casa. Primero, escuche el **Vocabulario útil.** Entonces (*Then*), lea la lista de acciones que son parte de la rutina de los compañeros. Luego, mientras (*while*) escucha la conversación, indique cuál de los compañeros tiene esa rutina: Antonio **(A)**, Diego **(D)** o Juan **(J)**. **¡OJO!** En unos casos hay más de una respuesta.

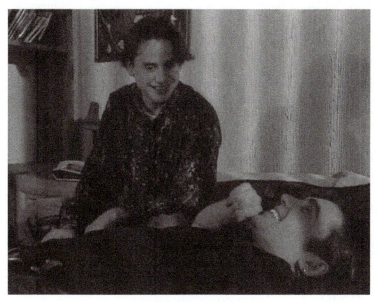

Diego y Antonio

Vocabulario útil

dime	tell me
almorzar	to eat lunch
la novia	girlfriend
entonces	then, next, therefore

	A	D	J
1. Se levanta a las seis y media.	☐	☐	☐
2. Se levanta a las siete.	☐	☐	☐
3. Se levanta a las siete y media.	☐	☐	☐
4. Se afeita.	☐	☐	☐
5. Almuerza en casa los lunes, miércoles y viernes.	☐	☐	☐
6. No almuerza en casa los martes y jueves.	☐	☐	☐
7. No vuelve a casa para almorzar.	☐	☐	☐

(Continúa.)

Paso 2. Ahora Ud. va a participar en una conversación similar entre Marcos y Alfonso. Primero, complete la conversación con palabras y frases de la lista a continuación. Verifique sus respuestas en el Apéndice antes de escuchar la conversación. Luego escuche lo que dice Marcos y conteste en voz alta con lo que dice Alfonso.

especial　　　　gracias　　　　por la tarde　　　　quién

MARCOS:　Bienvenido a nuestro apartamento, Alfonso.

ALFONSO:　_____,[1] Marcos.

MARCOS:　¿Tienes alguna pregunta acerca del (*about the*) horario (*schedule*)?

ALFONSO:　Pues, sí. ¿_____[2] prepara la comida (*food*) esta noche?

MARCOS:　Bueno, Lucas prepara la comida esta noche, yo cocino (*cook*) el jueves y tú vas a cocinar

　　　　el viernes.

ALFONSO:　Perfecto. No tengo clases el viernes _____,[3] y puedo preparar una cena

　　　　(*dinner*) _____.[4]

MARCOS:　¡Magnífico!

Paso 3. Ahora Ud. va a contestar algunas preguntas sobre su rutina. Lea y conteste las preguntas. Luego escuche una respuesta posible y repítala.

1. ¿A qué hora se levanta Ud.?

_____

2. ¿Vuelve a casa para almorzar?

_____

3. ¿Qué días almuerza en la cafetería?

_____

Un poco de todo

A. El próximo sábado. Complete las oraciones con la forma correcta del verbo para describir las actividades de Juan Carlos el próximo sábado.

Los sábados _____[1] a las nueve de la mañana, pero el sábado de la próxima
　　　　　　　(*yo:* levantarse)

semana _____[2] que _____[3] más temprano porque _____[4]
　　　　　(tener)　　　　　　　　(despertarse)　　　　　　　　　　　　　　　(querer)

ir a _____[5] al tenis con mi amigo Daniel. Casi siempre _____[6]
　　　(jugar)　　　　　　　　　　　　　　　　　　　　　　　　(*nosotros:* empezar)

a las nueve y media; si _____[7] el despertador[a] a las ocho y media y _____[8]
　　　　　　　　　　　(*yo:* poner)　　　　　　　　　　　　　　　　　　　　　　　(salir)

de casa a las nueve, _____[9] llegar a tiempo. Daniel y yo _____[10]
　　　　　　　　　　(poder)　　　　　　　　　　　　　　　　　　　(almorzar)

_____
[a]*alarm clock*

después de jugar al tenis. Si Daniel _____¹¹ el partido,^b _____¹²
  (perder)   (*él:* tener)

que pagar la cuenta;^c si yo _____¹³ el partido, yo _____¹⁴ que pagar.
                                    (perder)   (tener)

A las dos, _____¹⁵ a casa.
          (*yo:* volver)

_____

^b*match, game* ^c*bill*

B. *Listening Passage:* **Una casa hispana**

❖ **Antes de escuchar.** You are going to hear a passage about a house in a Hispanic country. Complete the sentences with information about your house or apartment. (If you live in a dorm, imagine that you are currently living in the house or apartment that you lived in with your family.) When a choice is given, circle the choice that is true for you.

Vocabulario útil

pareja   partner

1. Mi **casa / apartamento** tiene _____ alcoba(s) y _____ baño(s).

2. **Tiene / No tiene** sala.

3. **Tiene / No tiene** comedor.

4. Vivo allí con (mi) _____. (Vivo sol**o/a**).

5. El lugar en donde vivo **es / no es** típico de esta región o ciudad.

6. En la región donde vivo, **es necesario / no es necesario** tener calefacción (*heating*) en el invierno (*winter*).

7. Algo que (*Something that*) me gusta mucho de mi **casa / apartamento** es _____
   _____.

8. Algo que no me gusta es _____.

Listening Passage. Now you will hear a passage about Alma's house in El Salvador. First, listen to the **Vocabulario útil** and read the true/false statements in **Después de escuchar** to know what information to listen for. Then listen to the passage.

Vocabulario útil

las afueras	outskirts
bastante	rather
las recámaras	**las alcobas**
la sala de estar	**la sala**
juntos	together
los árboles	trees
el clima	climate
la calefacción	heating

(Continúa.)

Después de escuchar. Read the following true/false statements. Circle **C (cierto)** if the statement is true or **F (falso)** if it is false. If the information is not given in the passage, circle **ND (no lo dice)**. Correct the statements that are false.

1. C F ND En El Salvador, todos los edificios son de estilo colonial.

   _____

2. C F ND Alma vive en el centro de San Salvador.

   _____

3. C F ND Su casa es pequeña.

   _____

4. C F ND Alma y su familia almuerzan en el comedor.

   _____

5. C F ND La casa de Alma no tiene patio.

   _____

C. Un día típico para Miguel René. Ud. va a escuchar a un estudiante, Miguel René, hablar de su rutina normal. Primero, lea las siguientes frases para saber la información que Ud. necesita captar (*to get*) de la narración. Mientras escucha la narración, escriba información adicional que da (*gives*) Miguel René. Luego escriba oraciones completas con las frases.

1. levantarse a las _____

   _____

2. bañarse por la mañana/tarde/noche

   _____

3. ir a la universidad y tener clases

   _____

4. almorzar con _____

   _____

5. ir al trabajo

   _____

6. salir del trabajo a las _____

   _____

7. volver a casa antes/después de ir al gimnasio

   _____

CULTURA

A. Mapa. Identifique los países y las capitales en el siguiente mapa.

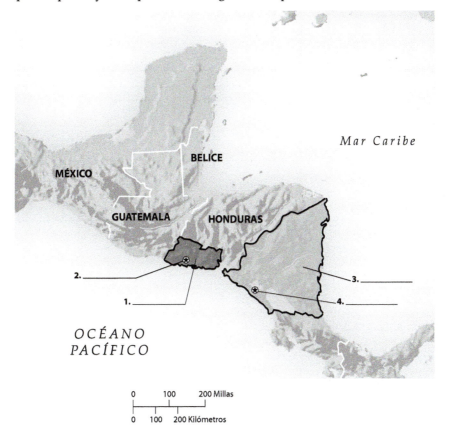

B. Comprensión. Complete las siguientes oraciones con palabras de la lista. Esta actividad se basa en información de las lecturas **Algo sobre...** (p. 143, 144 y 152) y **Lectura cultural** (p. 158) del libro de texto o del eBook.

bajareque   Centroamérica   costa   jardín   privado   volcanes

1. El lago de Nicaragua (o Cocibolca) es el lago más grande (*biggest*) de _____.

2. En Centroamérica hay casas de _____, un tipo de construcción que usa palos (*sticks*), barro (*mud*) y caña (*sugarcane*).

3. Casi todos (*almost all*) los países centroamericanos tienen _____ en los océanos Atlántico y Pacífico. El Salvador solo la tiene en el Pacífico.

4. Las casas de la época colonial en Nicaragua tienen techos de tejas (*tiled roofs*), un _____ en medio de la casa y un patio.

5. Los hispanos son muy hospitalarios (*hospitable*), pero también son _____ con sus huéspedes (*guests*).

6. Los _____ son un símbolo importante en el escudo (*shield*) de las banderas (*flags*) de Nicaragua y El Salvador.

PÓNGASE A PRUEBA

A. *Hacer, oír, poner, salir, traer, ver.* Complete la tabla.

INFINITIVO	yo	tú	nosotros/as	Uds., ellos/as
hacer			*hacemos*	
traer				*traen*
oír		*oyes*		
poner				
ver				
salir				

B. Present Tense of Stem-Changing Verbs

1. Escriba el cambio apropiado.

   a. empezar, perder e → _____

   b. dormir, almorzar o → _____

   c. pedir, servir e → _____

2. ¿Con qué sujetos no cambia la forma del verbo? _____ y _____

3. Complete las oraciones con los verbos y preposiciones entre paréntesis. **¡OJO!** No es necesario conjugar todos los verbos.

   a. (pensar, servir) ¿Qué _____ tú _____ en la fiesta?

   b. (empezar, a) Ahora yo _____ _____ entender.

   c. (volver, a) ¿Uds. van a _____ _____ entrar?

   4. (pedir) Voy a _____ otra Coca-Cola.

C. Reflexive Pronouns

1. Escriba el pronombre reflexivo apropiado.

   a. yo _____ levanto

   b. tú _____ acuestas

   c. él _____ despierta

   d. nosotros _____ divertimos

   e. Uds. _____ bañan

2. Cambie el plural por el singular.

   a. Nos acostamos tarde.

   _____

   b. ¿Cuándo se sientan a comer?

   (tú) _____

   c. Nos vestimos en cinco minutos.

   _____

PRUEBA CORTA

A. Actividades. Complete las oraciones con la forma apropiada de los verbos de la lista. Use cada verbo solo una vez (*once*). **¡OJO!** Algunos verbos se quedan (*remain*) en el infinitivo pero el pronombre reflexivo cambia.

Verbos: divertirse, dormirse, hacer, levantarse, oír, ponerse, salir, sentarse

1. Algunos (*Some*) estudiantes _____ en clase cuando están muy cansados

   (*tired*).

2. Prefiero _____ cerca del escritorio del profesor porque no

   _____ bien.

3. Yo _____ cuando salgo a bailar con mis amigos.

4. Si quieres llegar a tiempo, debes _____ temprano, como (*like*) a las seis

   de la mañana.

5. Para ir a un concierto al aire libre (*open-air*), ella _____ un suéter y *jeans*.

6. Siempre (tú) _____ muchas preguntas en clase, ¿verdad?

7. Los viernes por la noche mis amigos y yo _____ a comer en un

   restaurante y después vamos al cine.

❖ **B. Listas.** Complete las siguientes listas.

1. Escriba tres de las actividades que Ud. realiza (*that you do*) en la alcoba por la mañana:

   _____, _____ y _____

2. Escriba tres de las actividades que Ud. realiza en el baño después de despertarse:

   _____, _____ y _____

3. Escriba el nombre de tres de los muebles de su sala:

   _____, _____ y _____

(Continúa.)

4. Escriba el nombre de tres cosas o muebles que Ud. piensa comprar para su casa:

_____, _____ y _____

5. Escriba en qué cuartos de su casa realiza Ud. las siguientes actividades. Use oraciones completas.

almorzar: _____

dormir: _____

estudiar: _____

C. Definiciones. Va a escuchar unas definiciones. Primero, escuche el **Vocabulario útil.** Luego indique la palabra que se define en cada oración.

Vocabulario útil

el desayuno	breakfast
las comidas	meals

1. _____   **a.** la lámpara   **b.** el comedor   **c.** la cocina

2. _____   **a.** la sala   **b.** el baño   **c.** la alcoba

3. _____   **a.** el sofá   **b.** el armario   **c.** el lavabo

4. _____   **a.** el patio   **b.** el almacén   **c.** el garaje

5. _____   **a.** la cocina   **b.** el comedor   **c.** la sala

6. _____   **a.** la mesita   **b.** el plato   **c.** el sillón

7. _____   **a.** la cómoda   **b.** el estante   **c.** el jardín

D. Su rutina diaria. Hable de su rutina diaria, usando las palabras y frases dadas (*given*), según el modelo. Use yo como sujeto en todas las oraciones. Luego escuche la respuesta correcta y repítala.

> MODELO: (Ud. ve)   despertarse y levantarse
> (Ud. oye)   7:00 A.M.
> (Ud. dice)   Me despierto y me levanto a las siete de la mañana.
> (Ud. oye y repite)   Me despierto y me levanto a las siete de la mañana.

1. ducharse, vestirse y peinarse
2. hacer el desayuno (*breakfast*) y sentarse a comer
3. hacer la cama (*to make the bed*) y salir de casa
4. ir al gimnasio
5. hacer ejercicio
6. volver a casa y poner la tele
7. empezar a preparar la comida
8. por fin, acostarse / y dormirse inmediatamente

E. Se vende casa (*House for sale*). Va a escuchar un anuncio (*advertisement*) sobre una casa que se vende. Primero, escuche el **Vocabulario útil**. Luego escuche el anuncio y complete la tabla.

Vocabulario útil

mide	measures
los metros	meters
por	by (*as in 3 meters by 3 meters*)
estacionar	to park
las escuelas	schools
enfrente de	across from
el vecindario	neighborhood
la calle	Street

1.	el número de alcobas	
2.	el número de baños	
3.	¿Cuántos metros mide la sala?	
4.	Esta casa está...	cerca de _____ y enfrente de _____.
5.	la dirección (*address*) de la casa	calle _____ número _____

❖ PUNTOS PERSONALES

A. Su alcoba. Describa su alcoba. Mencione los muebles que hay y el color de las paredes y de la alfombra (si la hay [*if there is one*]). Luego use tres adjetivos para describir la alcoba en general.

_____

_____

_____

_____

B. Preguntas personales. Conteste con oraciones completas.

1. ¿Ve Ud. películas en casa o prefiere ir al cine?

_____

2. En clase, ¿hace Ud. muchas preguntas o prefiere estar callado/a (*quiet*)?

_____

3. ¿Qué cosas trae Ud. a clase en su mochila?

_____

(Continúa.)

4. ¿A qué hora almuerza Ud., generalmente?

_____

5. ¿Cuántas horas duerme Ud. los fines de semana?

_____

6. ¿Piensa Ud. estudiar otras lenguas extranjeras? ¿Cuáles?

_____

7. ¿Estudia Ud. por la noche? ¿A qué hora empieza a estudiar?

_____

8. ¿Pierde Ud. sus llaves con frecuencia?

_____

C. **Guided Composition.** Escriba sobre su día típico este semestre: ¿Qué hace y cuándo lo hace (_do you do it_)?

Paso 1. Antes de escribir, lea la lista de verbos y tache (_cross out_) los que no aplican a su día típico. Luego, para organizar los verbos que va a usar, indique **mañana (M), tarde (T)** o **noche (N)** al lado del (_next to_) infinitivo correspondiente. Ponga en secuencia cronológica los verbos de cada grupo.

acostarse	hacer	quitarse
afeitarse	ir	salir
almorzar	leer	sentarse a (comer, ...)
asistir	levantarse	tomar el desayuno (_breakfast_)
bañarse/ducharse	llamar por teléfono (a)	trabajar
despertarse	mirar	vestirse
dormirse	ponerse	volver
empezar a (estudiar, ...)		

POR LA MAÑANA   POR LA TARDE   POR LA NOCHE

_____   _____   _____

_____   _____   _____

_____   _____   _____

_____   _____   _____

_____   _____   _____

Paso 2. Ahora, en una hoja aparte (_on a separate sheet of paper_), escriba una composición de tres párrafos sobre su rutina diaria. Puede usar expresiones del **Vocabulario útil** y otras para describir cuándo hace estas actividades y para organizar la composición. Empiece cada párrafo con una de estas frases: **Por la mañana, Por la tarde,** y **Por la noche.**

Vocabulario útil

antes de	durante	primero, luego
con frecuencia, a veces	hasta	siempre, todos los días
después de	nunca	

D. Entrevista. Va a escuchar unas preguntas. Para cada pregunta, indique con **siempre**, **a veces** o nunca la frecuencia con que hace la actividad. Luego conteste cada pregunta por escrito con oraciones completas.

	SIEMPRE	A VECES	NUNCA
1.	☐	☐	☐
2.	☐	☐	☐
3.	☐	☐	☐
4.	☐	☐	☐
5.	☐	☐	☐
6.	☐	☐	☐

E. Mi diario. In your diary, write a description of your residence or that of your family. Be sure to include the following information.

- type of residence (house, apartment, dorm room, etc.) and size
- name of each room
- furniture in your bedroom and living room
- color of the walls and rug (if any)
- if there's a garage or yard, what it is like
- your favorite place in the residence and why

F. Intercambios. Escuche las siguientes preguntas y contéstelas por escrito (*answer them in writing*).

1.

_____

_____

_____

2.

_____

_____

_____

3.

_____

_____

_____

VOCABULARIO Preparación

 ## ¿Qué tiempo hace hoy?

A. ¿Qué tiempo hace? Ud. va a escuchar unas oraciones sobre los siguientes dibujos. Primero, mire los dibujos y escuche el **Vocabulario útil.** Luego escuche las oraciones. Dé (*Give*) el número del dibujo que corresponde a cada oración y repita la oración. Finalmente, escuche la respuesta (*answer*) correcta y repítala.

Vocabulario útil

pasear en bicicleta   to ride a bike

1.

MODELO: (Ud. oye) Hace mucho sol.

(Ud. ve) **5.**

(Ud. dice) Número 5: Hace mucho sol.

(Ud. oye y repite) Número 5: Hace mucho sol.

2.

3.

4.

5.

6.

7.

B. **Las personas y el tiempo.** Indique qué tiempo hace, según la descripción de cada persona.

1. Marta lleva impermeable y botas. _____

2. Joselito tiene frío y lleva abrigo, dos suéteres y botas. _____

3. Carmen tiene calor y lleva traje de baño. _____

4. Samuel lleva un suéter de lana, pero no lleva abrigo. _____

5. Todos llevan camiseta y pantalones y están en el parque. _____

6. Nadie (*No one*) hace ejercicio en el centro hoy. El aire está mal. _____
   _____

C. **¿Qué tiempo hace en estas ciudades?** Describa el clima en cada ciudad.

1. San José, Costa Rica

_____

2. la Ciudad de Panamá, Panamá

_____

3. Lima, Perú

_____

4. Londres (*London*), Reino Unido (*United Kingdom*)

_____

5. Chicago

_____

6. Ushuaia, Argentina

_____

7. la Ciudad de México, México

_____

Los meses y las estaciones del año

A. Los meses y las estaciones en el hemisferio norte. Complete las oraciones con las palabras apropiadas para hablar de los meses, las estaciones y el tiempo.

1. Los tres meses del verano son _____ , _____ y

_____ .

2. Diciembre es el primer mes de la estación de _____ .

3. Septiembre, octubre y noviembre son los tres meses del _____ .

4. En la primavera hace buen tiempo, pero también _____ mucho.

5. El _____ (*date*) se celebra el Día de la Independencia de los Estados Unidos.

6. Por lo general, _____ mucho en las montañas durante el invierno.

7. En el Canadá y los Estados Unidos, el Día de los Inocentes (*April Fools' Day*) es el

_____ (*date*).

8. Después de diciembre viene el mes de _____ , y después de abril viene

_____ .

9. La fecha del Día de los Enamorados (Día de San Valentín) es el _____ .

B. Fechas. Exprese las siguientes fechas en español, según el modelo. **¡OJO!** En español, la fecha se escribe (*is written*) y se dice (*is said*) con el día primero, después el mes y, al final, el año.

MODELO: 16/3/1982 → el dieciséis de marzo de mil novecientos ochenta y dos

1. 14/6/1925 _____

_____

2. 15/9/1566 _____

_____

3. 7/12/2015 _____

_____

4. 1/1/1777 _____

_____

5. 28/8/1994 _____

_____

C. ¿Cuál es la fecha? Una estudiante de intercambio quiere saber algunas (*some*) fechas. Primero, escuche el **Vocabulario útil,** luego escuche las preguntas de la estudiante y conteste con las fechas que se dan (*are provided*). **¡OJO!** Las fechas están en el orden que se usa en español: día, mes y año.

Vocabulario útil

el aniversario de bodas	wedding anniversary
el nacimiento	birth

MODELO:	(Ud. oye)	¿Cuál es la fecha de nacimiento de Nicolás? ¿Es el cuatro de mayo?
	(Ud. ve)	5/4/1998
	(Ud. dice)	No, es el cinco de abril de mil novecientos noventa y ocho.
	(Ud. oye y repite)	No, es el cinco de abril de mil novecientos noventa y ocho.

1. 22/7/2001
2. 30/4/1986
3. 11/2/1899
4. 4/7/1776
5. 15/9/1821

D. Estaciones favoritas

Paso 1. En esta conversación, cuatro amigos —Rubén, Tané, Miguel René y Karina— hablan de su estación favorita. Primero, escuche el **Vocabulario útil** y lea las siguientes oraciones, que están en el orden en que aparece (*appears*) la información en la conversación. Luego escuche la conversación y complete las oraciones con la información que falta (*is missing*).

Vocabulario útil

caluroso/a	warm-blooded
las flores	flowers
la lluvia	rain
marrón	(de) color café

Tané y Miguel René

Karina y Rubén

1. A Tané le gusta _____ porque _____. ¡Ella es puro trópico!

2. Miguel René prefiere _____ porque todo es _____, hay flores y no _____ mucho.

3. Karina prefiere _____ por las vacaciones.

4. A Rubén le gusta más _____, cuando las hojas (*leaves*) están _____ y se caen (*they fall*), y _____ es más melancólico.

Nota: Verifique sus respuestas del **Paso 1** en el Apéndice antes de empezar el **Paso 2.**

Paso 2. Ahora va a escuchar algunas (*some*) preguntas sobre la conversación. Conteste con la información del **Paso 1.** Luego escuche la respuesta correcta y repítala. Siga el modelo.

MODELO: (Ud. oye) **1.** ¿Por qué le gusta el verano a Tané?

(Ud. ve) **1.** A Tané le gusta *el verano* porque *no hay frío.* ¡Ella es puro trópico!

(Ud. dice) A Tané le gusta el verano porque no hay frío.

(Ud. oye y repite) A Tané le gusta el verano porque no hay frío.

2. ... **3.** ... **4.** ... **5.** ...

¿Dónde está? Las preposiciones (Part 2)

A. La clase de la profesora Ureña. Complete las oraciones con las preposiciones apropiadas para indicar dónde están las personas y cosas. **¡OJO!** Use las preposiciones solo una vez. Cambie la palabra **de** a **del** si es necesario.

a la derecha de	debajo de	encima de
a la izquierda de	delante de	entre
cerca de	detrás de	

1. La profesora está _____ los estudiantes.

2. Los papeles y el libro de texto de la profesora están _____ su escritorio.

3. La mochila de Antonia está _____ ella. (Continúa.)

4. Pámela se sienta muy _____ escritorio de la profesora.

5. El cuaderno de Alberto está _____ su lápiz.

6. El pizarrón blanco está _____ Sergio y Alberto.

7. Antonia se sienta _____ Sergio.

8. En el escritorio de la profesora, los papeles están _____ el bolígrafo y el libro de texto.

 B. **¿Dónde está?** Ud. va a oír algunas (*some*) descripciones. Primero, escuche el **Vocabulario útil.** Luego escuche las descripciones y diga (*say*) el nombre del país que se describe. Escuche la respuesta correcta y repítala.

Vocabulario útil

la costa   coast

MODELO: (Ud. oye) Este país está en la costa, al oeste de la Argentina.
              (Ud. dice) Es Chile.
     (Ud. oye y repite) Es Chile.

1. ... 2. ... 3. ... 4. ... 5. ...

C. ¿Dónde está el cuaderno con los exámenes?

Paso 1. Manolo no puede encontrar su cuaderno con los exámenes de sus estudiantes. Necesita la ayuda de Lola, su esposa. Primero, escuche el **Vocabulario útil** y lea la lista de lugares donde puede estar el cuaderno. Luego escuche la conversación entre Manolo y Lola. Mientras escucha, indique en qué lugares buscó (*looked for*) el cuaderno con los exámenes Lola.

Vocabulario útil

¿sabes?	do you know?
lo siento, querido	sorry, darling
no sé	I don't know
tal vez	maybe
dentro	inside
la entrada	entryway
la estantería	**el estante**
el portafolios	briefcase

Lugares

1. ☐ dentro de la mesita en la entrada
2. ☐ encima de la estantería
3. ☐ en la cocina
4. ☐ debajo de la cama
5. ☐ detrás de la televisión
6. ☐ detrás de la cómoda
7. ☐ en el portafolios de Manolo

Nota: Verifique sus respuestas al **Paso 1** en el Apéndice antes de empezar el **Paso 2.**

Paso 2. Ahora, cuando oiga (*you hear*) un lugar, diga quién (**Lola** o **nadie**) busca el cuaderno con los exámenes en ese lugar. **¡OJO!** Los lugares *no* están en el orden de la lista del **Paso 1.**

MODELO:	(Ud. oye)	dentro de la mesita en la entrada
	(Ud. ve) **1.** ☐	dentro de la mesita en la entrada
	(Ud. dice)	Nadie busca dentro de la mesita en la entrada.
	(Ud. oye y repite)	Nadie busca dentro de la mesita en la entrada.

2. ... **3.** ... **4.** ... **5.** ... **6.** ... **7.** ...

 # PRONUNCIACIÓN   *r* and *rr*

- The letter **r** has two pronunciations in Spanish: the trilled **r** (written as **rr** between vowels or as **r** at the beginning of a word), and the flap **r**, which appears in all other positions. Because mispronunciation or a lack of differentiation can affect the listener's interpretation of a word (as with **coro** [*chorus*] and **corro** [*I run*]), it is important to distinguish between these two pronunciations of the Spanish **r**.
- To pronounce the trill **r**, the tip of the tongue, under tension, strikes the area just behind the teeth several times in rapid succession. The sound is similar to what someone might make to imitate a brief machine gun pattern or a cat purring.
- The flap **r** is similar to the sound produced by the rapid pronunciation of *tt* and *dd* in the English words *Betty* and *ladder*.

A. **Repeticiones.** Escuche estos pares (*pairs*) de palabras y repita cada par.

petty / pero   *sadder* / Sara   *motor* / moro

B. **Más repeticiones.** Escuche las siguientes palabras, frases y oraciones. Imite al hablante (*speaker*) cuando las repita (*you repeat them*).

1. *flap:*   brazo   gracias   para   hora   triste
2. *trill:*   ruso   real   reportero   Roberto   rebelde
3. *trill:*   burro   corral   carro   barra   ahorro
4. el extranjero
   el precio del cuaderno
   el nombre correcto
   una mujer refinada
   las residencias
   Enrique, Carlos y Rosita
   Puerto Rico
   El perro está en el corral.
   Estos errores son raros.
   Soy el primo de Roberto Ramírez.

C. **¿R o rr?** Ud. va a oír algunas palabras. Indique la palabra que oye.

1. **a.** ahora   **b.** ahorra
2. **a.** caro   **b.** carro
3. **a.** coro   **b.** corro
4. **a.** coral   **b.** corral
5. **a.** pero   **b.** perro
6. **a.** cero   **b.** cerro

D. **Un sonido importante**

Paso 1. Deje de escuchar (*Stop listening*) y subraye (*underline*) los ejemplos del sonido (*sound*) rr.

1. Rosa
2. caro
3. guitarra
4. Rigoberta
5. rojo
6. un error horrible
7. un aroma raro
8. Raquel es rubia.
9. Federico es rico.

Nota: Verifique sus respuestas del **Paso 1** en el Apéndice antes de empezar el **Paso 2.**

Paso 2. Ahora, cuando oiga el número correspondiente, lea la palabra, frase u (*or*) oración del **Paso 1.** Luego escuche la pronunciación correcta y repítala.

> MODELO: (Ud. oye) Uno.
>   (Ud. ve) **1.** Rosa
>   (Ud. dice) Rosa
>   (Ud. oye y repite) Rosa

2. ...   3. ...   4. ...   5. ...   6. ...   7. ...   8. ...   9. ...

15. ¿Qué están haciendo? • Present Progressive: *Estar + -ndo*

A. Formas. Dé el gerundio del verbo.

MODELO: comprar → <u>comprando</u>

1. nevar _____

2. llover _____

3. hacer _____

4. leer _____

5. oír _____

6. dormir _____

7. preferir _____

B. La familia de Rigoberto. Describa lo que están haciendo los miembros de su familia, desde la perspectiva de Rigoberto. Use la forma apropiada del gerundio. **¡OJO!** Cuidado con los verbos que tienen un cambio en la raíz (*stem*).

1. Mi abuela está _____ (dormir) la siesta ahora.

2. Mi hermana María está _____ (pedir) veinte dólares para ir al cine.

3. Mi padre está _____ (servirse) un café.

4. Mis hermanos están _____ (leer) libros.

5. Mi madre está _____ (almorzar) con una amiga. Está _____

   (divertirse).

C. ¿Qué están haciendo Ud. y sus amigos? Ud. y sus amigos siempre hacen actividades muy diferentes. Cambie los infinitivos para mostrar (*show*) lo que están haciendo Uds. en este momento.

MODELO: David _____ (mandar) mensajes, pero yo _____

(estudiar) para un examen. →

David está mandando mensajes, pero yo estoy estudiando para un examen.

1. Luis _____ (jugar) al golf, pero Marta _____

   (escuchar) música.

2. Manolo _____ (mirar) la tele, pero Luisa

   _____ (vestirse) para salir.

3. Jaime _____ (leer) el periódico, pero María Elena

   _____ (hacer) ejercicio en el gimnasio.

4. Pepe _____ (acostarse), pero Ernesto _____

   (comer) una pizza.

D. ¿Qué están haciendo?

Paso 1. Ud. va a escuchar algunas oraciones sobre las actividades que están haciendo varias personas. Primero, escuche el **Vocabulario útil.** Luego empareje el número de cada oración con el dibujo (*drawing*) correspondiente.

Vocabulario útil

jugar a los videojuegos	to play videogames
pasear en bicicleta	to ride a bike
patinar en línea	to rollerblade

a. _____   b. _____   c. _____

d. _____   e. _____

Paso 2. Imagine que las personas en los dibujos todavía están haciendo estas actividades. Conteste las siguientes preguntas, según los dibujos del **Paso 1.** Luego escuche la respuesta correcta y repítala.

1. ...   2. ...   3. ...   4. ...   5. ...

E. **¿Qué está haciendo Lisaura?** Ud. va a describir lo que (*what*) Lisaura está haciendo en diferentes momentos del día. Primero, mire los dibujos y escuche el **Vocabulario útil.** Luego cuando oiga (*you hear*) el verbo o la frase que describe la acción de un dibujo, cambie el verbo al presente progresivo para describir lo que Lisaura está haciendo. Siga el modelo. **¡OJO!** Recuerde que en español no se usan los sujetos ni (*nor*) los pronombres personales con tanta (*as much*) frecuencia como (*as*) en inglés.

Vocabulario útil

maquillarse	to put on makeup
mirarse en el espejo	to look at oneself in the mirror

(Ud. oye)	despertarse
(Ud. dice)	Lisaura se está despertando. / Lisaura está despertándose.
(Ud. oye y repite)	Lisaura se está despertando. / Lisaura está despertándose.

1. ...   **2.** ...   **3.** ...   **4.** ...   **5.** ...   **6.** ...   **7.** ...

F. **¡Sé (*I know*) lo que estás haciendo!** Su amiga Amalia le va a decir (*is going to tell you*) dónde está ella y Ud. va a adivinar (*to guess*) lo que está haciendo en ese lugar. Primero, escuche la lista de actividades posibles. Luego escuche lo que dice Amalia. Escoja (*Choose*) un verbo de la lista y diga (*say*) lo que está haciendo. Finalmente escuche una respuesta posible y repítala.

Acciones: comer, estudiar, leer, mirar la tele, trabajar

MODELO: (Ud. oye) Estoy en mi alcoba.

(Ud. dice) Amalia, estás estudiando, ¿verdad?

(Ud. oye y repite) Amalia, estás estudiando, ¿verdad?

1. ...   **2.** ...   **3.** ...   **4.** ...

16. *Ser* o *estar* • Summary of the Uses of *ser* and *estar*

¿Recuerda Ud.?

Ser y *estar*. Empareje las preguntas con las respuestas apropiadas.

1. _____ ¿Cómo **está** Ud.?

2. _____ ¿Cómo **es** Ud.?

3. _____ ¿Cómo **es** tu hermana?

4. _____ ¿Cómo **está** tu hermana?

a. Está mejor (*better*), muchas gracias por tu interés.

b. ¡Estoy muy bien hoy!

c. Es muy inteligente pero un poco tímida.

d. Creo que soy paciente y simpático.

A. **¿Se usa *ser* o *estar*?**

Paso 1. Complete las oraciones con la forma apropiada de **ser** o **estar**.

a. Mi abuela _____ de España.

b. Mis padres _____ altos.

c. Miguel _____ el hijo de Julia.

d. La nieve _____ blanca.

e. ¡Mi café _____ frío!

f. ¿De quién _____ este dinero?

g. _____ las dos y media.

h. Tú _____ muy guapo esta noche.

i. ¿_____ Uds. ocupados?

j. Mis libros _____ en la mesa.

k. Nosotros _____ estudiantes.

Paso 2. Primero, escriba la letra de la oración del **Paso 1** que es ejemplo de cada uno de los siguientes usos. En algunos casos, hay (*there is*) más de una respuesta. Luego indique si se usa **ser** o **estar** en esas situaciones.

		SER	ESTAR
1.	_____ to tell where a person or thing is located	☐	☐
2.	_____ to indicate origin (with **de**)	☐	☐
3.	_____ to show possession (with **de**)	☐	☐
4.	_____ to show the norm or inherent qualities (with adjectives)	☐	☐
5.	_____ to show a change from the norm or to express temporary conditions (with adjectives)	☐	☐
6.	_____ to identify people or things	☐	☐
7.	_____ to express time	☐	☐

B. Minidiálogos. Complete los diálogos con la forma apropiada de **ser** o **estar**.

1. —¿De dónde _____ tú?

—_____ de San José, Costa Rica.

2. —¿De quién _____ estas cosas?

—Creo que _____ de Ana.

3. — Estos boletos (*tickets*) _____ para Uds. Vamos a entrar ahora, ¿eh? Las puertas del cine

ya _____ abiertas.

— Buena idea.

4. — Pablo, ya _____ la una y media. Tenemos que _____ en el aeropuerto a las dos y

_____ difícil encontrar (*to find*) un taxi a estas horas.

—Está bien. Vamos.

5. —Juan, tu cuarto _____ muy desordenado.

—Sí, mamá. (Yo) _____ de acuerdo, ¡pero la puerta _____ cerrada!

6. —La novia de Tito _____ cariñosa y alegre. ¿Y él?

—Él _____ muy formal y serio.

C. Preguntas y respuestas

Paso 1. Ud. va a escuchar las respuestas a algunas preguntas. Primero, lea las siguientes preguntas. Luego escuche las respuestas y seleccione la pregunta apropiada para cada respuesta.

1. a. ¿Cómo estás?   **b.** ¿Cómo eres?
2. a. ¿Cómo está Ud.?   **b.** ¿Cómo es?
3. a. ¿Dónde está?   **b.** ¿De dónde es Ud.?
4. a. ¿Dónde está el consejero?   **b.** ¿De dónde es el consejero?
5. a. ¿De quién es la blusa?   **b.** ¿De qué es la blusa?

Paso 2. Ahora, cuando oiga el número correspondiente, cambie la pregunta correcta del **Paso 1** al plural (por ejemplo, **yo → nosotros; tú/Ud. → Uds.; él/ella → ellos/ellas**). Escuche la pregunta correcta y repítala. Luego conteste la pregunta. Finalmente, escuche y repita una posible respuesta.

MODELO: (Ud. ve y oye)   **1.** ¿Cómo estás?

            (Ud. dice)   ¿Cómo están?

      (Ud. oye y repite)   ¿Cómo están?

            (Ud. dice)   Estamos bien.

      (Ud. oye y repite)   Estamos bien.

2. ...   **3.** ...   **4.** ...   **5.** ...

D. **Diálogo.** Complete el diálogo entre Mari y Anita con las formas apropiadas de **ser** o **estar**.

MARI: ¡Hola, Anita! ¿Cómo _____[1]?

ANITA: Todavía _____[2] un poco enferma de gripe.[a]

MARI: Ay, lo siento.[b] ¿Quiénes _____[3] esos chicos que _____[4] con tu hermano?

ANITA: _____[5] nuestros primos. _____[6] de la Argentina.

MARI: ¿Y esta guitarra? ¿De quién _____[7]?

ANITA: De mi prima Rosario. Ella _____[8] una guitarrista fabulosa. Canta y toca como[c]

          profesional.

MARI: ¿Cuánto tiempo van a _____[9] aquí?

ANITA: Solo dos semanas. ¿Por qué no vienes a casa el domingo? Vamos a dar[d] una fiesta.

MARI: Encantada, gracias.

---

[a]de... with the flu   [b]lo... I'm sorry   [c]like a   [d]have

E. **¿Cómo están?** Ud. va a describir algunos dibujos. Primero, mire los dibujos. Luego escuche cada pregunta y contéstela para describir el dibujo.

MODELO: (Ud. ve)   Verónica

          (Ud. oye)   ¿Está preocupada o enferma Verónica?

          (Ud. dice)   Verónica está preocupada.

    (Ud. oye y repite)   Verónica está preocupada.

Pedro   Josué   Luis

   Javier   Mariela

1. ...   **2.** ...   **3.** ...   **4.** ...

17. Describing • Comparisons

A. **¿Cómo se comparan?** Complete las comparaciones con **que** o **como**.

1. Hace más calor en el verano en San José _____ en mi país.

2. La primavera en las playas costarricenses es tan bella (*beautiful*) _____ el invierno en las

   montañas (*mountains*).

3. Costa Rica tiene tantas especies de pájaros (*birds*) _____ los Estados Unidos.

4. Los restaurantes tienen menos platos vegetarianos _____ los restaurantes en este país.

5. Me divierto aquí tanto _____ en mi país.

B. **Comparando a las personas.** Use **que** y **como** para comparar las cualidades indicadas de las personas nombradas (*named*). **¡OJO!** Preste (*Pay*) atención a la concordancia (*agreement*) de los adjetivos. Use los nombres de las personas en el orden dado (*given*).

Briana   Petra

MODELO: Briana / Petra (contento) → Briana está más contenta que Petra.

1. Briana / Petra (delgado) _____

2. Briana / Petra (simpático) _____

Ernesto   José   Julio

Mónica

Carmen   Carlitos   Inés

3. Ernesto / José (alto) _____

4. Carlitos / Julio (bajo) _____

5. Carmen / Mónica (extrovertido) _____

6. José / Ernesto (delgado) _____

7. Inés / Carlitos (joven) _____

8. Carmen / José (alegre) _____

C. La rutina de Alicia

Paso 1. La siguiente tabla presenta información sobre la rutina de Alicia. Primero, lea la tabla. Luego escuche algunas oraciones sobre su rutina. Indique si cada oración es cierta (**C**) o falsa (**F**), según la información de la tabla.

ACCIÓN	DE LUNES A VIERNES	LOS FINES DE SEMANA
levantarse	6:30 A.M.	9:30 A.M.
bañarse	7:15 A.M.	10:00 A.M.
trabajar	8 horas	1 hora
almorzar	20 minutos	30 minutos
divertirse	1 hora	8 horas
acostarse	11:00 P.M.	11:00 P.M.

1. C F   **2.** C F   **3.** C F   **4.** C F   **5.** C F

Paso 2. Ahora va a oír algunas preguntas sobre la rutina de Alicia. Conteste las preguntas con información de la tabla del **Paso 1.** Luego escuche la respuesta correcta y repítala.

1. ...   **2.** ...   **3.** ...   **4.** ...

D. En el centro. Conteste según el dibujo (*drawing*).

1. ¿Es el cine tan alto como la tienda Casa Montaño? _____

2. ¿Cuál edificio es más pequeño que todos los otros edificios? _____

3. ¿Cuál edificio es más alto que todos los otros edificios? _____

4. ¿Es el cine tan alto como el café? _____

5. ¿Es el hotel tan grande como el cine? _____

E. Comparaciones. Complete los diálogos con la forma comparativa.

> MODELO: —Yo leo dos libros al mes. ¿Y tú?
>
> —Yo leo más que tú. Leo más de cinco libros al mes.

1. —Yo estudio tres horas al día. ¿Y tú?

   —Yo estudio _____ tú. Estudio solo dos horas al día.

   —Sí, ¡pero tú siempre sales (*do*) _____ (*better than*) yo en los exámenes!

2. —Yo tengo veinte dólares. ¿Y tú?

   —Yo tengo _____ tú. Creo que tengo treinta. ¡Qué sorpresa! ¡En realidad (*Actually*), tengo

   _____ cincuenta dólares! Tengo cincuenta y cinco.

3. —Mi primo juega bien al tenis. ¿Y tú?

   —Creo que juego _____ él, porque siempre gano (*I win*).

4. —Este semestre tengo cuatro clases. ¿Y tú?

   —Yo también. Tengo _____ clases _____ tú, ¡y todas son difíciles!

F. Un desacuerdo. Imagine que Ud. y su amiga Lourdes nunca están de acuerdo. Primero, lea la declaración de Lourdes y escuche la corrección. Forme oraciones negativas para indicar que Ud. no está de acuerdo con lo que ella dice. Luego escuche y repita la respuesta correcta.

> MODELO: (Ud. ve)   Los amigos son más importantes que la familia.
>
>   (Ud. oye)   tan importantes
>
>   (Ud. dice)   No, los amigos son tan importantes como la familia.
>
> (Ud. oye y repite)   No, los amigos son tan importantes como la familia.

1. El invierno es más bonito que el verano.
2. Hace tanto calor en la Florida como en Alaska.
3. Hace más frío en Mineápolis que en Indianápolis.
4. Llueve tanto en el verano como en la primavera.
5. Hay tanta contaminación en México como en Costa Rica.

G. Vacaciones en el Caribe

❖ **Paso 1.** Complete las siguientes oraciones con palabras comparativas para expresar sus preferencias personales.

1. Me gusta bucear _____ _____ ir de compras.

2. Para mí, unas vacaciones en el Caribe son _____ interesantes _____ unas vacaciones de esquí.

3. En mi estado/provincia, llueve _____ en abril _____ en julio.

4. En el verano, tengo _____ tiempo de vacaciones _____ en el invierno.

Paso 2. Ud. va a escuchar una conversación entre Roberto y una agente de viajes. Primero, escuche el **Vocabulario útil** y la conversación. Luego complete las oraciones con información de la conversación. **Nota:** Todas las palabras que faltan (*are missing*) son palabras que forman comparaciones.

(Continúa.)

Vocabulario útil

no sé	I don't know
bucear	to scuba dive
viajar	to travel
una isla	island

1. Roberto quiere ir a una isla _____ _____ a una ciudad.

2. En el Caribe, hace _____ calor en los meses de invierno _____ en los meses de verano.

3. También, en el invierno llueve _____ _____ en el verano.

4. Viajar al Caribe en el verano es _____ barato _____ viajar en el invierno.

Nota: Verifique sus respuestas del **Paso 2** en el Apéndice antes de empezar el **Paso 3**.

Paso 3. Ahora Ud. va a oír algunas preguntas sobre lo que escribió en el **Paso 2**. Conteste con la información del **Paso 2**. Luego escuche la respuesta correcta y repítala.

1. ... 2. ... 3. ... 4. ...

Un poco de todo

A. **Un hermano increíble.** Complete la narración para describir al hermano del narrador. Escriba los números con letras. Cuando se presentan dos palabras entre paréntesis, escoja (*choose*) la más lógica.

Yo tengo _____[1] (21) años. Mi hermano Miguel tiene solo _____[2] (19), pero

_____[3] (ese / eso) chico es increíble. Estudia menos _____[4] (que / como) yo, pero

recibe mejores notas[a] _____[5] (de / que) yo. También gana[b] más dinero _____[6]

(de / que) yo, aunque[c] yo trabajo _____[7] (tanto / tan) _____[8] (como / que) él. En

realidad,[d] gana más _____[9] (de / que) _____[10] (200) dólares a la semana, pero

nunca tiene dinero _____[11] (porque / por qué) gasta[e] todo su dinero en ropa. ¡Le gusta

_____[12] (ser / estar) muy de moda! Por ejemplo, cree que necesita más _____[13]

(de / que) _____[14] (150) dólares para comprar tenis. Yo creo que es una tontería[f]

_____[15] (paga / pagar) tanto por unos zapatos.

B. *Listening Passage:* **Hablando del clima**

❖ **Antes de escuchar.** You will hear a passage about the climate in different regions of the Hispanic world. Before you listen to the passage, do the following activities.

Paso 1. Read the following statements about climate and circle **C** (**cierto**) if you think the statement might be true or **F** (**falso**) if you think it might be false. As you read the statements, try to infer what you will hear in the passage, as well as the specific information for which you need to listen.

1. **C F** En las regiones tropicales, por lo general hay una estación seca (*dry*) y una estación lluviosa (*rainy*).
2. **C F** En Latinoamérica no hace frío en ninguna (*any*) región.

---

[a]*grades* [b]*he earns* [c]*although* [d]*En... In fact* [e]*he spends* [f]*foolish thing*

3. **C F** En la mayor parte (*most*) de Sudamérica, las estaciones del año son opuestas a las de (*opposite to those of*) los países del hemisferio norte.
4. **C F** Hay climas muy variados en el mundo hispano.

Paso 2. You probably already know quite a bit about the climate of most of Latin America. That information will be fairly easy for you to recognize in the listening passage. Read the following multiple choice statements, and try to infer what type of information you will need to listen for regarding the person who will narrate the passage.

1. La persona que habla...
   a. es de Vermont.
   b. prefiere el frío del invierno.
   c. no quiere regresar a vivir en el Caribe.

2. A la persona que habla...
   a. le gusta la nieve porque es una experiencia nueva para él.
   b. no le gustan las estaciones lluviosas en los países tropicales.

Listening Passage. Now you will hear the passage, in which a young man talks about the climate in different regions of the Hispanic world. First, listen to the **Vocabulario útil,** then listen to the passage.

Vocabulario útil

se pone	turns
la luz	light
en cambio	on the other hand
en todo caso	at any rate
seco/a	dry
lluvioso/a	rainy
la mayor parte del tiempo	the majority of the time
suave	mild
agradable	pleasant

Después de escuchar. Here is another version of the statements you saw in **Paso 2** of **Antes de escuchar.** Circle **C** (**cierto**) if the statement is true or **F** (**falso**) if it is false, based on the information in the passage. Correct the statements that are false, then check your answers in the Appendix.

1. C F Nicanor es de Vermont.

   _____

2. C F A Nicanor no le gusta la nieve.

   _____

3. C F Nicanor quiere vivir en una región de clima tropical en el futuro.

   _____

4. C F En el mundo hispano hay climas muy variados.

   _____

5. C F En Sudamérica no hace frío en ninguna (*any*) región.

   _____

6. C F Cuando es verano en el hemisferio norte, también es verano en el hemisferio sur.

   _____

C. Entre amigos

Paso 1. Ud. va a escuchar las respuestas que unos amigos, Miguel René (de México), Rubén (de España) y Tané (de Cuba) dieron (*gave*) a tres preguntas. Primero, escuche el **Vocabulario útil,** luego escuche las respuestas. Después, indique a quién se refieren las siguientes oraciones: **M** (Miguel René), **R** (Rubén) o **T** (Tané). Miguel René siempre habla antes que Rubén.

Miguel René

Rubén

Tané

Vocabulario útil

eterno/a	permanent, eternal
disminuir (disminuye)	to decrease; to diminish
renacer	to be reborn
traer chamarra	**llevar chaqueta**

1. _____ En su país hay un eterno verano.

2. _____ En su país, las estaciones son muy variadas.

3. _____ En su país, hay mucha diferencia entre el norte y el sur.

4. _____ Prefiere el invierno porque le gusta más el frío que el calor.

5. _____ Le encanta ir a la playa en el verano.

6. _____ Prefiere la primavera porque hay un equilibrio de temperaturas.

7. _____ Su cumpleaños es en junio.

8. _____ Su cumpleaños es en noviembre.

9. _____ Su cumpleaños es en el último (*last*) mes del año.

Paso 2. Ahora Ud. va a participar en una entrevista similar en la que Ud. va a hacer el papel (*play the role*) de Karina, una estudiante venezolana. Primero, complete el diálogo con las siguientes frases y verifique sus respuestas en el Apéndice. Segundo, haga la entrevista: Escuche las preguntas de la entrevistadora y contéstelas en voz alta (*aloud*) con las respuestas de Karina. Luego escuche la pronunciación correcta y repita lo que oye.

me encantan (*I love*) las vacaciones   en mi país   llueve   es en otoño

ENTREVISTADORA: ¿Cómo es el clima de tu país?

KARINA: _____,[1] Venezuela, hace mucho calor. Normalmente

es un clima tropical y muy pocos días _____.[2]

ENTREVISTADORA: ¿Cuál es tu estación favorita del año y por qué?

KARINA: Mi estación favorita del año es el verano, porque _____.[3]

ENTREVISTADORA: ¿Cuándo es tu cumpleaños?

KARINA: Mi cumpleaños es el 10 de noviembre. _____.[4]

CULTURA

A. Mapa. Identifique el país y la capital en el siguiente mapa.

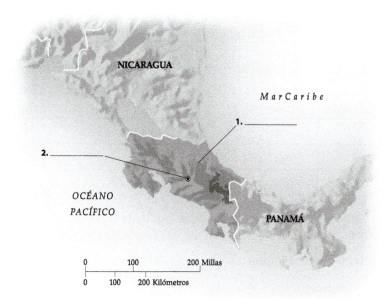

B. Comprensión. Complete las siguientes oraciones con palabras de la lista. Esta actividad se basa en la información de las lecturas **Nota cultural** (p. 169), **Algo sobre...** (p. 175, 180 y 185) y **Lectura cultural** (p. 194). **¡OJO!** No se usan todas las palabras.

capital	desierto	habitantes	sur
colores	diversidad	lluviosa	temperaturas
democracia	fechas	playa	transporte

1. El Niño es un fenómeno meteorológico que está caracterizado por _____ más calientes de lo normal (*warmer than normal*) en la zona ecuatorial del Pacífico.

2. Desde 1948, Costa Rica ha disfrutado de paz (*has enjoyed peace*) y _____.

3. Fundada (*founded*) en 1738, San José es la _____ de Costa Rica y tiene una población de 288.000 _____.

4. Costa Rica tiene dos temporadas: una seca (*dry*) y otra _____ que ocurre entre mayo y noviembre.

5. Las carretas son un método de _____ tradicional y su uso se asocia con las plantaciones de café. En Costa Rica, las decoran con bellos diseños y _____.

6. El _____ de Atacama en Chile es el más seco del mundo.

7. España tiene una gran _____ climática y geográfica. Tiene la zona más caliente de Europa en el _____ del país, y en el norte tiene una de las cordilleras más altas del continente.

PÓNGASE A PRUEBA

A. **Present Progressive:** *Estar* + *-ndo*. Complete la tabla con la forma correcta del gerundio.

VERBO	GERUNDIO	VERBO	GERUNDIO
cepillarse		hablar	*hablando*
divertirse		leer	
dormir	*durmiendo*	poner	
escribir		servir	
estudiar		tener	*teniendo*

B. *¿Ser o estar?* Empareje las oraciones de la columna izquierda con los usos apropiados de **ser** y **estar** de la columna derecha.

1. _____ Estamos muy ocupados.

2. _____ Son las nueve.

3. _____ Ella está en Costa Rica.

4. _____ El reloj es de Carlos.

5. _____ Gracias, estoy bien.

6. _____ Ella es de Costa Rica.

7. _____ Marta es alta y morena.

8. _____ Están mirando la tele.

9. _____ Es importante salir ahora.

   a. to tell time
   b. with **de** to express origin
   c. to tell location of a person or thing
   d. to form generalizations
   e. with the present participle to form the progressive
   f. with adjectives to express a change from the norm or to express conditions
   g. with adjectives to express the norm or inherent qualities
   h. to speak of one's health
   i. with **de** to express possession

C. **Comparaciones.** Indique las palabras correctas para completar las comparaciones.

1. Paulina es (más / tanta) bonita (que / como) su hermana.

2. Tengo (tan / tantos) problemas (que / como) tú.

3. Este libro es bueno, pero el otro es (más bueno / mejor).

4. Tú cantas (tan / tanto) bien (que / como) Gloria.

5. Mis hermanos tienen (tantos / menos) clases (que / como) yo.

6. Las botas cuestan más (que / de) cien dólares

PRUEBA CORTA

A. **¿Qué están haciendo todos?** Escriba oraciones en el presente progresivo.

1. (yo) mirar / programa _____

2. Juan / leer / periódico _____

3. Marta / servir / café / ahora _____

4. niños / dormir _____

5. ¿almorzar (tú) / ahora? _____

B. **¿*Ser* o *estar*?** Complete las oraciones con la forma apropiada de **ser** o **estar**, según el contexto.

1. —Buenas tardes. ¿Cómo _____ Ud., señorita?

   —_____ bien, gracias.

2. —¿De dónde _____ (tú), Pablo?

   —_____ de Bogotá, Colombia.

3. —¿En qué clase _____ Uds.?

   —_____ en la clase de Español 1.

4. —¿Qué te pasa? (*What's the matter with you?*) ¿_____ enferma?

   —No, solo _____ cansada.

5. —Carlitos, debes ponerte otra camisa. Esa _____ sucia.

C. **Arturo y Roberto.** Mire los dibujos. Luego escriba oraciones completas con las palabras en el orden dado (*order given*) para comparar a los dos chicos.

Arturo 17 años

Roberto 15 años

1. Arturo / perros / Roberto _____

2. Arturo / gordo / Roberto _____

3. Arturo / no / moreno / Roberto _____

4. Roberto / menor / Arturo _____

5. los perros de Arturo / grande / el perro de Roberto _____

_____

D. Hablando de viajes. Imagine que Ud. va a viajar (*travel*) a varios lugares este año. Conteste las preguntas que oye con las palabras indicadas. **¡OJO!** Las preguntas no van a ser idénticas a las del modelo. Cambie sus respuestas, según las preguntas que oye.

MODELO:
(Ud. ve) Detroit, 30/3: fresco
(Ud. oye) ¿Cuándo sale Ud. para Detroit?
(Ud. dice) Salgo el treinta de marzo.
(Ud. oye y repite) Salgo el treinta de marzo.
(Ud. oye) ¿Y qué tiempo hace allá?
(Ud. dice) Hace fresco.
(Ud. oye y repite) Hace fresco.

1. Acapulco, 15/7: calor
2. Aspen, 1/12: nevando
3. La Argentina, 10/1: sol
4. Chicago, 24/5: viento

E. Algunas diferencias entre países. Ud. va a oír algunas oraciones sobre la siguiente tabla de información recopilada (*compiled*) de www.internetworldstats.com. Primero, lea la tabla. Luego indique si las oraciones son ciertas (**C**) o falsas (**F**), según la información de la tabla.

PAÍS	POBLACIÓN (HABITANTES)	ÁREA EN KILÓMETROS CUADRADOS (*SQUARE*)	NÚMERO DE USUARIOS DEL INTERNET
COSTA RICA	4.576.562	51.090	2.000.000
GUATEMALA	13.824.463	108.894	2.280.000
MÉXICO	113.724.226	1.967.138	34.900.000
NICARAGUA	5.666.301	129.454	600.000

1. C F   2. C F   3. C F   4. C F   5. C F   6. C F

❖ PUNTOS PERSONALES

A. ¿Qué hace Ud.? Complete las oraciones para expresar lo que hace Ud. cuando hace los tiempos que se mencionan. Use la forma apropiada de las expresiones de la lista o sea (*be*) creativo/a. **¡OJO!** ¡Tenga cuidado (*Be careful*) con los pronombres reflexivos!

almorzar en el parque
hacer ejercicio afuera (*outside*)
ir al cine / a la biblioteca / a un café / de compras
pasar el día en el centro comercial
estar molesto/a
ponerse otro suéter
preferir quedarse en casa
quedarse en cama
tener sueño / ganas de ir a la playa
¿ ?

1. Cuando llueve, yo _____.

2. Cuando hay mucha contaminación, yo _____.

3. Cuando hace calor, yo _____.

4. Cuando tengo frío, yo _____.

5. Cuando hace buen tiempo, yo _____.

B. **Aquí me siento yo.** Escriba un párrafo en el que indica dónde se sienta Ud. generalmente en la clase de español y dónde se sientan otros compañeros de clase.

Vocabulario útil

a mi derecha/izquierda
al lado de
delante/detrás de (mí, Jim, ¿ ?)
lejos/cerca de

_____

_____

_____

_____

_____

C. **Opiniones personales.** Complete las oraciones lógicamente. Use **más/menos... que, tan... como** o **tanto/a/os/as... como** cuando sea (*it is*) apropiado. Cuando hay dos posibilidades, escoja (*choose*) la que quiere usar.

1. Soy _____ alto/a _____ mi padre/madre.

2. La salud (*Health*) es _____ importante _____ el dinero.

3. Mi cuarto está _____ limpio _____ el cuarto de mi mejor amigo/a.

4. Yo tengo _____ clases _____ mi mejor amigo/a. Mi amigo tiene _____

   (número) clases y yo tengo _____ (número).

5. Mi _____ es más serio/a que mi _____.

6. Yo soy _____ estudioso/a _____ mi mejor amigo/a.

7. Yo estudio _____ horas al día _____ mi hermano.

D. **Guided Composition.** En una hoja aparte (*On a separate sheet of paper*), escriba dos párrafos (*paragraphs*) sobre unas vacaciones futuras (pueden ser verdaderas o imaginarias). Use las preguntas como guía para la composición. No se olvide de que Ud. no debe escribir una lista de respuestas sino (*but rather*) una composición coherente. Puede usar las siguientes palabras y otras para conectar las ideas de su composición y hacerla más interesante: **por eso, y, aunque** (*although*), **también, luego** y **porque.**

Nota: En español, para expresar *because* al comienzo de una oración, no se comienza la oración con **porque,** sino con **como** (*since*). Por ejemplo, se puede combinar las oraciones **Hace calor** y **Voy a llevar un traje de baño** de las siguientes maneras.
Como hace calor, voy a llevar un traje de baño. *Since it's hot, I'm going to take a swimsuit.*
Voy a llevar un traje de baño porque hace calor. *I'm going to take a swimsuit because/since it's hot.*

Primer párrafo: ¿En que mes piensa Ud. ir de vacaciones este año? ¿Adónde va a ir? ¿Con quién(es) va? ¿Cuánto tiempo piensan Uds. estar allí? ¿Dónde van a quedarse? (en un hotel, un apartamento, en la casa de unos amigos, ¿ ?)

Segundo párrafo: ¿Qué tiempo hace en ese lugar en la estación cuando piensa ir? (¿Llueve con frecuencia? ¿Nieva mucho? ¿Hay contaminación?) ¿Qué ropa piensa Ud. llevar? ¿Qué cosas quiere hacer durante el día? ¿Y durante la noche? ¿En qué fecha piensan Uds. volver?

E. Entrevista. Ud. va a oír algunas preguntas. Para contestar las preguntas, complete las siguientes oraciones con información que es cierta para Ud.

1. En _____ (nombre de ciudad), donde yo vivo, en verano,

   _____. En invierno, _____.

2. En el verano, _____.

   Me gusta porque _____.

3. (No) Soy _____. Por ejemplo, soy

   _____ que _____ (miembro de su familia).

4. Este semestre/trimestre _____

   _____.

F. Mi diario. En su diario, escriba Ud. sobre tres cosas que hace o que le gusta hacer en cada estación del año.

Vocabulario útil

celebrar mi cumpleaños
esquiar   to ski
ir a la playa
nadar   to swim
quedarme en casa
visitar a mis abuelos/amigos

> MODELO: En las vacaciones de primavera me gusta visitar a mis amigos en Denver. Si (*If*) todavía hay nieve, me gusta esquiar un día de las vacaciones. Si no hay nieve...

G. Intercambios. Escuche las siguientes preguntas y contéstelas por escrito.

1. _____

2. _____

3. _____

4. _____

Capítulo 7

¡A comer!

VOCABULARIO Preparación

La comida y las comidas

A. La comida. Complete las oraciones con palabras apropiadas de la lista a continuación.

agua	helado	lechuga	té
camarones	huevos	pan	tomate
carne	jugo	papas fritas	verduras
galletas	langosta	queso	
hambre	leche	sed	

1. En los Estados Unidos, un desayuno típico para mucha gente (*people*) es dos _____

   con jamón y _____ tostado con mermelada. Y para beber: _____

   de naranja, café, _____ o _____ fría.

2. Dos de los mariscos favoritos son los _____ y la _____.

3. Las especialidades de McDonald's son las hamburguesas y las _____.

4. Es bueno para la salud (*health*) beber ocho vasos de _____ cada día.

5. De (*For*) postre, ¿prefiere Ud. pastel, flan o _____ de vainilla o chocolate?

6. Un vegetariano no come _____; prefiere las _____ y las frutas.

7. El sándwich de jamón y _____ es una comida popular para el almuerzo.

8. La ensalada típica se hace (*is made*) con _____ y _____.

9. Cuando los niños vuelven a casa después de un día largo en la escuela, tienen

   _____.

10. Cuando tengo _____, bebo agua fría.

B. Definiciones

Paso 1. Ud. va a oír algunas definiciones. Indique la letra de la palabra definida en cada oración.

1. **a.** la zanahoria   **b.** los huevos
2. **a.** la lechuga   **b.** la langosta
3. **a.** la leche   **b.** el vino blanco
4. **a.** un postre   **b.** un sándwich
5. **a.** el almuerzo   **b.** la cena
6. **a.** los espárragos   **b.** el agua mineral

Paso 2. Ahora, basándose en (*based on*) las respuestas correctas del **Paso 1**, dé las respuestas a las definiciones que oye. Use la forma apropiada del verbo ser en sus respuestas.

MODELO: (Ud. oye)   Es algo que normalmente se come para el desayuno.

                 (Ud. dice)   Son los huevos.

         (Ud. oye y repite)   Son los huevos.

1. ...   **2.** ...   **3.** ...   **4.** ...   **5.** ...

C. Identificaciones. Identifique los siguientes alimentos (*foods*) cuando oiga el número correspondiente. Use el artículo definido correcto (**el, la, los, las**) en sus respuestas. Luego escuche la respuesta correcta y repítala.

1.

2.

3.

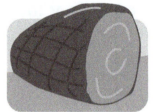

4.

5.

6.

7.

8.

D. ¡A categorizar! Ud. va a oír los nombres de algunas comidas. Primero, escuche la lista de categorías, luego escuche las palabras. Repita cada comida y diga a qué categoría pertenece (*it belongs*). Después, escuche la respuesta correcta y repítala.

Categorías: una bebida, un tipo de carne, una fruta, un marisco, un postre, una verdura

MODELO: (Ud. oye)   el té

                 (Ud. dice)   El té es una bebida.

         (Ud. oye y repite)   El té es una bebida.

1. ...   **2.** ...   **3.** ...   **4.** ...   **5.** ...

E. **Comida típica panameña**

Paso 1. Ud. va a escuchar una entrevista con el dueño de un restaurante panameño. Primero, escuche el **Vocabulario útil.** Luego escuche la entrevista y complete las siguientes oraciones.

Vocabulario útil

actualmente	currently
el maíz	corn
el platillo	dish
sería(n)	would be
los frijoles de palo	pigeon beans
el sancocho	**sopa que tiene variantes por toda Latinoamérica**
la gallina	hen
asado/a	grilled
platicar	to chat
la cebolla	onion
el ají (los ajíes)	chile (pepper)
el pimiento	bell pepper
el otoe	type of root vegetable
el ñame	yam
faltar	to lack
para que sepa	so that it tastes

1. El entrevistado se llama Maír Citón Moreno y es de _____.

2. El Sr. Citón es propietario de un _____ especializado en comida

   _____.

3. Entre los platillos más típicos de su país están el _____ de frijoles de palo, el

   sancocho de gallina, los _____ y las _____ asadas.

4. En la opinión del Sr. Citón, el plato que más identifica a los panameños a nivel nacional es el

   _____.

Paso 2. Ahora escuche la entrevista otra vez. Mientras escucha, indique todos los ingredientes del sancocho de gallina que menciona el Sr. Citón.

☐ arroz	☐ cebolla	☐ gallina
☐ ajíes	☐ cerdo	☐ maíz
☐ ajo (*garlic*)	☐ frijoles de palo	☐ ñame
☐ otoe	☐ pavo	☐ tortillas asadas
☐ papa	☐ pimientos	☐ yuca
☐ pasta	☐ tamales	☐ zanahorias

¿Qué sabe Ud. y a quién conoce?

A. *¿Saber o conocer?* ¿Se usa **saber** o **conocer** para hablar de lo siguiente (*the following*)? Escriba el infinitivo del verbo que se debe usar.

1. _____ el número de teléfono

2. _____ a una persona

3. _____ un lugar

4. _____ la dirección de un lugar

5. _____ el título de una película o libro

6. _____ hacer algo (hablar español, tocar un instrumento)

7. _____ el nombre de una persona

B. **El restaurante El Canal.** Complete las oraciones con la forma apropiada de los verbos entre paréntesis.

MARCO ANTONIO: ¿ _____¹ (*tú:* Saber) dónde está el restaurante El Canal?

JAVIER: ¡Cómo no! (*Of course!*) Ceci y yo _____² (conocer) muy bien a los dueños.

MARCO ANTONIO: Yo _____³ (conocer) a su hija Lucía, pero no _____⁴ (saber) la

dirección del restaurante. Lucía dice (*says*) que sus padres _____⁵ (saber)

cocinar mejor que nadie (*anyone*).

JAVIER: Ceci _____⁶ (saber) su número de teléfono si quieres llamar. Debes

_____⁷ (conocer) a toda la familia. Todos son muy simpáticos.

C. *¿Saber o conocer?* Complete las oraciones con la forma apropiada de **saber** o **conocer**, según el sentido (*meaning*).

1. Ellas no _____ a mi primo.

2. Yo no _____ a qué hora llegan del teatro.

3. ¿(Tú) _____ tocar el piano?

4. Necesitan _____ a qué hora vas a venir.

5. (Nosotros) _____ a los padres de Paquita, pero yo no _____ al resto de su familia.

6. Queremos _____ al presidente del club.

D. **Los amigos de Rosa**

Paso 1. Ud. va a oír un breve (*brief*) párrafo sobre lo que saben hacer los amigos de Rosa y a quiénes y qué conocen. Primero, escuche el **Vocabulario útil**, luego escuche el párrafo. Después, marque las casillas (*checkboxes*) apropiadas. Una respuesta ya se ha completado (*has been completed*).

Vocabulario útil

les gustan	they like
los deportes	sports
ninguno	none, not any
probar	to try

	BAILAR	A JUAN	JUGAR AL TENIS	A LOS PADRES DE ROSA	LA CIUDAD
Enrique sabe/conoce...	☑	☐	☐	☐	☐
Roberto sabe/conoce...	☐	☐	☐	☐	☐
Susana sabe/conoce...	☐	☐	☐	☐	☐

Nota: Verifique sus respuestas del **Paso 1** en el Apéndice antes de empezar el **Paso 2**.

Paso 2. Ahora Ud. va a oír algunas (*some*) preguntas. Contéstelas con la información del **Paso 1**. Luego escuche las respuestas correctas y repítalas.

1. ... **2.** ... **3.** ... **4.** ...

PRONUNCIACIÓN   *d*

The Spanish letter **d** has two pronunciations.

- At the beginning of a phrase or sentence and after **n** or **l**, it is pronounced similarly to the English *d* as in *dog*, as a stop. That is, no air is allowed to escape between the tongue and the ridge behind the teeth. This sound is represented as [d].
- In all other positions, the letter **d** is pronounced like the English sound *th* in *another* but softer, as a fricative. That is, some air is allowed to escape when the **d** is pronounced. This sound is represented as [ð].

A. Repeticiones. Escuche las siguientes palabras y repítalas.

[d]	diez	¿dónde?	venden	condición	falda	el doctor
[ð]	adiós	seda	ciudad	usted	cuadros	la doctora

B. Oraciones. Escuche las siguientes oraciones y repítalas. Preste (*Pay*) atención a la pronunciación de la **d** y también a la entonación.

¿Dónde está el dinero?   ¿Qué estudia Ud.?
Dos y diez son doce.   Venden de todo, ¿verdad?

C. A escoger. Ud. va a oír algunas palabras que contienen (*contain*) la letra **d**. Escoja (*Choose*) la letra del sonido de la **d** que oye en cada palabra.

1. **a.** [d]   **b.** [ð]

2. **a.** [d]   **b.** [ð]

3. **a.** [d]   **b.** [ð]

4. **a.** [d]   **b.** [ð]

5. **a.** [d]   **b.** [ð]

D. La d fricativa [ð]

Paso 1. Primero, repase (*review*) las reglas (*rules*) de pronunciación de la **d**. Luego subraye (*underline*) solo los ejemplos del sonido de la d fricativa [ð] en las siguientes palabras, frases y oraciones.

1. el día
2. adónde
3. ustedes

4. personalidad
5. verdad
6. venden de todo

7. Perdón, Diego.
8. Buenos días, Adela.
9. ¿Dónde está el doctor?

Paso 2. Ahora, cuando oiga el número correspondiente, lea cada palabra, frase u (*or*) oración. Luego escuche la pronunciación y repítala.

1. ... **2.** ... **3.** ... **4.** ... **5.** ... **6.** ... **7.** ... **8.** ... **9.** ...

GRAMÁTICA

18. Expressing *what* or *who(m)* • Direct Objects: The Personal *a;* Direct Object Pronouns

A. **Correspondencias.** Empareje (*Match*) los sustantivos y pronombres personales con los pronombres del complemento directo (*direct object pronouns*) correspondientes. **¡OJO!** Algunos pronombres del complemento directo se usan más de una vez.

_____ **1.** la galleta

_____ **2.** los camarones

_____ **3.** el pescado

_____ **4.** tú

_____ **5.** Elena y Mónica

_____ **6.** los dueños

_____ **7.** Ana

_____ **8.** Diego y yo

_____ **9.** yo

a. lo

b. la

c. los

d. las

e. nos

f. te

g. me

B. Esperando a Marilena

Paso 1. Pablo y Marta tienen planes para cenar en un restaurante elegante con su amiga Marilena. Primero, lea su conversación y subraye (*underline*) los complementos directos.

PABLO: No veo _____[1] el dueño y no conozco _____[2] los camareros. Todos son nuevos.

CAMARERO: Buenas noches, señores. ¿ _____[3] quién buscan Uds.?

PABLO: Buscamos _____[4] la Srta. Estrada. Creo que no está aquí todavía.

CAMARERO: ¿Quieren Uds. sentarse mientras (*while*) esperan?

PABLO: Gracias, podemos esperar _____[5] nuestra amiga en la mesa. Mis padres

conocen _____[6] este restaurante. Creen que es muy bueno.

MARTA: ¿Por qué no llamas _____[7] el camarero ahora? Quiero ver _____[8]

el menú mientras esperamos _____[9] Marilena.

PABLO: Ahí viene. ¡Hola, Marilena!

Paso 2. Ahora complete el diálogo del **Paso 1** con la **a** personal, cuando sea (*whenever it is*) necesario. Cuando la **a** precede el artículo definido **el,** tache (*cross out*) el artículo y escriba **al.**

C. La dieta de Sebastián

Paso 1. Sebastián está a dieta y necesita comer bien. Empareje las oraciones de la columna a la izquierda con las comidas y bebidas de la columna a la derecha que forman parte de la dieta de Sebastián.

1. _____ Los come con frecuencia.
2. _____ Le gusta tomarlo solo en ocasiones especiales.
3. _____ Las prefiere comer crudas (*raw*).
4. _____ La bebe todos los días.

a. las verduras
b. la leche
c. los mariscos
d. el vino

Verifique sus respuestas del **Paso 1** en el Apéndice antes de empezar el **Paso 2.**

Paso 2. Ahora traduzca (*translate*) al inglés las oraciones del **Paso 1.**

1. _____
2. _____
3. _____
4. _____

D. El cumpleaños de Felipe. César Eco habla con un amigo de los planes para la fiesta de cumpleaños de su amigo Felipe. César contesta todas sus preguntas sobre la fiesta, pero con mucha repetición. Vuelva a escribir (*Rewrite*) Ud. sus respuestas con pronombres del complemento directo.

> MODELOS: —¿Quién llama a Felipe?
>
> —Yo llamo a Felipe. → Yo lo llamo.
>
> —¿Quién va a llevar las sillas?
>
> —Pepe va a llevar las sillas. (*two ways*) →
>
> —Pepe va a llevarlas. / Pepe las va a llevar.

1. —¿Quién prepara el pastel?
   —Yo preparo el pastel.

   _____

2. —¿Quién va a comprar los refrescos?
   —Yo voy a comprar los refrescos. (*two ways*)

   _____

   _____

3. —¿Quién va a hacer las galletas?
   —Dolores va a hacer las galletas. (*two ways*)

   _____

   _____

4. —¿Quién trae los discos?
   —Juan trae los discos.

   _____

5. —¿Quién invita a los primos de Felipe?
   —Yo invito a los primos de Felipe.

   _____

E. ¿Quién ayuda con la fiesta? Lea las preguntas sobre las preparaciones para la fiesta. En las respuestas, escriba un pronombre del complemento directo de la lista y la forma apropiada del verbo **ayudar**.

> MODELOS: —¿Quién me ayuda a limpiar el apartamento? ¿Tú? → Sí, yo te ayudo.
>
> PRONOMBRE DEL COMPLEMENTO DIRECTO: la, los, me, te

1. ¿Quién me ayuda con la cena? ¿María y tú?

   Sí, María y yo _____.

2. ¿Te puedo ayudar con las bebidas?

   Sí, _____ puedes _____.

3. ¿Quién ayuda a Isabel con las decoraciones?

   Yo _____.

4. ¿Quién nos ayuda a César y a mí con los platos?

   Marcos y Ceci _____.

F. En la cocina. Imagine que Ud. está preparando la cena y su amigo Pablo está ayudando a Ud. Conteste sus preguntas de manera positiva o negativa, según las indicaciones y use el pronombre del complemento directo apropiado. Luego escuche la respuesta correcta y repítala. **¡OJO!** Recuerde que hay más de una respuesta posible con respecto a (*with respect to*) la posición del pronombre del complemento directo.

MODELO: (Ud. oye) ¿Tienes que preparar la carne ahora?

(Ud. ve) no

(Ud. dice) ¿La carne? No, no la tengo que preparar todavía (*yet*).

(¿La carne? No, no tengo que prepararla todavía.)

(Ud. oye y repite) ¿La carne? No, no la tengo que preparar todavía.

(¿La carne? No, no tengo que prepararla todavía.)

1. no **2.** sí **3.** sí **4.** no

G. Planes para mañana. Imagine que se encuentra con (*run into*) su amigo Manuel y que Uds. hacen planes para reunirse (*get together*) mañana. Primero, escuche el **Vocabulario útil,** luego escuche las preguntas de Manuel. Conteste las preguntas con las siguientes palabras y el pronombre de complemento directo apropiado, si es necesario. Después, escuche una respuesta posible y repítala.

Vocabulario útil

¡regio!	great!
¿me puedes buscar?	can you pick me up?

1. esta noche **4.** 4:00
2. mañana **5.** café La Rioja
3. sí

H. La compra para una cena especial

Paso 1. La Srta. Castillo va al mercado para comprar los ingredientes que necesita para hacer una cena especial. Ud. va a escuchar una conversación entre ella y el vendedor, el Sr. Valderrama. Primero, escuche el **Vocabulario útil,** luego escuche la conversación. Después, indique por escrito (*in writing*) si ella necesita los siguientes ingredientes y para qué los necesita. Siga (*Follow*) los modelos.

Vocabulario útil

¿Qué le doy?	What can I get for you?
el ceviche	a Latin American dish made with raw fish or shellfish marinated in lemon juice
el consejo	(*piece of*) advice
la cebolla	onion
¿A cuánto está... ?	How much is . . . ?
colón (colones)	**la moneda** (*currency*) **de Costa Rica**

MODELOS: ¿pasta? → No, no la necesita.

¿limones? → Sí, los necesita. Los necesita para el ceviche.

1. ¿pescado? _____

2. ¿arroz? _____

3. ¿tomates? _____

4. ¿zanahorias? _____

5. ¿langosta? _____

6. ¿cebollas? _____

(Continúa.)

7. ¿atún? _____

8. ¿camarones? _____

Paso 2. Ahora complete las siguientes oraciones con información de la conversación.

1. Mariela quiere preparar una cena especial para impresionar a _____

_____ .

2. A su novio no le gusta el _____ .

3. A su novio le gustan muchísimo los _____ .

4. A Mariela le gustan las _____ .

5. Las zanahorias van bien con las _____ .

6. Mariela también compra _____, pero ella no menciona cómo _____ piensa usar.

I. En casa de la familia Buendía. Conteste las preguntas según los dibujos (*drawings*). Use los pronombres del complemento directo.

1. ¿A qué hora despierta el despertador (*alarm clock*) a los padres?

_____

2. ¿Quién levanta al bebé? _____

3. ¿Quién lo baña? _____

4. ¿Quién divierte al bebé con una pelota (*ball*)? _____

5. ¿Qué hace la madre con el bebé antes de darle de comer (*feeding him*)?

_____

6. ¿Quién acuesta al bebé? _____

J. ¿Qué acaban de hacer estas personas? Escriba oraciones sobre lo que acaban de hacer las siguientes personas.

MODELO: Diego, después de un partido (*game*) de tenis →
Acaba de jugar al tenis. *o* Acaba de mirar un partido.

1. María y Pablo, después de ir a un concierto de música rock

   _____

2. Ana, después de su fiesta de cumpleaños

   _____

3. los miembros de la familia Ruiz, en un restaurante

   _____

4. el camarero, al final de la comida

   _____

5. el Sr. Ruiz, después de recibir la cuenta

   _____

19. Expressing Negation • Indefinite and Negative Words

¿Recuerda Ud.?

Palabras indefinidas y negativas. Complete las siguientes oraciones lógicamente con palabras de la lista.

nunca   siempre   también

1. Me gustan mucho los cereales. Por eso _____ los como por la mañana.

2. Tomo café con el desayuno. Si no tiene prisa, mi compañero toma café _____.

3. _____ ceno después de las diez de la noche porque me acuesto temprano.

A. Correspondencias. Empareje las palabras de la columna izquierda con las palabras indefinidas y negativas correspondientes de la columna derecha.

1. algo _____   **a.** ningún

2. alguien _____   **b.** nunca, jamás

3. siempre _____   **c.** nada

4. también _____   **d.** nadie

5. algún _____   **e.** tampoco

B. ¿Pesimista u (*or*) optimista?

Paso 1. Su amigo Federico es muy pesimista y siempre contesta en forma negativa. Conteste las preguntas como si Ud. fuera (*as if you were*) él. Use la forma negativa de las palabras indicadas.

Vocabulario útil

contigo   with you
conmigo   with me

MODELO: —¿Sirven *algo* bueno esta noche? → —No, no sirven nada bueno.

1. —¿Vas a hacer *algo* interesante este fin de semana?

   —No, _____.

2. —¿*Siempre* sales con *alguien* los sábados?

   —No, _____.

3. —¿Tienes *algunos* amigos nuevos en la universidad? (**¡OJO!** Recuerde usar el singular.)

   —No, _____.

4. —¿*Algunas* de esas chicas son tus amigas? (**¡OJO!**)

   —No, _____.

5. —¿*Alguien* cena contigo *a veces*?

   —No, _____.

Paso 2. Evita, la novia de Federico, es una persona positiva. Escriba las reacciones positivas de Evita ante (*in response to*) los comentarios de Federico.

1. —No quiero comer nada. La comida aquí es mala.

   —Pues, yo sí _____.

2. —Nadie viene a atendernos (*wait on us*).

   —Pero aquí viene _____.

3. —Nunca cenamos en un restaurante bueno.

   —Yo creo que _____.

4. —No hay ningún plato sabroso en el menú.

   —Pues, aquí veo _____.

 C. Descripciones. Ud. va a oír dos preguntas sobre cada uno de los siguientes dibujos. Primero, escuche el **Vocabulario útil**, luego escuche las preguntas. Conteste, según lo que ve en los dibujos. Después escuche la respuesta correcta y repítala.

Vocabulario útil

la pantalla   screen

MODELOS: (Ud. ve)

(Ud. oye)   ¿Hay alguien en el salón de clase?

(Ud. dice)   Sí, hay alguien en el salón de clase. Hay una profesora.

(Ud. oye y repite)   Sí, hay alguien en el salón de clase. Hay una profesora.

(Ud. oye)   ¿Hay algunas calculadoras en la mesa?

(Ud. dice)   No, no hay ninguna calculadora en la mesa.

(Ud. oye y repite)   No, no hay ninguna calculadora en la mesa.

1.

2.

3.

4.

D. **¡No hay comida en casa!**

Paso 1. Ud. va a escuchar una conversación entre Manolo y Lola sobre la comida en casa. Primero, escuche el **Vocabulario útil**, luego escuche la conversación.

Vocabulario útil

las compras	the grocery shopping
el aniversario de bodas	wedding anniversary

Paso 2. Ahora, cuando oiga la oración, diga lo contrario (*opposite*), según lo que dijeron (*said*) Manolo y Lola en la conversación. Luego escuche la respuesta correcta y repítala.

MODELO: (Ud. oye) No comemos mucho en esta familia.

(Ud. dice) Comemos mucho en esta familia.

(Ud. oye y repite) Comemos mucho en esta familia.

1. ... **2.** ... **3.** ... **4.** ...

E. **¡Por eso no come nadie allí!** Ud. va a oír algunas preguntas sobre un restaurante que no es muy popular. Conteste con el negativo doble. Luego escuche la respuesta correcta y repítala.

MODELO: (Ud. oye) ¿Sirven algunos postres especiales?

(Ud. dice) No, no sirven ningún postre especial.

(Ud. oye y repite) No, no sirven ningún postre especial.

1. ... **2.** ... **3.** ... **4.** ... **5.** ...

20. Influencing Others • Commands (Part 1): Formal Commands

¿Recuerda Ud.?

Mandatos. Ud. ya ha visto (*have already seen*) mandatos (*commands*) formales con mucha frecuencia. Traduzca (*Translate*) los siguientes mandatos al inglés. Luego escriba en español el infinitivo del verbo.

	TRADUCCIÓN	INFINITIVO (ESPAÑOL)
1. **Escuche** la conversación	*Listen to the conversation.*	*escuchar*
2. **Lea** las oraciones.		
3. **Conteste** las preguntas.		
4. **Escriba** un párrafo		

A. Tabla. Complete la tabla con las formas indicadas.

INFINITIVO	YO (PRESENTE DE INDICATIVO)	MANDATO	
		UD.	UDS.
hablar	*hablo*	*hable*	*hablen*
comer		*coma*	
escribir	*escribo*		
buscar		*busque*	
conocer			
dar			
divertir	*divierto*		
empezar	*empiezo*		
estar			
ir	*voy*		
oír			*oigan*
perder	*pierdo*		
saber			
ser		*sea*	
salir			
traer			*traigan*
volver		*vuelva*	

B. Durante las vacaciones. El siguiente folleto (*flyer*), distribuido por el gobierno (*government*) español, da consejos (*advice*) sobre cómo preparar su casa antes de salir de vacaciones. Léalo y complete los siguientes pasos. No preste atención al vocabulario que no sabe Ud., sino que (*rather*) trate de (*try to*) entender las ideas básicas del folleto.

Vocabulario útil

el buzón	mailbox
los escondites	hiding places
la confianza	trust

(Continúa.)

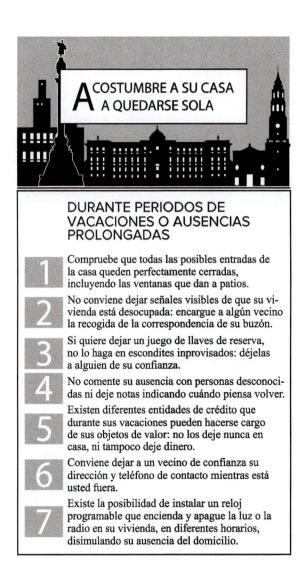

A COSTUMBRE A SU CASA
A QUEDARSE SOLA

DURANTE PERIODOS DE VACACIONES O AUSENCIAS PROLONGADAS

1. Compruebe que todas las posibles entradas de la casa queden perfectamente cerradas, incluyendo las ventanas que dan a patios.

2. No conviene dejar señales visibles de que su vivienda está desocupada: encargue a algún vecino la recogida de la correspondencia de su buzón.

3. Si quiere dejar un juego de llaves de reserva, no lo haga en escondites inprovisados: déjelas a alguien de su confianza.

4. No comente su ausencia con personas desconocidas ni deje notas indicando cuándo piensa volver.

5. Existen diferentes entidades de crédito que durante sus vacaciones pueden hacerse cargo de sus objetos de valor: no los deje nunca en casa, ni tampoco deje dinero.

6. Conviene dejar a un vecino de confianza su dirección y teléfono de contacto mientras está usted fuera.

7. Existe la posibilidad de instalar un reloj programable que encienda y apague la luz o la radio en su vivienda, en diferentes horarios, disimulando su ausencia del domicilio.

Paso 1. Busque en el folleto los mandatos que corresponden a los siguientes infinitivos y escríbalos en el espacio indicado.

MODELO: acostumbrar → acostumbre

1. comprobar _____

2. encargar _____

3. no hacerlo _____

4. dejarlas _____

5. no comentar _____

6. no dejar _____

7. no dejarlos _____

Paso 2. Ahora empareje cada consejo del folleto con su descripción correspondiente en inglés.

_____ 1. **Consejo 1**

_____ 2. **Consejo 2**

_____ 3. **Consejo 3**

_____ 4. **Consejo 4**

_____ 5. **Consejo 5**

a. Ask a neighbor to pick up your mail.

b. Don't leave notes indicating when you will return.

c. Don't leave objects of value or money in your house.

d. Leave an extra set of keys with someone you know.

e. Make sure that your house is well locked.

 C. ¿Qué acaban de decir? Ud. va a oír algunos mandatos. Escriba el número de cada mandato que oye al lado del dibujo correspondiente. **¡OJO!** Hay un dibujo extra.

a. _____

b. _____

c. _____

d. _____

e. _____

f. _____

D. Consejos. Sus amigos tienen los siguientes problemas. Déles (*Give them*) consejos apropiados con un mandato formal.

MODELO: Estamos cansados. → Entonces (*Then*) descansen.

1. Tenemos hambre. _____

2. Tenemos sed. _____

3. Mañana tenemos un examen. _____

4. Las ventanas están abiertas y tenemos frío. _____

5. Siempre llegamos tarde. _____

6. Somos impacientes. _____

E. ¡Qué amigos tan buenos! Sus amigos Emilio y Mercedes están ayudando a la hora de cenar. Primero, lea el **Vocabulario útil,** luego lea sus preguntas. Conteste las preguntas con mandatos afirmativos o negativos según sea apropiado (*as appropriate*). Cambie los sustantivos del complemento directo por pronombres, según el modelo.

Vocabulario útil

cortar   to cut

MODELO: —¿Lavamos (*Shall we wash*) los platos ahora? →
          —Sí, lávenlos ahora. (No, no los laven todavía.)

1. —¿Cortamos el pan ahora? —Sí, _____

2. —¿Preparamos la ensalada ahora? —No, _____

3. —¿Servimos la cena ahora? —No, _____

4. —¿Llamamos a tu papá ahora? —Sí, _____

5. —¿Hacemos el café ahora? —No, _____

6. —¿Traemos las sillas ahora? —Sí, _____

F. Profesor(a) por un día... Imagine que Ud. es profesor(a) por un día y necesita darles (*give them*) mandatos a sus estudiantes. Primero, escuche el verbo que necesita, luego forme un mandato de **Uds.** con el verbo y la frase correspondiente. Después, escuche la respuesta correcta y repítala.

MODELO: (Ud. ve)   los libros
              (Ud. oye)   cerrar
              (Ud. dice)   Cierren los libros.
         (Ud. oye y repite)   Cierren los libros.

1. los ejercicios   4. la tarea en clase
2. el capítulo siete   5. en clase mañana
3. el diálogo

G. La dieta del Sr. Morales. El Sr. Morales está a dieta, y Ud. es su médico/a. Cuando el Sr. Morales le pregunte (*asks you*) si puede comer ciertas comidas, conteste sus preguntas con mandatos afirmativos o negativos, según las indicaciones. Use pronombres de complemento directo en sus respuestas.

MODELO: (Ud. oye) ¿Puedo comer este chocolate?

       (Ud. ve) No, ...

      (Ud. dice) No, no lo coma.

   (Ud. oye y repite) No, no lo coma.

1. No, ... **2.** No, ... **3.** No, ... **4.** Sí, ... **5.** Sí, ...

H. Un nuevo restaurante. Ud. va a oír un anuncio para un restaurante nuevo. Primero, escuche la lista de acciones, luego escuche el anuncio. Después, indique **Sí** o **No**, según lo que se menciona (*is mentioned*) en el anuncio.

		SÍ	**NO**
1.	hacer reservaciones	☐	☐
2.	vestirse formalmente	☐	☐
3.	pedir el pescado	☐	☐
4.	pedir una hamburguesa	☐	☐
5.	llegar temprano	☐	☐
6.	pagar con tarjeta de crédito	☐	☐
7.	pagar al contado (*in cash*)	☐	☐

Un poco de todo

A. Por teléfono. Complete el diálogo entre Ana y Pablo con las palabras apropiadas entre paréntesis.

ANA: Oye, Pablo, ¿no _____[1] (conoces / sabes) tú _____[2] (a / al / el) profesor Vargas?

PABLO: No, no _____[3] (él / lo) _____[4] (sé / conozco). ¿Por qué?

ANA: Es profesor de historia. El viernes va a dar una conferencia[a] sobre la función de la mujer en la Revolución mexicana. ¿No quieres ir? Yo _____[5] (sé / conozco) que va a ser muy interesante.

PABLO: ¡Qué lástima![b] Casi _____[6] (siempre / nunca) tengo tiempo libre[c] los viernes, pero este viernes tengo varios compromisos.[d]

ANA: Pues, yo no tengo mucho tiempo libre _____[7] (también / tampoco), pero voy a asistir. _____[8] (Al / El) Sr. Vargas siempre usa imágenes fascinantes y tengo ganas de verlas.

---

[a]dar... *give a lecture* [b]¡Qué... *What a shame!* [c]*free* [d]*engagements*

B. *Listening Passage:* **La vida social en los bares y los cafés de España**

❖ **Antes de escuchar.** You are going to hear a passage about the importance of bars and cafés in Spain. Many aspects of social life and nightlife in Spain are different from those of this country. Before you listen to the passage, read the following statements and check the ones that you think apply to Spain but not to this country.

1. ☐ Hay muchos bares. ¡A veces hay dos en la misma calle (*same street*)!

2. ☐ La familia entera (*entire*), padres y hasta (*even*) hijos pequeños, puede ir a un bar.

3. ☐ Por lo general, no sirven comida en un bar.

4. ☐ En los bares, es costumbre pedir tapas: pequeños platos de comidas diversas.

Listening Passage. Now you will hear the passage. First, listen to the **Vocabulario útil**, then listen to the passage.

Vocabulario útil

dar un paseo	**caminar**
encontrarse	to meet up, get together
el estilo	style

Después de escuchar. Complete the sentences with words from the following list, then check your answers in the Appendix.

amigos   bar   café   calle   estilos   familia   música   tapas   tradicionales

1. En España, los españoles van con frecuencia a un _____ o a un

   _____ para encontrarse con los _____ y la familia.

2. Es normal ver a una _____ con niños pequeños en un bar español.

3. Hay bares y cafés de muchos _____ en España: Hay *pubs*, con

   _____ y también hay bares _____.

4. En España, hay un bar en cada _____, ¡y a veces más!

5. En los bares españoles, sirven _____, que son pequeños platos de comidas

   diversas.

C. **La cena de aniversario**

Paso 1. Ud. va a escuchar una conversación entre Manolo y Lola, quienes celebran su aniversario de bodas (*wedding*) en un restaurante, y su camarero. Primero, escuche el **Vocabulario útil** y lea las siguientes oraciones. Luego escuche el diálogo y complete las oraciones.

Vocabulario útil

Rioja	*a wine-producing region in northern Spain*
el agua mineral con gas	sparkling water
la gamba	**el camarón**
poco asado/a	rare (*meat*)
el ajo	garlic
la copa	after-dinner drink

1. De beber, Lola y Manolo piden _____ y _____.

2. De comer, Lola pide _____ para empezar. De segundo plato

   (*As a second course*), pide _____.

3. De primero, Manolo pide _____ y de segundo plato pide

   _____.

4. De postre, ¿Lola y Manolo piden algo? Lola y Manolo _____.

5. Como es su aniversario, el restaurante les invita a (*treats them to*) una _____.

6. En la opinión de Manolo, este restaurante es _____ y la comida es

   _____.

Paso 2. Ahora Ud. va a participar en un diálogo similar al del **Paso 1** en el que Ud. hace el papel del cliente en un restaurante. Primero, complete el diálogo con las siguientes frases y verifique sus respuestas en el Apéndice. Segundo, haga el diálogo en voz alta (*aloud*) y conteste cada pregunta que oye. Luego escuche la pronunciación correcta y repítala.

un coctel de camarones   el flan de naranja   los tacos de pollo   un vino blanco

CAMARERA: ¿Sabe ya lo que desea de comer?

CLIENTE: Sí. Favor de traerme _____.[1]

CAMARERA: Sí, cómo no. ¿Y para empezar? Tenemos una gran variedad de antojitos (*appetizers*) que

seguramente le van a gustar.

CLIENTE: Bueno, tráigame _____,[2] por favor.

CAMARERA: ¿Algo de postre?

CLIENTE: Sí, quiero _____,[3] por favor.

CAMARERA: Muy bien. ¿Y para beber?

CLIENTE: ¿Me puede traer _____[4]?

CAMARERA: Sí. Se lo traigo en seguida.

Ahora haga el diálogo en voz alta.

CULTURA

A.   **Mapa.** Identifique el país, la capital y el cuerpo (*body*) de agua en el siguiente mapa.

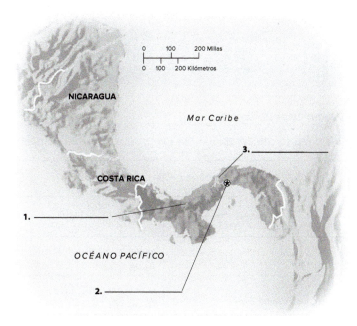

B. Comprensión. Complete las siguientes oraciones con palabras de la lista. Esta actividad se basa en información de las lecturas **Nota cultural** (p. 204), **Algo sobre...** (p. 206, 213 y 218) y **Lectura cultural** (p. 226) del libro de texto o del eBook. **¡OJO!** No se usan todas las palabras.

la arquitectura	las empanadas	salsa
el arroz	el Estrecho de Magallanes	sopa
el canal de Panamá	frutas	las tortillas
los emberás	el maíz	verduras

1. _____, una comida fundamental en las cocinas latinoamericanas, fue introducido en América por (*by*) los españoles.

2. Rubén Blades es uno de los cantautores (*singer-songwriters*) de _____ más conocidos (*most well-known*) en todo el mundo.

3. La parte antigua de la Ciudad de Panamá mezcla (*mixes*) _____ colonial con el estilo de las casas antillanas (*de las islas Antillas*).

4. Las casas de _____, un pueblo amerindio de Panamá, están en alto (*raised up*).

5. El sancocho es un tipo de _____ típica de los países caribeños. Lleva carne, _____ y legumbres (*beans*).

6. La chicha panameña es un tipo de bebida que se hace con _____ panameñas, como el coco, la guanábana y el maracuyá.

7. _____ son una comida que consiste en una masa de pan rellena (*filled*) de algo dulce o salado.

8. _____ une (*unites*) el mar Caribe con el océano Pacífico.

PÓNGASE A PRUEBA

A. Los pronombres del complemento directo

1. Complete la tabla con la forma apropiada del los pronombres del complemento directo.

	COMPLEMENTO DIRECTO		COMPLEMENTO DIRECTO
me	*me*	*us*	
you (*fam. sing.*)			
you (*form. sing., m.*), him, it (*m.*)		*you* (*form. pl., m.*), *them* (*m.*)	*los*
you (*form. sing., f.*), her, it (*f.*)		*you* (*form. pl., f.*), *them* (*f.*)	

2. Escriba de nuevo (*Rewrite*) la oración con el pronombre del complemento directo apropiado para reemplazar (*replace*) el complemento directo subrayado (*underlined*).

    a. Yo traigo <u>el postre</u>. _____

    b. ¡Traiga <u>el postre</u>! _____

    c. ¡No traiga <u>el postre</u>! _____

    d. Estamos esperando <u>al camarero</u>. (*two ways*)

       _____

       _____

    e. Voy a llamar <u>al camarero</u>. (*two ways*)

       _____

       _____

B. Las palabras negativas. Escriba la forma negativa de las siguientes palabras o frases.

    1. alguien _____   **4.** algo _____

    2. también _____   **5.** algunos detalles (**¡OJO!**)

    3. siempre _____   _____

C. Mandatos formales. Complete la tabla con la forma apropiada de los mandatos formales.

VERBO	MANDATO FORMAL	VERBO	MANDATO FORMAL
pensar	Ud.	**ser**	*sea* Ud.
volver	Ud.	**buscar**	Ud.
dar	Ud.	**estar**	Ud.
servir	*sirva* Ud.	**saber**	Ud.
ir	Ud.	**decir**	Ud.

PRUEBA CORTA

A. *¿Saber o conocer?* Escriba la forma apropiada de **saber** o **conocer.**

—Yo no _____[1] a la novia de Juan. ¿La _____[2] tú?

—No muy bien, pero (yo) _____[3] que ella se llama María Elena y que

_____[4] tocar bien la guitarra.

B. Palabras negativas. Escriba las oraciones en la forma afirmativa.

    1. No quiero comer nada. _____

    2. No busco a nadie. _____

    3. No hay nada para beber. _____

    4. —No conozco a ninguno de sus amigos. _____

       —Yo tampoco. _____

C. **Los pronombres del complemento directo.** Conteste las preguntas con pronombres del complemento directo.

1. —¿Vas a pedir la ensalada de fruta?

   —No, _____.

2. —¿Quieres aquellas zanahorias con la comida?

   —Sí, _____.

3. —¿Tomas café por la noche?

   —No, _____.

4. —¿Quién prepara la cena en tu casa?

   —(Yo) _____.

D. **El mandato formal.** Escriba la forma apropiada del mandato formal plural del verbo indicado.

1. _____ (*Uds.:* Comprar) tomates y lechuga.

2. No _____ (*Uds.:* hacer) ensalada hoy.

3. _____ (*Uds.:* traer) dos sillas, por favor.

4. No _____ (*Uds.:* poner) tanto aceite en la comida.

5. Juan no está aquí todavía. _____ (*Uds.:* Llamarlo) ahora.

6. ¿El vino? No _____ (*Uds.:* servirlo) todavía.

E. **Hablando de un nuevo restaurante.** Combine las palabras que se dan (*are provided*) y las que oye para formar oraciones. Cuando hay dos posibilidades, escoja (*choose*) el verbo o la palabra correcta. Cambie los verbos según el sujeto que se da. Luego escuche la respuesta correcta y repítala. **¡OJO!** Si el sujeto está entre paréntesis, no lo incluya (*include*) en la oración.

   MODELO: (Ud. ve)   (yo) saber / conocer

                    (Ud. oye)   un buen restaurante

                    (Ud. dice)   Conozco un buen restaurante.

          (Ud. oye y repite)   Conozco un buen restaurante.

1. (el restaurante) llamarse
2. (el restaurante) ser / estar
3. (yo) saber / conocer
4. (yo) saber / conocer
5. Ellos lo / la acabar de abrir
6. (ellos) preparar
7. Los / Las cocinan
8. no hay algo / nada
9. Siempre / Nunca

PUNTOS PERSONALES

❖ **A. Preguntas personales**

Paso 1. Conteste estas preguntas sobre sus hábitos y preferencias con respecto a (*with respect to*) la comida.

1. ¿Dónde y a qué hora almuerza Ud. generalmente?

_____

2. Cuando Ud. vuelve a casa después de sus clases o después de trabajar y tiene hambre, ¿qué le apetece (*do you feel like*) merendar? ¿fruta? ¿galletas? ¿un sándwich? ¿ ?

Me apetece merendar _____.

3. Por lo general, ¿qué come Ud.: pescado, pollo o carne?

_____

Paso 2. Conteste las siguientes preguntas. Use pronombres del complemento directo, cuando sea (*whenever it is*) posible.

1. ¿Sabe Ud. cocinar bien?

_____

2. ¿Conoce Ud. a la familia de su mejor amigo/a?

_____

3. ¿Conoce Ud. bien a los estudiantes de su clase de español?

_____

4. ¿Tiene Ud. algunos planes para el fin de semana?

_____

5. Escriba dos cosas que Ud. **nunca** hace los sábados.

Vocabulario útil

afeitarse
despertarse temprano
estudiar
ir al cine
quedarse en casa
salir a bailar

_____

_____

B. Gustos personales y tradiciones nacionales

Paso 1. Ud. va a oír una entrevista con Karina, Rubén y Tané. Los amigos hablan de sus gustos personales en cuanto a (*in terms of*) la comida y también de sus tradiciones nacionales. Primero, escuche el **Vocabulario útil,** luego escuche la entrevista. Mientras escucha, fíjese en (*pay attention to*) las comidas que mencionan los tres amigos y complete la tabla. Escuche la entrevista tres veces, fijándose en las respuestas de solo una persona cada vez que escucha.

Vocabulario útil

la arepa	*similar to a corn tortilla, but thicker and made of white corn; typical of Venezuela and Colombia*
todo lo que provenga del mar	anything that comes from the sea
el pulpo	octopus
el platillo	small dish
el pabellón criollo	*dish with black beans, white rice, meat, and plantains*
la carne mechada	*meat similar to pot roast*
la tajada	plantain
el puerco	pork

		KARINA	TANÉ	RUBÉN
1.	COMIDA FAVORITA			
2.	EN SU FAMILIA, ¿QUIÉN COCINA?			
3.	PLATILLOS TRADICIONALES			
4.	HORA DE DESAYUNAR			
5.	HORA DE ALMORZAR			
6.	HORA DE CENAR			
7.	PAÍS DE ORIGEN			

❖ **Paso 2.** Ahora Ud. va a oír las mismas preguntas de la entrevista. Contéstelas por escrito (*in writing*) con información que es verdadera (*true*) para Ud. **¡OJO!** Las preguntas no están en el mismo orden que en la entrevista.

1. _____

   _____

2. _____

   _____

3. _____

   _____

4. _____

   _____

❖ **C. Guided Composition**

Paso 1. En una hoja aparte (*On a separate sheet of paper*), conteste las siguientes preguntas sobre uno de sus restaurantes favoritos.

1. ¿Cómo se llama el restaurante? ¿Dónde está?
2. ¿Qué clase de comida sirven? ¿Cómo es la comida? ¿Es rica? ¿barata? ¿cara?
3. ¿Muchas personas conocen este restaurante o es una joya escondida (*hidden gem*)?
4. De los platos principales que sirven, ¿cuál es su favorito? ¿Qué lleva el plato? (Es decir [*That is to say*], dé algunos de los ingredientes principales.) ¿Cómo se prepara? ¿Qué viene con el plato principal? (¿Viene una verdura? ¿papas o arroz? ¿pan?)
5. ¿El restaurante ofrece (*offer*) platos del día con precios especiales? Dé ejemplos de algunos especiales del día.

Vocabulario útil

lo/la/los/las fríen	they fry it/them
asar	to grill
hervir (hervido) (e → ie)	to boil (boiled)
hornear	to bake
al horno	baked, roasted
bastante cocido/a	medium
bien cocido/a	well done
crudo/a	raw

Paso 2. En una hoja aparte, escriba sobre su restaurante favorito. Organice y combine en dos párrafos sus respuestas del **Paso 1**. **¡OJO!** Para conectar ideas, use expresiones como: **por eso, como...** (*since . . .*), **porque, aunque** (*although*) y **luego**.

❖ **D. Mi diario.** En su diario, escriba un párrafo sobre un desayuno o un almuerzo típico para Ud. Mencione las comidas y las bebidas que toma y a qué hora y con quién come. También mencione dónde desayuna o almuerza generalmente.

Vocabulario útil

el tocino	bacon
los fideos	noodles
el pavo	turkey
las papitas	potato chips

❖ **E. Intercambios.** Escuche las siguientes preguntas y contéstelas por escrito.

1. _____

   _____

2. _____

   _____

3. _____

   _____

4. _____

   _____

Capítulo 8 De viaje

VOCABULARIO   Preparación

De viaje

A. **Un viaje en avión.** Complete las oraciones con la forma apropiada de las palabras de la lista. Use cada expresión solo una vez.

asistente de vuelo   escala   subir
bajarse   extranjero   vuelo
cola   ida y vuelta
control de seguridad   pasajero
demora   pasaporte
equipaje   salida

1. Generalmente, es más barato comprar un boleto de _____ que dos boletos de ida

   solamente (*only*).

2. Quiero un vuelo sin _____; no quiero tener que _____ del avión.

3. Si voy al _____, es necesario tener un _____.

4. Después de llegar al aeropuerto, un maletero me ayuda a facturar el _____.

5. Antes de llegar a la puerta de embarque, hay que pasar por el _____.

6. En la sala de espera, hay muchos _____ que esperan su vuelo.

7. Anuncian que el _____ número 68 de AeroMéxico con destino a Santo

   Domingo está atrasado. Hay una _____ de media hora.

8. Cuando por fin anuncian la _____ de nuestro avión, los pasajeros hacemos

   _____ para _____ al avión.

9. Media hora después que el avión despega (*takes off*), los _____ sirven el desayuno.

   ¡Y qué hambre tengo!

B. Andrés viaja a Santo Domingo. Complete las oraciones con una palabra apropiada para describir el viaje de Andrés.

1.

Andrés está comprando un

_____ electrónico. Lo paga

con una _____ de crédito.

2.

Andrés está facturando su

_____ en el aeropuerto.

Recibe su tarjeta de _____

de la empleada.

3.

Los pasajeros están pasando por el

_____ de

_____.

4.

Todos están haciendo _____

antes de subir al avión. El número de la

puerta de _____ es 23.

5.

En el avión, una madre y sus hijos están

sentados (*seated*) en los

_____ al lado de Andrés.

6.

Andrés está en la _____ de

un aeropuerto internacional. La agente

necesita ver su _____.

C. Definiciones

Paso 1. Ud. va a escuchar algunas definiciones. Indique la letra de la palabra que se define. **¡OJO!** Hay más de una respuesta correcta en algunos casos.

1. **a.** el avión   **b.** la playa   **c.** el mar (*sea*)
2. **a.** el billete   **b.** la estación de trenes   **c.** el aeropuerto
3. **a.** el hotel   **b.** el restaurante   **c.** la llegada
4. **a.** el puerto   **b.** el mar   **c.** las montañas (*mountains*)
5. **a.** la cabina   **b.** el maletero   **c.** el tren

Paso 2. Ahora recree (*recreate*) las definiciones que escuchó en el **Paso 1** con las indicaciones que oye y las respuestas correctas del **Paso 1**.

MODELO: (Ud. oye) Uno. se puede tomar el sol

(Ud. ve) **1. a.** el avión **(b.)** la playa **(c.)** el mar

(Ud. dice) En la playa y en el mar se puede tomar el sol.

(Ud. oye y repite) En la playa y en el mar se puede tomar el sol.

2. ... **3.** ... **4.** ... **5.** ...

 D. Identificaciones. Identifique los objetos o las personas cuando oiga el número correspondiente. Empiece cada respuesta con **Es el...** , **Es la...** o **Son...** .

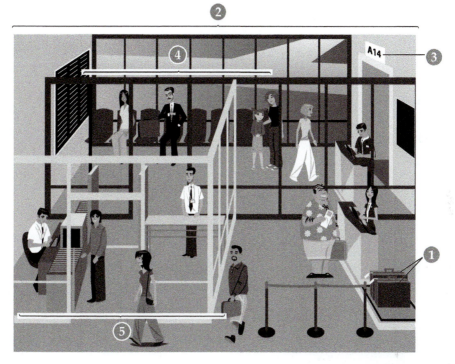

1. ... **2.** ... **3.** ... **4.** ... **5.** ...

E. Un viaje en tren

Paso 1. Juan Carlos va a hacer un viaje en tren. Primero, escuche el **Vocabulario útil.** Luego escuche la conversación entre Juan Carlos y la vendedora (*salesperson*) de billetes en la estación de trenes.

Vocabulario útil

parece	it seems
faltan todavía...	that's still . . . away
De veras, lo siento.	I'm really sorry.
no hay remedio	there's nothing I can do (about it)
a la hora en punto	exactly on time
la guía	guidebook
no importa	it doesn't matter
el pueblo	**ciudad pequeña**

(Continúa.)

Paso 2. Ahora complete el párrafo con la forma apropiada de las palabras de la lista para resumir (*summarize*) la conversación. **¡OJO!** No se usan todas las palabras.

atrasado/a	facturar	salir
autobús	ida	subir
billete	parada	tarjeta
cabina	pedir	tren
cambiar (*to change*)	puesto	viaje
cola	quejarse	vuelta

Juan Carlos está en una estación de _____.[1] En la ventanilla de ventas[a] (él)

_____[2] un _____[3] de _____[4] y _____[5] a Tarma.

El tren normalmente _____[6] a las dos y media, pero hoy está _____.[7] Por

eso, Juan Carlos _____[8] sus planes y decide ir a Chincheros, otro pueblo que él quiere

visitar para la guía turística que piensa escribir.

[a]ventanilla... *ticket sales window*

De vacaciones

A. Las vacaciones

Paso 1. Identifique los objetos y lugares en el dibujo. Use el artículo definido.

1. _____   4. _____

2. _____   5. _____

3. _____

Paso 2. Use el presente progresivo para explicar lo que están haciendo los miembros de la familia en el dibujo.

MODELO: El padre → El padre está sacando fotos (de la madre).

1. La madre _____

2. Las hijas _____

3. El hijo _____

4. Toda la familia _____

B. Unas vacaciones inolvidables (*unforgettable*). Cecilia va a hablar de las vacaciones inolvidables que tuvo (*she had*). Primero, escuche el **Vocabulario útil** y la descripción de sus vacaciones. Luego indique si cada oración es cierta (**C**) o falsa (**F**), según la información que oye.

Vocabulario útil

hace un año	a year ago
el pueblo	**ciudad pequeña**
conseguir	to get
pudimos	we managed
estábamos	we were
tuvimos que hacernos cargo de	we had to take care of
armamos	we set up
el árbol	tree
había	there were
la gente	people
teníamos	we had

1. C F Cecilia y su amiga pasaron (*spent*) el verano en las montañas.

2. C F Los padres de las muchachas pagaron (*paid for*) el viaje.

3. C F Cecilia y su amiga pasaron un mes en el Uruguay.

4. C F Había otra gente joven en la playa donde se quedaron (*stayed*) Cecilia y su amiga.

Nota comunicativa: Other Uses of *se*

¿Cuánto sabe Ud. de estas cosas? Complete cada oración con una frase apropiada con **se**.

se come   se factura   se habla   se muestra (*one shows*)   se permite

1. _____ portugués en el Brasil.

2. _____ el equipaje en el mostrador.

3. No _____ fumar en el avión.

4. _____ el pasaporte en la aduana.

5. _____ mucho en un crucero.

- In Spanish, the letter **g** followed by **e** or **i** has the same sound as the letter **j** followed by any vowel. This sound, represented as [x], is similar to the English *h*. The pronunciation of this sound varies, depending on the region or country of origin of the speaker. Note the difference in the pronunciation of the following words by speakers from Spain and the Caribbean.

    Jorge   jueves   general   álgebra

- When the letter **g** is followed by the vowels **a**, **o**, or **u**, or by the combination **ue** or **ui**, its pronunciation is somewhat similar to the pronunciation of the English letter *g*. However, just as you've seen with the letters **b** and **d** in Spanish, there are two pronunciations of this letter, depending on its position in the word or phrase.

- At the beginning of a word, after a pause, or after the letter **n**, the Spanish **g** is pronounced as a stop. That is, no air is allowed to escape over the back of the tongue when it is pronounced. This sound, equivalent to the letter *g* in the English word *get*, is represented as [g]. Listen to the pronunciation of the following words.

    tengo   gusto   gastar   Miguel   Guillermo

- In all other positions, the Spanish **g** is a fricative, represented as [ɣ]. It has a softer sound, produced by allowing some air to escape when it is pronounced. There is no exact equivalent for this variant in English. Listen to the pronunciation of the following words.

    agua   laguna   diálogo   legal   igual

A. Repeticiones: El sonido [x]. Repita las siguientes palabras. Imite lo que oye.

[x] **1.** general   gigante   geranio

[x] **2.** jamón   Juana   jipijapa

Ahora, cuando oiga el número correspondiente, lea las siguientes palabras. Luego escuche la pronunciación correcta y repítala.

[x] **3.** gimnasio   **4.** giralda   **5.** rojo   **6.** pasaje

B. Repeticiones: El sonido [g]. Repita las siguientes palabras. Imite lo que oye.

[g] **1.** ángulo   gordo   gato   guerra   guitarra

Ahora, cuando oiga el número correspondiente, lea las siguientes palabras. Luego escuche la pronunciación correcta y repítala.

[g] **2.** gorila   **3.** grande   **4.** guerrilla   **5.** Guevara

C. Repeticiones: El sonido [ɣ], la g fricativa. Repita las siguientes palabras. Imite lo que oye.

[ɣ] **1.** abrigo   hago   juego   algodón   el gusto

Ahora, cuando oiga el número correspondiente, lea las siguientes palabras. Luego escuche la pronunciación correcta y repítala.

[ɣ] **2.** agua   **3.** la gota   **4.** la guerrilla   **5.** las guitarras

D. Repeticiones: Combinaciones. Repita las siguientes palabras, frases y oraciones. Imite lo que oye.

1. [g]/[ɣ]   un grupo / el grupo   gracias / las gracias   un gato / el gato   un gorila / el gorila
2. [x]/[g]   gigante   jugos   juguete
3. [g]/[x]   aguja   garaje
4. ¡Qué ganga!
5. Domingo es guapo y delgado.
6. Tengo algunas amigas guatemaltecas.
7. La guitarra de Guillermo es de Gijón.

E. Oraciones. Escriba las oraciones que oye.

1. _____
2. _____
3. _____
4. _____

F. Sonidos importantes: [g] o [x]

Paso 1. Indique el sonido que se usa en cada una de estas palabras.

	[g]	[x]			[g]	[x]
1. jirafa	☐	☐	5. guapo		☐	☐
2. gusto	☐	☐	6. general		☐	☐
3. Geraldo	☐	☐	7. largo		☐	☐
4. guía	☐	☐	8. La Giralda		☐	☐

Paso 2. Ahora, cuando oiga el número correspondiente, lea las palabras del **Paso 1.** Luego escuche la pronunciación y repítala.

1. ... 2. ... 3. ... 4. ... 5. ... 6. ... 7. ... 8. ...

GRAMÁTICA

¿Recuerda Ud.?

Avoiding Repetition. In **Gramática 18 (Cap. 7),** you learned how to use direct object pronouns to avoid repetition. To what or to whom do the direct object pronouns in the following exchange refer?

ANA: ¿Puedes traer las otras sillas?

CARLOS: Sí, **las** traigo del coche ahora. (**las** = _____[1])

ANA: Si quieres, **te** ayudo. (**te** = **a ti** [_____[2]])

CARLOS: Gracias, **te** espero en el coche. (**te** = **a ti** [_____[3]])

21. Expressing *to who(m)* or *for who(m)* • Indirect Object Pronouns; *Dar* and *decir*

A. Los pronombres del complemento indirecto. Complete la tabla con los pronombres apropiados.

to/for me	*me*	to/for us	
to/for you (*fam. sing.*)		to/for you (*fam. plur.*)	*os*
to/for you (*form. sing.*), him, her		to/for you (*pl.*), them	

B. ¿A quién? Complete las oraciones con los pronombres apropiados del complemento indirecto.

1. Mis padres _____ dan dinero (a mí).

2. _____ mando mensajes a mi amigo.

3. La profesora _____ explica la gramática (a nosotros).

4. _____ muestro fotos a mis abuelos.

5. ¿_____ entregamos la tarea a Ud., profesor?

6. No, no _____ voy a prestar mi carro (a ti).

C. Formas verbales. Complete las oraciones con la forma apropiada de los verbos **dar** y **decir.** Use el presente de indicativo.

(**dar**): Hoy es el cumpleaños de Ana y todos lo celebramos con una fiesta. ¿Qué regalos le

_____[1] nosotros? Carmela le _____[2] una blusa, los padres de Ana le _____[3]

un impermeable, tú le _____[4] un suéter y yo le _____[5] un teléfono.

(**decir**): ¡No estamos de acuerdo! Yo _____[6] que quiero salir, Jorge _____[7] que tiene

que estudiar, Anita y Memo _____[8] que no tienen suficiente dinero y tú _____[9] que

estás cansado. ¿Qué les (nosotros) _____[10] a los otros?

D. Necesito consejos. Pregúntele a un amigo lo que Ud. debe hacer en las siguientes situaciones.

MODELO: Mañana es el cumpleaños de mi novio/a. (¿comprar / flores?) →
¿Le compro flores?

1. Mi hermano necesita $25 para ir a un concierto. (¿prestar / dinero?)

_____

2. Mi amigo está triste hoy. (¿contar / un chiste?)

_____

3. Teresa y Manuela van a España este semestre. (¿ofrecer / mi maleta?)

_____

4. Tengo problemas en la clase de cálculo. (¿pedir ayuda / profesor?)

_____

5. Julio y Tomás quieren otra cerveza. (¿servir / más?)

_____

E. Las vacaciones de primavera

Paso 1. Escuche la conversación entre Javier y sus padres sobre las vacaciones de primavera de él. Luego llene los espacios en blanco con el pronombre de complemento indirecto apropiado o una frase con **a,** según el modelo.

MODELO: (Ud. ve) **1.** Javier nunca _____ pide dinero _____ durante el semestre.

(Ud. escribe) **1.** Javier nunca les pide dinero a sus padres durante el semestre.

2. Pero para las vacaciones de primavera, Javier _____ pide _____ dinero para el pasaje de avión.

3. La madre de Javier siempre _____ dice _____ que Javier es muy trabajador.

4. Los padres de Javier _____ van a dar un cheque _____ para el pasaje.

Paso 2. Ahora mire las oraciones del **Paso 1.** Cuando oiga un complemento indirecto con el número correspondiente, cambie la oración para reflejar (*reflect*) el nuevo complemento. Luego escuche la respuesta correcta y repítala.

MODELO: (Ud. ve) **1.** Javier nunca les pide dinero *a sus padres* durante el semestre.

(Ud. oye) **1.** a su hermano Manolo

(Ud. dice) Javier nunca le pide dinero a su hermano Manolo durante el semestre.

(Ud. oye y repite) Javier nunca le pide dinero a su hermano Manolo durante el semestre.

2. ... **3.** ... **4.** ...

F. Una cena en casa. Diga para quién las siguientes personas hacen las siguientes cosas. Luego escuche la respuesta correcta y repítala.

MODELO: (Ud. ve) Mi padre sirve el guacamole.

(Ud. oye) a nosotros

(Ud. dice) Mi padre nos sirve el guacamole.

(Ud. oye y repite) Mi padre nos sirve el guacamole.

1. Mi madre sirve la sopa.

2. Ahora ella prepara la ensalada.

3. Mi hermano trae el café.

4. Rosalinda da postre.

G. ¿Qué hacen estas personas? Cuando oiga un nombre, diga lo que hacen las siguientes personas para el aniversario de los señores Moreno. Conjugue los verbos que se dan y use los pronombres de complemento indirecto apropiados. Luego escuche la respuesta correcta y repítala.

MODELO: (Ud. oye) Ana

(Ud. ve) dar un libro *al Sr. Moreno*

(Ud. dice) Ana le da un libro al Sr. Moreno.

(Ud. oye y repite) Ana le da un libro al Sr. Moreno.

1. regalar una botella de vino *al Sr. Moreno*

2. regalar dos suéteres *a los Sres. Moreno*

3. mandar una tarjeta *a los Sres. Moreno*

4. dar flores *a la Sra. Moreno*

5. comprar un bolso *a la Sra. Moreno*

H. Reservaciones

Paso 1. La Sra. Velasco necesita hacer reservaciones para un viaje a las Islas Galápagos. En esta conversación, ella habla con su agente de viajes, el Sr. Gómez. Primero, escuche el **Vocabulario útil.** Luego escuche la conversación.

Vocabulario útil

¿cómo le fue... ?	how did . . . go?
todo salió bien	it all went well
Ud. viajó	you traveled
fui	I went
fue una experiencia inolvidable	it was an unforgettable experience
arreglar	to arrange
me gustaría	I would like

Paso 2. Ahora combine elementos de cada columna para formar por lo menos (*at least*) siete oraciones completas sobre el diálogo. Hay muchas opciones posibles.

SUJETO	+	PRONOMBRE + VERBO	+	A + COMPLEMENTO INDIRECTO	+	COMPLEMENTO DIRECTO
Elisa el Sr. Gómez		le dice le explica le hace le pide le pregunta		a Elisa al Sr. Gómez		una reservación de avión para las Islas Galápagos qué días quiere viajar cuánto tiempo piensa quedarse allí cuánto cuesta el boleto de avión si él conoce las Galápagos que el viaje a las Galápagos con su esposa fue inolvidable si ella necesita una reservación de hotel también

1. _____

2. _____

3. _____

4. _____

5. _____

6. _____

7. _____

¿Recuerda Ud.?

Los gustos. Conteste las preguntas para expresar sus gustos y preferencias.

1. ¿A Ud. le gusta la leche? Sí, (No, no) _____.

2. ¿A Ud. le gusta viajar al extranjero? Sí, (No, no) _____.

3. ¿A Ud. le gusta nadar en el mar? Sí, (No, no) _____.

4. ¿A Ud. le gusta hacer *camping*? Sí, (No, no) _____.

22. Expressing Likes and Dislikes • *Gustar* (Part 2)

A. Tabla. Complete la tabla con el pronombre del complemento indirecto (**me, te, le, nos les**) y la forma apropiada del verbo **gustar** (**gusta, gustan**).

1. A mí _____ _____ la playa.	4. A nosotros _____ _____ nadar.
2. ¿A ti _____ _____ las playas de Costa Rica?	5. ¿A Uds. _____ _____ esquiar?
3. ¿A Ud. _____ _____ la playa?	6. ¿A Uds. _____ _____ los viajes largos?

B. Preferencias en los vuelos. Complete las oraciones con la forma apropiada de **gustar** y el pronombre del complemento indirecto apropiado.

MODELO: A mí me gusta llegar temprano al aeropuerto.

1. ¿A ti _____ _____ sentarte en el pasillo?

2. A muchas personas no _____ _____ hacer paradas.

3. A mí también _____ _____ los vuelos directos.

4. A nosotros no _____ _____ la comida que sirven en la clase turística, pero a Jorge

   _____ _____ todo.

5. ¿Y qué línea aérea _____ _____ a Uds.?

C. Los gustos de la familia de Ernesto. Forme oraciones completas para decir qué lugares o actividades les gustan a los diferentes miembros de la familia de Ernesto. Haga todos los cambios necesarios. ¡OJO! No se olvide de escribir **a** antes del complemento indirecto.

MODELO: su padre / gustar / la playa → A su padre le gusta la playa.

1. su padre / gustar / vacaciones en las montañas

   _____

2. su madre / encantar / cruceros

   _____

3. sus hermanos / gustar / deportes (*sports*) acuáticos

   _____

4. nadie / gustar / viajar en autobús

   _____

5. Ernesto / encantar / sacar fotos

   _____

D. **¿Vacaciones para toda la familia?** Su familia no puede decidir adónde ir para sus vacaciones y Ud. necesita tomar (*to make*) unas decisiones. Primero, escuche la lista de lugares, luego escuche lo que le gusta a cada miembro de la familia. Diga adónde le gustaría ir a cada miembro, según los lugares que se dan (*are given*). Después, escuche la respuesta correcta y repítala. Hay más de una respuesta posible en algunos casos.

Lugares: Disneylandia, la Florida, Nueva York, las playas de México, quedarse en casa, Roma

MODELO: (Ud. oye)   A mi padre le gusta mucho jugar al golf.

                    (Ud. dice)   Le gustaría ir a la Florida.

        (Ud. oye y repite)   Le gustaría ir a la Florida.

1. ...   **2.** ...   **3.** ...   **4.** ...   **5.** ...

E. **¿Qué le gusta y qué no le gusta?** Ud. va a hablar de lo que le gusta y lo que no le gusta. Primero, escuche el **Vocabulario útil.** Luego escuche las situaciones o lugares y diga lo que le gusta y lo que no le gusta de las siguientes situaciones o lugares usando palabras del **Vocabulario útil.** Luego escuche una respuesta posible y repítala.

Vocabulario útil:

hablar con los amigos	**el calor**	**las fiestas**
hacer cola	**la comida**	**las flores**
jugar al voleibol	**las clases**	**los insectos**
nadar	**los exámenes**	**los perros**
viajar		

MODELO: (Ud. oye)   ¿En el verano?

                   (Ud. dice)   Me gusta nadar. No me gusta el calor.

        (Ud. oye y repite)   Me gusta nadar. No me gusta el calor.

1. ...   **2.** ...   **3.** ...   **4.** ...   **5.** ...

F. **Entrevista con una agente de viajes.** Ud. va a oír una entrevista con Heidi Luna, una agente de viajes hondureña a quien le gusta mucho su trabajo. Primero, escuche el **Vocabulario útil,** luego escuche la entrevista. Después, combine elementos de cada columna para formar por lo menos (*at least*) cinco oraciones verdaderas (*true*) según la entrevista.

Vocabulario útil

para que les ayudemos	so that we help them
divertido/a	fun
la mayoría	the majority
la gente	people
de hecho	in fact

a Heidi a sus clientes	**+**	le(s) gusta(n) le(s) encanta(n)	**+**	su trabajo viajar a *Disney World* viajar algunos destinos de México y Sudamérica Canadá como destino turístico

1. _____

2. _____

3. _____

4. _____

5. _____

23. Talking about the Past (Part 1) • Preterite of Regular Verbs and of *dar, hacer, ir,* and *ser*

A. El pretérito. Escriba la forma apropiada del pretérito de los verbos.

INFINITIVO	YO	TÚ	UD.	NOSOTROS	UDS.
hablar	*hablé*				
volver		*volviste*			
vivir			*vivió*		
dar				*dimos*	
hacer					*hicieron*
ser/ir	*fui*				
jugar		*jugaste*			
sacar			*sacó*		
empezar				*empezamos*	

B. ¿Qué hicieron estas personas? Complete las oraciones con la forma apropiada de los infinitivos. **¡OJO!** Recuerde (*Remember*) los cambios ortográficos como *almorcé, empecé, hizo,* etcétera.

yo: Hoy _____¹ (volver) de la universidad a la una de la tarde. _____²

(Hacerme) un sándwich y lo _____³ (comer) sentadoª delante de la televisión.

Cuando _____ (terminar), _____⁵ (meterᵇ) la ropa sucia en la

lavadora.ᶜ Antes de salir para el trabajo, le _____⁶ (dar) comida al perro.

ª*seated*   ᵇ*to put*   ᶜ*washing machine*

tú: ¿Por qué no _____¹ (asistir) a tu clase de música esta mañana?

_____² (acostarse) tarde? ¿Ya _____³ (empezar) a estudiar para

el examen? ¿Adónde _____⁴ (ir) anoche? ¿_____⁵ (salir) con

alguien interesante? ¿A qué hora _____⁶ (volver) a casa?

Eva: El año pasado, Eva _____¹ (ir) a vivir a Escociaª con su esposo. Después de

varios meses, _____² (matricularse [*to enroll*]) en la Universidad de Edimburgo y

_____³ (empezar) a estudiar para enfermera.ᵇ Durante el verano

_____⁴ (regresar) a Vermont para visitar a sus abuelos por una semana.

Luego _____⁵ (viajar) a California, donde _____⁶ (ver) a

muchos de sus amigos y lo _____⁷ (pasar) muy bien.ᶜ

ª*Scotland*   ᵇ*para... to be a nurse*   ᶜ*lo... she had a good time*

(Continúa.)

mi amiga y yo: El verano pasado, mi amiga Sara y yo _____[1] (pasar) dos meses en

Europa. _____[2] (Vivir) con una familia francesa en Aix-en-Provence,

donde _____[3] (asistir) a clases en la universidad. También

_____[4] (hacer) algunos viajes cortos. _____[5]

(Visitar) la costa del sur de Francia, _____[6] (caminar[a]) por las

playas de Niza,[b] _____[7] (comer) muchos mariscos y

_____[8] (ver) a varias personas famosas allí.
_____

[a]*to walk*   [b]*Nice*

dos científicos: Mi papá y otro profesor de astronomía _____[1] (ir) a Chile en

enero de 1986 para observar el cometa Halley. _____[2] (Salir) de

Los Ángeles en avión y _____[3] (llegar) a Santiago doce horas

después. De allí _____[4] (viajar) a un observatorio en los

Andes donde _____[5] (ver) el cometa todas las noches y

_____[6] (sacar) muchas fotos. La comida y el vino chilenos les

_____[7] (gustar) mucho y _____[8] (volver) de su

viaje muy contentos.

C. ¿Qué hizo Antonio anoche (*last night*)?

Paso 1. Ud. va a oír algunas oraciones que describen lo que hicieron Antonio y Cecilia anoche. Primero, escuche el **Vocabulario útil** y mire los dibujos (*drawings*). Luego escuche las oraciones y escriba el número de cada oración sobre (*above*) el dibujo correspondiente.

Vocabulario útil

dejar de + *inf.*	to stop (*doing something*)
caminar	to walk
hasta	to

a. _____

b. _____

c. _____

d. _____

e. _____

f. _____

g. _____

h. _____

Paso 2. Ahora Ud. va a describir lo que hicieron Antonio y Cecilia anoche. Cuando oiga el número correspondiente, use los dibujos, las oraciones que escuchó en el **Paso 1** y las siguientes palabras y frases para describir cada acción. Luego escuche la respuesta correcta y repítala.

MODELO: (Ud. oye) **1.**

(Ud. ve) **1.**  anoche / dejar de estudiar / salir

(Ud. dice) Anoche, Antonio dejó de estudiar y salió.

(Ud. oye y repite) Anoche, Antonio dejó de estudiar y salió.

2.  ir a un club / bailar mucho con...

3.  hablar mucho en...

4. darle su número de teléfono a...

5. después de salir del club, / caminar juntos hasta...

6. preguntarle a... / «¿Quieres salir este sábado?»

7. contestarle que sí

8. 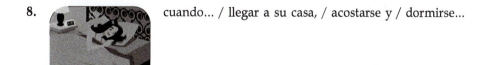 cuando... / llegar a su casa, / acostarse y / dormirse...

D. ¿Quién hizo qué? Va a oír algunas preguntas sobre lo que Ud. y sus amigos hicieron anoche (*last night*). Primero, mire los dibujos, luego escuche las preguntas. Contéstelas, según los dibujos. Luego escuche la respuesta correcta y repítala.

MODELO: (Ud. oye) ¿Quiénes bailaron?

(Ud. ve)

(Ud. dice) Araceli y Lorenzo bailaron.

(Ud. oye y repite) Araceli y Lorenzo bailaron.

Tomás

Sabina

Cristina Rafael

Marco Elena

yo

1. ... **2.** ... **3.** ... **4.** ... **5** ...

E. Las últimas vacaciones

Paso 1. En este diálogo, la Sra. Velasco habla con su agente de viajes, el Sr. Gómez, sobre sus vacaciones en las Islas Galápagos. Primero, escuche el **Vocabulario útil** y la conversación. Luego indique las oraciones que son ciertas. Preste (*Pay*) atención a los detalles.

Vocabulario útil

caminar	to walk
sobre todo	above all
espero que sí	I hope so
por supuesto	of course
placer	pleasure
Que le vaya bien.	I hope all goes well.
Hasta la próxima.	Until next time.

¿Cierto?

1. ☐ La Sra. Velasco le preguntó al Sr. Gómez qué hicieron sus hijos durante las vacaciones en las Galápagos.
2. ☐ Los Sres. Velasco hicieron muchas actividades en su viaje a las Galápagos.
3. ☐ La Sra. Velasco le pidió permiso (*asked permission*) al Sr. Gómez para llamarlo otra vez si tiene más preguntas.
4. ☐ El Sr. Gómez fue a las Islas Galápagos con su esposa.
5. ☐ Los Sres. Gómez no descansaron nada (*at all*) durante su estancia (*stay*) en las Galápagos.
6. ☐ El Sr. Gómez no sacó ninguna foto, porque le dio su cámara a su hija.
7. ☐ La Sra. Gómez tomó el sol.
8. ☐ A la Sra. Gómez no le gusta nadar.

Paso 2. Ahora haga una lista de por lo menos cinco de las actividades que los Sres. Gómez hicieron durante su viaje a las Islas Galápagos. Use el pretérito.

Los Sres. Gómez...

1. _____
2. _____
3. _____
4. _____
5. _____

Un poco de todo

A. De vacaciones en Miami. Complete la narración para describir unas vacaciones en Miami. Use la forma apropiada del infinitivo y escriba los números en palabras. Cuando se presentan dos palabras entre paréntesis, escoja (*choose*) la más lógica.

El verano pasado _____[1] (*yo:* ir) a Miami con dos amigos para pasar unos días de

vacaciones. Yo _____[2] (comprar) un billete electrónico en línea[a] y _____[3]

(pagar) con mi tarjeta de crédito. Mi billete solo _____[4] (costar) _____[5]

(223) dólares. Como[b] siempre llevo _____[6] (mucha / poca) ropa, solo _____[7]

(llevar) una maleta pequeña y un bolso. Mis amigos y yo _____[8] (pasar) por el control de

seguridad sin _____[9] (ninguna / ningún) problema. Del aeropuerto _____[10]

(Continúa.)

(*nosotros:* ir) al hotel en taxi. La primera cosa que _____¹¹ (*nosotros:* hacer) fue ponernos el traje de baño y tomar el sol en la playa. _____¹² (*yo:* Sacar) _____¹³ (algunas / algunos) fotos y a las siete y media _____¹⁴ (*nosotros:* salir) a cenar a El Toledano, un restaurante cubano en la Calle Ocho muy recomendado por el hotel. Todos _____¹⁵ (comer) el arroz con pollo, la especialidad de la casa. Deᶜ postre, todos _____¹⁶ (comer) también el flan. _____¹⁷ (Les / Nos) gustó muchísimo. Y así pasó el primer día.

ᵃen... *online*   ᵇ*Since*   ᶜ*For*

B. *Listening Passage:* **Un anuncio turístico**

Antes de escuchar. You will hear a travel ad about an excursion to Mexico. Before you listen to the ad, do the following activity.

Find out how much you know about Mexico's tourist attractions by answering the following questions. As you read the questions, try to infer the information the passage will give you, as well as the specific information for which you will need to listen. How much do you know? Check your answers in the Appendix and find out.

1. ¿Conoce Ud. México? Indique los lugares que se encuentran en México.

☐ la Basílica de Guadalupe   ☐ el Museo Nacional de Antropología
☐ Cartagena   ☐ las pirámides de Teotihuacán
☐ Guadalajara   ☐ el río Amazonas
☐ Isla Mujeres   ☐ ruinas mayas
☐ las Islas Galápagos   ☐ el Salto (*Falls*) Ángel
☐ el lago Maracaibo   ☐ Sevilla
☐ Machu Picchu   ☐ Taxco
☐ Museo del Prado   ☐ el Yucatán

2. _____ ¿Sabe Ud. que la Ciudad de México es una de las ciudades más grandes del mundo, más grande aun (*even*) que Nueva York? ¿Cuál es su población aproximada?

   a. 29 millones de habitantes (57 millones si incluye los suburbios)
   b. 9 millones de habitantes (20 millones si incluye los suburbios)
   c. 2,5 millones de habitantes (8 millones si incluye los suburbios)
   d. 0,8 millones de habitantes (5,5 millones si incluye los suburbios)

3. _____ ¿Sabe Ud. el nombre de algunos de los pueblos indígenas (*native*) de México? Los olmecas, los toltecas, los zapotecas y los mixtecas son menos famosos que otros. ¿Cuáles son los dos más famosos?

   a. los incas y los navajos
   b. los aztecas y los incas
   c. los mayas y los navajos
   d. los aztecas y los mayas

Listening Passage. Now you will hear the travel ad. First, listen to the **Vocabulario útil.** Then listen to the ad once to get a general idea of the content. Afterwards, listen again for activities that tourists can do on the trip.

Vocabulario útil

lindo/a	**bonito/a**	**relajarse**	to relax
el reino	kingdom	**broncearse**	to get a tan
la bahía	bay	**el submarinismo**	snorkeling
bello/a	**bonito/a**	**saborear**	to taste
la plata	silver	**tentador(a)**	tempting
la artesanía	craft	**la reserva**	reservation
la calidad	quality		

Después de escuchar. Now indicate the activities available for tourists on the advertised trip.

Los turistas en esta excursión pueden...

1. ☐ broncearse.

2. ☐ hacer submarinismo.

3. ☐ escalar (*climb*) unas montañas muy altas.

4. ☐ comprar objetos de plata.

5. ☐ nadar en dos playas, por lo menos (*at least*).

6. ☐ ver las ruinas de Machu Picchu.

7. ☐ visitar un museo antropológico.

8. ☐ visitar ruinas mayas.

 C. Vacaciones

Paso 1. Ud. va a oír las respuestas de Rubén, Karina y Miguel René a tres preguntas diferentes relacionadas con las vacaciones, pero no va a oír las preguntas. Primero, escuche el **Vocabulario útil** y las respuestas de los estudiantes. Luego escriba tres preguntas apropiadas para las respuestas que dan los amigos.

Rubén   Karina   Miguel René

Vocabulario útil

tirarse	to "lay out"
disfrutar (de)	to enjoy; to take advantage of
pasear	to go for a stroll
el partido de fútbol	soccer game
sencillo/a	simple, unpretentious
relajarse	to relax
la brisa	breeze
patinar	to skate
último/a	last

Ahora escriba las preguntas.

1. _____

2. _____

3. _____

(Continúa.)

❖ **Paso 2.** Ahora va a escuchar las preguntas de la entrevista, pero esta vez dirigidas (*addressed*) a Ud. Conteste por escrito las preguntas que oye.

1. _____

2. _____

3. _____

CULTURA

A. **Mapa.** Identifique el país y la capital en el siguiente mapa.

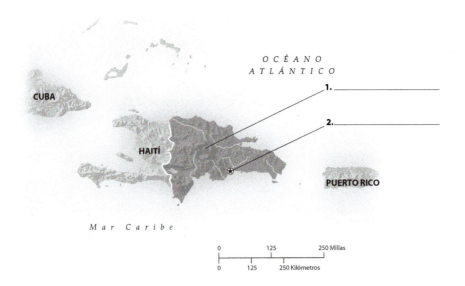

B. **Comprensión.** Complete las siguientes oraciones con palabras de la lista. Esta actividad se basa en información de las lecturas **Algo sobre...** (p. 238, 245 y 255) y **Lectura cultural** (p. 260) del libro de texto o del eBook. **¡OJO!** No se usan todas las palabras.

el casabe	Madrid	música
los colmados	las Mariposas	Punta Cana
el extranjero	monumentos	
el güiro	las playas	

1. En la República Dominicana, _____ son tiendas que son un punto de encuentro

   (*meeting place*) para la gente del barrio (*neighborhood*).

2. _____ es una especie de tortilla que se hace con la yuca (*manioc*).

3. Las fotos de las tres hermanas Mirabal, también conocidas como _____, aparecen en los billetes (*bills*) de 200 pesos dominicanos.

4. En la República Dominicana, un lugar de gran atracción turística por sus playas y clima es _____.

5. En Santo Domingo, hay una hermosa (*beautiful*) zona colonial con museos, casas antiguas y otros _____ históricos.

6. El merengue es un tipo de _____ de origen dominicano que incluye instrumentos como el acordeón, _____, la tambora, el piano y los instrumentos de viento.

PÓNGASE A PRUEBA

A. Los pronombres del complemento indirecto, *dar* y *decir*

1. Escriba el pronombre **le** en la posición apropiada en las siguientes oraciones.

   a. Siempre ____ digo la verdad a mi amiga.

   b. ____ estoy diciendo la verdad a mi amiga.

      o estoy diciéndo____ la verdad a mi amiga.

   c. ____ voy a decir la verdad a mi amiga.

      o voy a decir____ la verdad a mi amiga.

   d. (*mandato afirmativo, Ud.:* **decir**) ¡_____ la verdad a su amiga!

   e. (*mandato negativo, Ud.:* **decir**) ¡_____ la verdad a su amiga!

2. Complete la siguiente tabla con los verbos en el presente de indicativo.

INFINITIVO	YO	TÚ	ÉL	NOSOTROS/AS	ELLOS/ELLAS
dar		*das*			
decir				*decimos*	

B. *Gustar*. Escriba oraciones con las siguientes palabras.

1. ¿(a ellos) gustar / viajar? _____

2. a mí / no / gustar / quejarse _____

3. Juan / gustar / aeropuertos _____

C. El pretérito de los verbos regulares y de *dar, hacer, ir* y *ser*

Complete la tabla con las formas apropiadas de los verbos en el pretérito.

INFINITIVO	YO	TÚ	ÉL	NOSOTROS	ELLOS
dar		*diste*			
hablar			*habló*		
hacer				*hicimos*	
ir/ser	*fui*				
salir					*salieron*

PRUEBA CORTA

A. **Complementos indirectos.** Complete las oraciones con el pronombre del complemento indirecto apropiado.

1. Yo _____ compré un regalo. (a mi madre)

2. Ellos _____ escribieron una carta la semana pasada. (a nosotros)

3. Nosotros _____ compramos boletos para un concierto. (a nuestros amigos)

4. Roberto siempre _____ pide favores. (a mí)

5. ¿Qué _____ dieron tus padres para tu cumpleaños? (a ti)

B. **Hablando de gustos.** Use la forma apropiada de **gustar** y del complemento indirecto.

1. A mi padre no _____ _____ los asientos cerca de la puerta.

2. A mis mejores amigos _____ _____ viajar solos.

3. A mí no _____ _____ la comida que sirven en el avión.

4. A todos nosotros _____ _____ los vuelos sin escalas.

5. Y a ti, ¿adónde _____ _____ ir de vacaciones?

C. **Hablando del pasado.** Complete las oraciones con la forma apropiada del pretérito del verbo entre paréntesis.

1. ¿A quién le _____ (*tú*: mandar) las tarjetas postales?

2. Ayer _____ (*yo*: empezar) a hacer las maletas a las once.

3. Mi hermano _____ (hacer) un viaje al Caribe.

4. ¿_____ (*Uds.*: ir) en clase turística?

5. ¿_____ (*tú*: Oír) el anuncio (*announcement*) para subir al avión?

6. Ellos _____ (volver) de su viaje el domingo pasado.

7. Juan no me _____ (dar) el dinero para el boleto.

D. De vacaciones. Cuando oiga el número correspondiente y una acción, haga oraciones con las palabras que se dan para describir unas vacaciones en Cancún. Use el pretérito de los verbos. Si el sujeto está entre paréntesis, no lo use. Luego escuche la respuesta correcta y repítala.

MODELO: (Ud. ve) **1.** mi familia y yo / de vacaciones

          (Ud. oye) **1.** ir

          (Ud. dice) Mi familia y yo fuimos de vacaciones.

   (Ud. oye y repite) Mi familia y yo fuimos de vacaciones.

2. el agente de viajes / un viaje a Cancún
3. (nosotros) / a Cancún en avión
4. el avión / escalas
5. (nosotros) / al hotel sin problemas
6. el recepcionista / un cuarto con balcón
7. mis hermanos / en la piscina
8. (yo) / el sol
9. nuestra madre / fotos
10. nuestro padre / tarjetas postales a nuestros amigos

◆ PUNTOS PERSONALES

A. Encuesta

Paso 1. Va a oír algunas preguntas. Indique **Sí** o **No**, según lo que es verdad para Ud.

SÍ   NO

1. ☐ ☐
2. ☐ ☐
3. ☐ ☐
4. ☐ ☐
5. ☐ ☐
6. ☐ ☐
7. ☐ ☐
8. ☐ ☐

Paso 2. Ahora escuche las preguntas otra vez (*again*). Conteste las preguntas por escrito (*in writing*) con sus respuestas del **Paso 1.**

MODELOS: (Ud. oye) Uno. ¿Les presta Ud. dinero a sus amigos?

        (Ud. ve) Sí ☑

   (Ud. escribe) Sí, les presto dinero a mis amigos.

   o (Ud. ve) No ☑

   (Ud. escribe) No, no les presto dinero a mis amigos.

2. _____

3. _____

4. _____

(Continúa.)

5. _____

6. _____

7. _____

8. _____

B. **Cosas que pasaron el semestre/trimestre pasado.** Use las siguientes frases para decir lo que hizo Ud. para alguien o lo que alguien hizo para Ud. el semestre/trimestre pasado. Use el pretérito y el pronombre de complemento indirecto apropiado. Escriba oraciones afirmativas o negativas, según lo que es verdad para Ud.

MODELO: escribir una carta → Les escribí una carta a mis abuelos.

(No le escribí a nadie.)

(Nadie me escribió a mí.)

1. mandar tarjetas postales _____

2. regalar flores _____

3. recomendar un restaurante _____

4. ofrecer ayuda _____

5. prestar una maleta _____

6. hacer un pastel _____

C. **Preguntas personales.** Conteste con oraciones completas.

1. ¿Le gustaría viajar en crucero? ¿Adónde?

_____

2. ¿Viajó Ud. en tren o en autobús a otro estado el año pasado?

_____

3. ¿Qué medio de transporte prefiere Ud. cuando hace un viaje largo?

_____

4. ¿Tiene miedo de ir en avión o de viajar en barco?

_____

D. **Guided Composition.** Imagine que Ud. acaba de recibir un regalo de 5.000 dólares de su abuela (tía) rica. Le mandó el dinero para un viaje extraordinario. En otro papel, escríbale a su benefactor una carta de unas 100 palabras con la descripción de sus planes. Incluya la siguiente información.

1. ¿Adónde piensa ir y en qué mes va a salir?

2. ¿Cómo va a viajar?

3. ¿Qué ropa va a llevar?

4. ¿Qué piensa hacer en ese lugar?

5. ¿Cuánto tiempo piensa estar de viaje?

6. ¿Va a viajar solo/a o con otra persona (otras personas)?

7. ¿Dónde piensa quedarse?

MODELO:

Querida _____,

¡Mil gracias por el regalo tan fenomenal! Te escribo para darte detalles de mis planes para el viaje...

Un abrazo y muchos recuerdos cariñosos (*fond regards*) de tu (nieto/a, sobrino/a)...

E. **Mi diario.** En su diario, escriba sobre unas vacaciones que Ud. o un amigo / una amiga tomó. Incluya (*Include*) la siguiente información:

- adónde y con quién fue
- cuándo y cómo viajó
- qué tiempo hizo durante las vacaciones (llovió mucho, nevó, hizo mucho calor, ...)
- cuánto tiempo pasó allí
- qué cosas interesantes hizo
- lo qué le gustó más (o menos) de ese lugar
- si le gustaría volver a ese lugar

Vocabulario útil

esquiar	to ski
hace un año (semana, mes)	a year (week, month) ago

F. **Intercambios.** Escuche las siguientes preguntas y contéstelas por escrito.

1. _____

_____

2. _____

_____

3. _____

_____

4. _____

_____

Capítulo 9 — Los días festivos

VOCABULARIO — Preparación

Una fiesta de cumpleaños para Javier

A. En una fiesta. Empareje las definiciones con las palabras. **¡OJO!** No se usan todas las palabras.

_____ **1.** la comida que sirven en una fiesta, normalmente en pequeñas porciones.

_____ **2.** la persona que da una fiesta

_____ **3.** no asistir a una fiesta

_____ **4.** las personas que vienen a la fiesta

_____ **5.** estar en el mismo lugar con otras personas

_____ **6.** lo opuesto a (*opposite of*) divertirse

_____ **7.** el postre que se come en una fiesta de cumpleaños

_____ **8.** una de las cosas que recibe una persona que cumple años

_____ **9.** una bebida que se toma cuando hay una celebración

_____ **10.** representan el número de años que una persona cumple

a. ¡Felicitaciones!
b. la anfitriona
c. el champán
d. las botanas
e. los invitados
f. el pastel
g. la tarjeta
h. las velas
i. faltar
j. gastar
k. pasarlo mal
l. reunirse

B. ¿Cuánto sabe Ud. de los días festivos? Complete las oraciones con el día festivo apropiado.

el Día de la Raza (*Columbus Day / Hispanic Awareness Day*)
el Día de los Muertos (*Day of the Dead*)
la Navidad
la Nochebuena
la Nochevieja
la Pascua judía (*Passover*)

1. El día antes del primero de enero se llama _____.

2. El 25 de diciembre, los cristianos celebran _____.

3. _____ conmemora la huida (*escape*) de los judíos (*Jews*) de Egipto.

4. Muchos católicos asisten a la Misa del Gallo (*Midnight Mass*) el día antes de la Navidad, que se conoce como _____.

5. _____ se celebra el 2 de noviembre.

6. _____ se celebra el 12 de octubre.

C. Asociaciones. Ud. va a oír algunas descripciones. Indique la fiesta o la celebración que se asocia con cada descripción. **¡OJO!** Hay más de una respuesta correcta en algunos casos.

1. _____
   a. la Navidad
   b. el Día de la Raza (*Columbus Day / Hispanic Awareness Day*)
   c. el cumpleaños

2. _____
   a. el Cinco de Mayo
   b. la Pascua
   c. el Día del Canadá

3. _____
   a. el Día de los Reyes Magos (*Day of the Magi (Three Kings) / Epiphany* [Jan. 6])
   b. el Día de Acción de Gracias (*Thanksgiving*)
   c. el Día de los Muertos (*Day of the Dead*)

4. _____
   a. el Día de San Patricio
   b. el Día de los Reyes Magos
   c. el día del santo (*saint's day* [*the saint for whom one is named*])

5. _____
   a. el Cuatro de Julio
   b. Janucá (*Hanukkah*)
   c. la Semana Santa (*Holy Week, the week ending on Easter Sunday*)

D. ¿Una fiesta típica?

Paso 1. Ud. va a oír la descripción de una reunión (*gathering*) reciente (*recent*) de la familia de Sara. Primero, escuche el **Vocabulario útil** y la descripción. Luego escuche las siguientes oraciones e indique si son ciertas (**C**) o falsas (**F**), según lo que dice Sara. Si la información no se dio en la descripción, indique **ND** (No lo dice).

Vocabulario útil

portarse (mal)	to behave (badly)
el angelito	little angel
esta vez	this time
Dios	God
fueran	would be, were

1. C F ND Según lo que dice <u>Sara</u>, las fiestas de su familia normalmente son *muy divertidas*.
2. C F ND A la tía Eustacia *le gusta discutir* con el padre de <u>Sara</u>.
3. C F ND Normalmente, los primos de <u>Sara</u> *se portan mal* en las fiestas familiares.
4. C F ND <u>Sara</u> nunca *lo pasa bien* en las fiestas familiares.
5. C F ND Los hermanos de <u>Sara</u> *discuten mucho* con sus padres.

Paso 2. Ahora cambie el nombre de **Sara** a **Antonio** para describir las fiestas familiares de Antonio. Sustituya (*Substitute*) las palabras en cursiva de las oraciones del **Paso 1** por la información que oye.

MODELO: (Ud. ve) **1.** Según lo que dice <u>Sara</u>, las fiestas familiares normalmente son *muy divertidas*.

(Ud. oye) **1.** en un hotel

(Ud. dice) Según lo que dice Antonio, las fiestas familiares normalmente son en un hotel.

(Ud. oye y repite) Según lo que dice Antonio, las fiestas familiares normalmente son en un hotel.

2. ... **3.** ... **4.** ... **5.** ...

E. **La quinceañera de Amanda.** Lea el siguiente párrafo. Luego conteste las preguntas con oraciones completas. Use pronombres de complemento directo e indirecto si es posible.

El 14 de septiembre es el cumpleaños de Amanda. Va a cumplir 15 años. Para celebrarlo, sus padres van a hacerle una quinceañera, la fiesta tradicional para las jóvenes que cumplen esa edad. Esta es una fiesta en la que[a] los padres a veces gastan mucho dinero. Para no gastar tanto, sus padres van a hacer la fiesta en casa, no en un hotel o restaurante. Los padres de Amanda ya le compraron un vestido elegante para la ocasión e invitaron a sus parientes y a los mejores amigos de su hija. Va a haber[b] cien invitados, y todos van a regalarle algo a Amanda. Todos los parientes van a ayudar a preparar botanas, como empanadas y croquetas[c] de jamón, y platos principales como arroz con pollo y chiles rellenos. De postre,[d] va a haber un magnífico pastel de cumpleaños y flan. Además,[e] tres amigos de ella van a tocar la guitarra y cantar en su honor. Amanda está muy emocionada.[f] Sin duda,[g] la quinceañera va a ser una fiesta muy divertida.[h]

---

[a]la... *which* [b]*to be* [c]*balls of meat or potato coated in breadcrumbs and deep-fried* [d]De... *For dessert* [e]*In addition* [f]*excited* [g]Sin... *Without a doubt* [h]*fun*

1. ¿Por qué van a hacerle sus padres una fiesta a Amanda?

_____

2. ¿Cómo se llama esa fiesta tradicional? _____

3. ¿Dónde va a ser la fiesta? _____

4. ¿Por qué decidieron los padres hacer la fiesta en ese lugar?

_____

5. ¿Cuántos invitados van a ir a la fiesta?

_____

6. ¿Qué van a hacer todos los invitados para Amanda?

_____

7. ¿Quiénes van a preparar la comida? _____

8. ¿Que tipo de botanas van a preparar? _____

F. **Entrevista cultural.** Ud. va a oír una entrevista con Rocío en la que (*in which*) habla de su trabajo y de algunas celebraciones cubanas. Primero, escuche el **Vocabulario útil** y luego la entrevista. Después, complete el párrafo con información de la entrevista.

Vocabulario útil

el globo	balloon
la serpentina	paper streamer
el payaso	clown
disfrutar	to enjoy
el arroz con gris	rice cooked with black beans
la yuca con mojo	manioc (cassava) with citrus-garlic sauce
el buñuelo con almíbar	fried pastry covered in syrup

Rocío es de _____,[1] _____.[2] Pero ahora vive en

_____.[3] Trabaja en una _____[4] que vende

artículos _____[5] de _____.[6]

En su país, en las fiestas de _____[7] hay _____[8]

para beber y se come cake. Y para los niños hay payasos, globos y piñatas.

El día festivo favorito de Rocío es la _____[9] porque toda la familia

se reúne y se hace una gran _____[10] con _____[11]

típica cubana. Un plato típico es la carne de puerco _____.[12]

Las emociones y los estados afectivos

A. **Un día emocional.** Hoy es un día emocional. Empareje las oraciones con las imágenes correspondientes.

a.

b.

c.

d.

e.

f.

_____ **1.** Ana llora.

_____ **2.** Carmen y Martín se enojan.

_____ **3.** Javier se pone rojo.

_____ **4.** Julia se siente nerviosa.

_____ **5.** Los niños se portan mal.

_____ **6.** Patricia empieza a reírse.

B. **¿Cómo reaccionan los profesores y los estudiantes?** Escriba cómo reaccionan los profesores y los estudiantes con la forma apropiada de los verbos de la lista.

discutir	ponerse (irritado/a,	quejarse
enfermarse	nervioso/a, rojo/a, triste)	recordar
enojarse	portarse	reírse

1. Cuando Julián no contesta bien en clase, se ríe porque se pone nervioso. Cuando

   yo no _____ la respuesta correcta, yo _____.

2. Cuando nos olvidamos de entregar (*turn in*) la tarea a tiempo, los profesores

   _____.

3. Cuando llega la época de los exámenes, algunos estudiantes _____

   porque no duermen lo suficiente (*enough*). Y todos _____ porque

   dicen que tienen muchísimo trabajo.

4. Generalmente los estudiantes universitarios son responsables y _____

   bien en clase.

5. A los profesores no les gusta _____ con los estudiantes sobre las

   notas que les dan.

C. **Enfáticamente.** Complete las oraciones con la forma **–ísimo/a** del adjetivo apropiado.

cansado/a	difícil	rico/a
caro/a	largo/a	

1. La novela *Guerra y paz* (War and Peace) del autor ruso Tolstoi es _____.

2. Carlos Slim Helú, Bill Gates y Warren Buffett son _____.

3. Después de correr diez kilómetros me siento _____.

4. Una villa en Italia es _____.

5. Las preguntas del último examen fueron _____.

D. **Reacciones.** Describa cómo reaccionan estas personas en las siguientes situaciones, según las indicaciones. Use **cuando** en cada oración. Luego escuche la respuesta correcta y repítala.

MODELO: (Ud. ve) Mi novio olvida el cumpleaños de su madre.

(Ud. oye) ponerse triste

(Ud. dice) Mi novio se pone triste cuando olvida el cumpleaños de su madre.

(Ud. oye y repite) Mi novio se pone triste cuando olvida el cumpleaños de su madre.

(Continúa.)

1. Los abuelos juegan con sus nietos.

2. Marta ve una película triste.

3. Nosotras sacamos buenas notas.

4. Tengo que hacer cola.

5. Los estudiantes tienen demasiada (*too much*) tarea.

PRONUNCIACIÓN   c and *qu*

- The [**k**] sound in Spanish can be written two ways: before the vowels **a, o,** and **u** it is written as **c;** before **i** and **e,** it is written as **qu.** Note that the *kw* sound, spelled in English with *qu* (as in *quaint* and *quince*), is spelled in Spanish with **cu,** not **qu: cuando, cuento.** The letter **k** itself appears only in words that have come to Spanish from other languages.
- Unlike the English [**k**] sound, the Spanish sound is not aspirated; that is, no air is allowed to escape when it is pronounced. Compare the following pairs of English words in which the first [**k**] sound is aspirated and the second is not.

can / scan   cold / scold   kit / skit

A. Repeticiones

Paso 1. Repita las siguientes palabras, imitando al hablante (*speaker*). No se olvide (*Don't forget*) de pronunciar el sonido [**k**] sin aspiración.

1.	casa	cosa	rico	loca	roca
2.	¿quién?	Quito	aquí	¿qué?	pequeño	querosén
3.	kilo	kilogramo	kilómetro	karate

Paso 2. Cuando oiga el número correspondiente, lea las siguientes palabras y oraciones en voz alta. Luego escuche la pronunciación correcta y repítala.

1.	paquete	4.	¿por qué?	7.	¿Quién compró los camarones?
2.	quinceañera	5.	cuaderno	8.	Carolina no come con Carlos.
3.	química	6.	comida	9.	Ricardo quiere ir a Querétaro.

B. El sonido [k].
Escriba las palabras que oye. **¡OJO!** Fíjese en los sonidos y no se distraiga (*don't get distracted*) por las palabras desconocidas (*unknown*) que oye.

1. _____

2. _____

3. _____

4. _____

5. _____

6. _____

24. Talking about the Past (Part 2) • Irregular Preterites

¿Recuerda Ud.?

El pretérito. You have already learned the irregular preterite stem and endings for the verb **hacer**. All of the verbs presented in **Gramática 24** have irregular stems and use the same endings as **hacer**. Review the preterite endings for regular verbs and those for **hacer** by completing the following chart.

hablar: yo habl _____   nosotros habl _____   Ud. habl _____   ellos habl _____

comer: yo com _____   nosotros com _____   Ud. com _____   ellos com _____

vivir: yo viv _____   nosotros viv _____   Ud. viv _____   ellos viv _____

hacer   yo hic _____   nosotros hic _____   Ud. hiz _____   ellos hic _____

A. **Formas verbales.** Escriba la forma indicada de los verbos.

INFINITIVO	YO	TÚ	UD.	NOSOTROS	UDS.
estar		estuviste		estuvimos	
	tuve				tuvieron
			pudo	pudimos	
poner	puse			pusimos	
		quisiste	quiso		quisieron
saber					supieron
venir		viniste			
decir			dijo	dijimos	
	traje				trajeron

B. **¿Qué pasó ayer?**

Paso 1. Va a oír algunas oraciones sobre lo que pasó ayer. Primero, escuche las oraciones. Luego escriba el número de la oración y el nombre de cada persona en el dibujo (drawing) debajo del dibujo correspondiente.

a. ____   b. ____   c. ____

_____   _____   _____

d. ____   e. ____

_____   _____

Nota: Verifique sus respuestas del **Paso 1** en el Apéndice antes de empezar el **Paso 2.**

Paso 2. Ahora va a oír algunas preguntas. Contéstelas, según los dibujos del **Paso 1.** Luego escuche la respuesta correcta y repítala.

MODELO: (Ud. oye) **1.** ¿Quién tuvo que hacer su maleta para un viaje?
                 (Ud. ve)

                 e. 1 - Ricardo

        (Ud. dice) Ricardo tuvo que hacer su maleta para un viaje.

   (Ud. oye y repite) Ricardo tuvo que hacer su maleta para un viaje.

2. ...   **3.** ...   **4.** ...   **5.** ...

C. Situaciones. Complete las oraciones con el pretérito de los verbos entre paréntesis.

Durante la Navidad: La familia Román _____[1] (tener) una reunión[a] familiar muy bonita para la Navidad. Todos sus hijos _____[2] (estar) presentes. _____[3] (Venir) de Denver y Dallas, y _____[4] (traer) regalos para todos. Su mamá pensaba[b] hacer una gran cena para la Nochebuena, pero todos le _____[5] (decir) que no. Por la noche todos _____[6] (ir) a un restaurante muy elegante donde _____[7] (comer) bien, _____[8] (poder) escuchar música y _____[9] (pasarlo) bien.

_____
[a]*gathering*   [b]*was planning*

Otro terremoto[a] en California: Esta mañana _____[1] (*nosotros:* saber) que _____[2] (haber) un terremoto en California. Lo _____[3] (*yo:* oír) primero en la radio y luego lo _____[4] (*yo:* leer) en el periódico. Algunas casas _____[5] (dañarse[b]), pero en general, este terremoto no _____[6] (hacer) mucho daño.[c] Un experto _____[7] (decir): «No _____[8] (ser) el primero ni va a ser el último».

_____
[a]*earthquake*   [b]*to be damaged*   [c]*damage*

D. Después del examen. Jorge y Manuel hablan en la cafetería. Complete las oraciones con la forma apropiada de los verbos entre paréntesis.

JORGE: ¿Cómo _____[1] (estar) el examen?

MANUEL: ¡Terrible! No _____[2] (poder) contestar las últimas tres preguntas porque no _____[3] (tener) tiempo. ¿Por qué no _____[4] (ir) tú?

JORGE: _____[5] (Querer) ir, pero _____[6] (estar) enfermo todo el día. ¿Qué preguntas _____[7] (hacer) el profesor?

MANUEL: Muchas, pero ahora no recuerdo ninguna. ¿_____[8] (*Tú:* Saber) que Claudia _____[9] (tener) un accidente y tampoco _____[10] (ir) al examen?

JORGE: Sí, me lo _____[11] (decir) María Inés esta mañana... Bueno, tengo que irme... ¡Caramba! ¿Dónde _____[12] (poner) mi cartera?

MANUEL: ¿No la _____[13] (traer) otra vez? Yo solo _____[14] (traer) dos dólares. Vamos a buscar a Ernesto. Él siempre tiene dinero.

25. Talking About the Past (Part 3) • Preterite of Stem-Changing Verbs

A. Formas verbales. Escriba la forma indicada de los verbos.

INFINITIVO	YO	TÚ	UD.	NOSOTROS	UDS.
divertirse		*te divertiste*		*nos divertimos*	
sentir			*sintió*	*sentimos*	
dormir	*dormí*				
conseguir		*conseguiste*			
reírse			*se rio*		
vestir	*vestí*				*vistieron*

B. Situaciones. Complete las oraciones con la forma apropiada del pretérito de uno de los verbos de la lista, según el significado de la oración.

      dormirse   sentarse

1. Yo _____ delante de la televisión y poco después _____.

2. —¿A qué hora _____ Uds. a comer?

   —A las nueve y media. Y después de trabajar tanto, ¡nosotros casi _____ en la mesa!

3. Mi esposo se despertó a las dos y no _____ otra vez hasta las cinco de la mañana.

      reírse   sentir (*to regret*)   sentirse

4. Esa película fue tan divertida (*funny*) que (nosotros) _____ toda la noche. Solo

   Jorge no _____ mucho porque no la comprendió.

5. Rita y Marcial _____ mucho haber faltado (*having missed*) a tu fiesta, pero Rita se

   enfermó y _____ tan mal que se quedó en la cama todo el fin de semana.

C. Una mala noche

Paso 1. Cambie al pretérito los verbos indicados para describir la noche horrible de Juan.

Juan *entra*[1] en el restaurante y *se sienta*[2] a comer con unos amigos. *Pide*[3] una cerveza y el camarero le *sirve*[4] inmediatamente, pero después de tomar dos tragos[a] *se siente*[5] mal, *se levanta*[6] y *se despide*[7] de todos rápidamente. *Vuelve*[8] a casa y no *duerme*[9] en toda la noche.

1. _____ *entró* _____

2. _____

3. _____

4. _____

5. _____

6. _____

7. _____

8. _____

9. _____

---

[a]*sips*

Paso 2. Esta vez la mala noche fue suya (*yours*). Complete el párrafo con la forma apropiada de los verbos en el pretérito. **¡OJO!** Tenga cuidado (*Be careful*) con los pronombres.

Yo _____[1] (entrar) en el restaurante y _____[2] (sentarse) a comer con unos

amigos. _____[3] (*yo:* Pedir) una cerveza y el camarero _____[4] (servirme)

inmediatamente, pero después de tomar dos tragos _____[5] (sentirse) mal,

_____[6] (levantarse[6]) y _____[7] (despedirse) de todos rápidamente.

_____[8] (Volver) a casa y no _____ (dormir) en toda la noche.

D. La fiesta sorpresa (*surprise party*)

Paso 1. Ud. va a oír un breve párrafo narrado por Ernesto sobre una fiesta sorpresa. Primero, mire la tabla, luego escuche el párrafo. Después, indique en la tabla las acciones de cada persona.

PERSONA	VESTIRSE ELEGANTEMENTE	SENTIRSE MAL	DORMIR TODA LA TARDE	PREFERIR QUEDARSE EN CASA
Julia				
Verónica				
Tomás				
Ernesto (el narrador)				

Nota: Verifique sus respuestas del **Paso 1** en el Apéndice antes de empezar el **Paso 2**.

Paso 2. Ahora va a oír algunas oraciones sobre la narración del **Paso 1**. Indique si son ciertas (**C**) o falsas (**F**), según la narración. Si la información no se dio, indique **ND** (No lo dice).

1. C F ND   4. C F ND
2. C F ND   5. C F ND
3. C F ND

E. ¿Qué le pasó a Antonio? Raquel invitó a Antonio a una fiesta en su casa. Antonio le dijo a Raquel que él asistiría (*would attend*), pero todo le salió mal. Escuche las frases y diga lo que le pasó a Antonio. Luego escuche la respuesta correcta y repítala.

MODELO: (Ud. oye) **1.** no recordar
                (Ud. ve) **1.** llevar los refrescos
                (Ud. dice) No recordó llevar los refrescos.
        (Ud. oye y repite) No recordó llevar los refrescos.

2. la dirección de Raquel
3. muy tarde a la fiesta
4. en la fiesta
5. enfermo después de la fiesta
6. muy tarde
7. mal esa noche
8. a las cinco de la mañana
9. a clases de todos modos (*anyway*)

26. Avoiding Repetition • Expressing Direct and Indirect Object Pronouns Together

---

¿Recuerda Ud.?

Direct and Indirect Object Pronouns. Cambie las frases indicadas (**a Ud., a nosotros, a ellos,** etcétera) y los complementos indicados por pronombres. Luego identifique la clase de pronombre (C.D. = complemento directo; C.I. = complemento indirecto). Siga los modelos.

modelos: No dice la verdad. (*a Uds.*) → No les dice la verdad. (C.I.)

No dice *la verdad.* → No la dice. (C.D.)

1. Yo traigo el café. (*a Ud.*) _____

2. Yo traigo *el café* ahora. _____

3. Ellos compran los boletos hoy. (*a nosotros*) _____

4. Ellos compran *los boletos* hoy. _____

5. No hablo mucho. (*a ellas*) _____

6. No conozco bien *a tus primas.* _____

7. Queremos dar una fiesta. (*a mis padres*) _____

8. Pensamos dar *la fiesta* en casa. _____

A. ¡Promesas, promesas!

Paso 1. Lea las siguientes promesas típicas. Luego empareje las preguntas con las promesas correspondientes.

_____ 1.   Te lo pago mañana.

_____ 2.   Te las traigo esta noche.

_____ 3.   Me los prometieron para esta tarde.

_____ 4.   Se la devuelvo (*return*) a José mañana.

a. ¿El dinero?
b. ¿La bicicleta?
c. ¿Las botanas?
d. ¿Los pasteles?

Paso 2. Aquí hay más promesas. Complete las oraciones con un complemento directo e indirecto.

Recuerde:

le **les** { lo, la, los, las	→ **se** { lo, la, los, las

---

1. ¿Las flores? José _____ _____ trae (a nosotros) pronto.

2. ¿El champán? _____ _____ traen (a ti) esta tarde.

3. ¿Los regalos? _____ _____ doy a Isabel esta noche.

4. ¿Las fotos? _____ _____ mando a Uds.

B. Durante la cena

Paso 1. Durante la cena, su hermano le pregunta acerca de (*about*) la comida que sobra (*that is left*). Indique la comida a la que (*to which*) él se refiere en cada pregunta.

MODELO: (Ud. oye)   ¿Hay más? ¿Me la pasas, por favor?

(Ud. ve)   la sopa   el pan   el pescado

(Ud. indica)   (la sopa)

1. las galletas   la fruta   el helado
2. la carne   el postre   los camarones
3. la leche   el vino   las arvejas
4. las papas fritas la cerveza   el pastel

Paso 2. Ahora va a oír las preguntas de su hermano otra vez. Contéstelas, según el modelo. Luego escuche la respuesta correcta y repítala.

MODELO: (Ud. oye)   ¿Hay más? ¿Me la pasas, por favor? →

(Ud. ve)   (la sopa)

(Ud. dice)   ¿La sopa? Claro que (*Of course*) te la paso.

(Ud. oye y repite)   ¿La sopa? Claro que te la paso.

1. ...   2. ...   3. ...   4. ...

C. Una fiesta sorpresa para Lupita

Paso 1. Ud. va a oír una descripción de la fiesta sorpresa que Olivia hizo recientemente para su amiga Lupita. Mientras escucha, escriba las palabras que faltan (*are missing*).

El viernes pasado, mis amigos y yo dimos una fiesta sorpresa para Lupita, una de nuestras amigas. Yo

escribí las invitaciones y _____ _____[1] mandé a todos. Carmen hizo un pastel y _____ _____[2]

dio antes de la fiesta. Anita preparó una comida elegante y _____ _____[3] sirvió en el comedor.

Arturo y Patricio sacaron muchas fotos y _____ _____[4] regalaron a Lupita. Todos llevamos regalos

y _____ _____[5] presentamos a Lupita al final de la fiesta. ¡Lupita nos dijo que fue una fiesta

maravillosa!

Nota: Verifique sus respuestas del **Paso 1** en el Apéndice antes de empezar el **Paso 2**.

Paso 2. Ahora va a oír algunas preguntas sobre la narración del **Paso 1**. Conteste cada pregunta, luego escuche la respuesta correcta y repítala.

1. ...   2. ...   3. ...   4. ...   5. ...   6. ...

D. La herencia (*inheritance*). Imagine que un pariente rico murió y les dejó (*he left*) varias cosas a Ud. y a diferentes personas e instituciones. ¿Qué le dejó a quién?

Ana y Ernesto

Marta

Memo

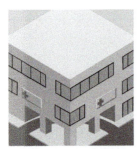
la Cruz Roja

la biblioteca

yo

MODELO: ¿A quién le dejó su ropa? → Se la dejó a la Cruz Roja.

1.   ¿A quién le dejó su coche? _____

2.   ¿A quién le dejó su nueva cámara? _____

3.   ¿A quién le dejó sus libros? _____

4.   ¿A quién le dejó sus muebles? _____

5.   ¿A quién le dejó su camioneta? _____

6.   ¿A quién le dejó los $20.000 dólares? _____

 E. ¿Dónde está? Carolina quiere pedirle prestadas (*borrow*) algunas de las cosas que Ud. tiene. Dígale a quién ya le prestó Ud. las cosas que Carolina quiere.

MODELO: (Ud. oye)   Oye, ¿dónde está tu diccionario?

                    (Ud. ve)   Se (lo/la) presté a Nicolás. Él (lo/la) necesita para un examen.

                (Ud. dice)   Se lo presté a Nicolás. Él lo necesita para un examen.

        (Ud. oye y repite)   Se lo presté a Nicolás. Él lo necesita para un examen

1.   Se (lo/la) presté a Nicolás. Él (lo/la) necesita para un viaje.
2.   Se (los/las) presté a Teresa. Ella (los/las) necesita para ir a una fiesta.
3.   Se (la/las) presté a Juan. Él (la/las) necesita para escribir una composición.
4.   Se (lo/la) presté a Nina. Ella (lo/la) necesita para ir al parque.

🎧 **F.** **En una tienda de ropa.** Ud. va a oír un diálogo en el que (*in which*) un empleado de una tienda de ropa atiende (*helps*) a una clienta y luego a un cliente. Primero, escuche el **Vocabulario útil**, luego escuche el diálogo. Después, indique si las siguientes oraciones se refieren al cinturón, a los pantalones o al recibo (*receipt*).

Vocabulario útil

probarse	to try on (*clothing*)
quisiera	I would like
devolver	to return (*something*)
el recibo	receipt
reembolsar	to refund
el reembolso	refund
Qué pena.	What a shame.
cambiar	to exchange

1.	Puede probárselos allá.	cinturón	pantalones	recibo
2.	¿Por qué quiere devolverlo?	cinturón	pantalones	recibo
3.	No lo tengo.	cinturón	pantalones	recibo
4.	Me lo regalaron para mi cumpleaños.	cinturón	pantalones	recibo
5.	¿Puede cambiármelo?	cinturón	pantalones	recibo

G. **Preguntas y más preguntas.** Escriba una respuesta para cada pregunta. Use los pronombres del complemento directo y complemento indirecto juntos.

> MODELO: —¿Quién te regaló esta novela?
> — *Me la regaló* mi tía

1. —¿Quién te dio estas flores?

_____ mi amigo Samuel.

2. —¿A cuántas personas les mandaste las invitaciones de la fiesta?

_____ a treinta personas por lo menos.

3. —¿Puedo pedirte un favor?

—¡Claro que puedes _____!

4. —Profesora, ¿le damos a Ud. la tarea ahora?

—Sí, por favor, _____ ahora.

Un poco de todo

A. **Un mensaje para un amigo**

Paso 1. Complete el mensaje que Gerardo le escribe a un amigo que vive en La Habana. Use el pretérito de los verbos entre paréntesis. Cuando se presentan dos palabras entre paréntesis, escoja (*choose*) la más lógica.

Hola Pepe,

La semana pasada _____[1] (*yo:* hacer) un viaje corto a La Habana para reunirme con

Felipe Rubio, un director de _____[2] (nuestro) compañía. _____[3] (Ser)

imposible verte ese día porque la reunión[a] _____[4] (ser) muy _____[5] (corta /

baja) y luego él me _____[6] (invitar) a comer con otros miembros de la compañía. El día

siguiente _____[7] (*yo:* tener) otras reuniones que _____[8] (también / tampoco)

(Continúa.)

_____⁹ (terminar) muy tarde. Quería[b] visitarte, pero _____¹⁰ (saber) por Luis

Dávila que estabas[c] de viaje. Cuando _____¹¹ (*yo: encontrarse*[d]) con Luis, le

_____¹² (dar) unas fotos de la última vez que _____¹³ (*nosotros: estar*) juntos,

y _____¹⁴ (le / lo) _____¹⁵ (pedir) que te _____¹⁶ (las / los)

diera[e] a ti.

Espero verte durante mi próxima visita. Recibe un fuerte abrazo[f] de tu amigo,

Gerardo

---

[a]*meeting* [b]*I wanted* [c]*you were* [d]*to meet up* [e]*he give* [f]*hug*

Paso 2. Conteste las preguntas con oraciones completas.

1. ¿Por qué fue Gerardo a La Habana?

   _____

2. ¿Por qué no pudo ver a Pepe el primer día?

   _____

3. ¿Cómo supo que Pepe estaba de viaje?

   _____

4. ¿A quién le dio las fotos?

   _____

B. *Listening Passage:* **El Carnaval**

Antes de escuchar. Antes de escuchar la selección sobre las celebraciones de carnaval, indique si las oraciones describen **una fiesta al aire libre** (*outdoor*) o **una celebración religiosa solemne**.

	UNA FIESTA AL AIRE LIBRE	UNA CELEBRACIÓN RELIGIOSA SOLEMNE
1. La gente bebe, come, canta y baila.	☐	☐
2. La gente es seria.	☐	☐
3. La gente no se habla mucho.	☐	☐
4. La gente reza (*pray*).	☐	☐
5. La gente se divierte hasta altas (*late*) horas de la noche.	☐	☐
6. Se celebra en las calles.	☐	☐

Listening Passage. You will hear a passage about carnival celebrations (**los carnavales**). First, listen to the **Vocabulario útil.** Next, listen to the passage once to get a general idea of the content. Then listen again for details.

Vocabulario útil

la Cuaresma	Lent	**caricaturesco/a**	cartoonish, satirical
aun	even	**durar**	to last
la gente	people	**pagano/a**	pagan
la máscara	mask	**se mezclan**	are blended
el disfraz	costume	**de maravilla**	great, wonderfully
el monstruo	monster		

Después de escuchar. Ahora indique si las siguientes oraciones son **ciertas** (**C**) o **falsas** (**F**).

_____ **1.** La fiesta de carnaval ocurre justo antes de empezar la Cuaresma.

_____ **2.** El carnaval es una tradición exclusivamente europea.

_____ **3.** Las celebraciones de carnaval pueden durar toda la noche.

_____ **4.** Las celebraciones de carnaval en todo el mundo tienen muchas semejanzas.

_____ **5.** Para el narrador, Mardi Gras es el carnaval más impresionante.

_____ **6.** En el Brasil, hace frío y viento durante la época de carnaval.

_____ **7.** El narrador lo pasó bien en el Carnaval de Río de Janeiro el año pasado.

C. Charlando (*Chatting*) y preparando una fiesta

Paso 1. Ud. va a oír una conversación entre Miguel René y Rubén, quienes charlan mientras preparan una fiesta. Primero, escuche el **Vocabulario útil**. Luego escuche la conversación e indique todos los temas que mencionan.

Rubén y Miguel René

Vocabulario útil

colgar (cuelgo) (gu)	to hang
el globo	balloon
para que la genta sepa	so that people know
juntarse	**reunirse (me reúno)**
las uvas de la suerte	the lucky grapes
nos agarramos de	we hold
el segundo	second

1. ☐ una fiesta para María
2. ☐ la celebración del Día de la Independencia
3. ☐ las tradiciones de la Nochevieja
4. ☐ la importancia de la familia

Paso 2. En el **Paso 3**, Ud. va a participar en una conversación similar a la del **Paso 1** en la que (*in which*) Ud. va a hacer el papel (*play the role*) de Enrique, quien habla con su amigo Juan sobre una fiesta que ellos están planeando para su amiga Ana. Primero, complete la conversación con las siguientes frases.

celebra tu familia la Navidad	gastamos mucho dinero
comemos las doce uvas de la suerte	le va a encantar

(Continúa.)

JUAN: Creo que los adornos (*decorations*) para la fiesta están quedando muy bien.

ENRIQUE: ¡De acuerdo! Creo que a Ana _____.[1]

JUAN: Estos preparativos me recuerdan mucho a la Navidad.

ENRIQUE: ¿Cómo _____[2]?

JUAN: Pues nos juntamos toda la familia, hay mucho que comer, muchos regalos,... ¿Y tu familia?

ENRIQUE: Pues cosas similares, y siempre _____.[3]

JUAN: ¿Y hacen algo especial para la Nochevieja?

ENRIQUE: Sí. Tenemos una cena especial, y a la medianoche _____

_____.[4]

JUAN: ¡Ah! Esa es la costumbre española, ¿verdad?

Nota: Verifique sus respuestas del **Paso 2** en el Apéndice antes de empezar el **Paso 3.**

Paso 3. Ahora haga el papel de Enrique en la conversación completa del **Paso 2.** Después de leer en voz alta cada línea del diálogo de Enrique, escúchela y repítala.

CULTURA

A. **Mapa.** Identifique el país y la capital en el siguiente mapa.

B. Comprensión. Complete las oraciones con palabras de la lista. Esta actividad se basa en la información de las lecturas **Nota cultural** (p. 270), **Algo sobre...** (p. 269, 280 y 285) y **Lectura cultural** (p. 288). **¡OJO!** No se usan todas las palabras.

africanos	el merengue	parrandas	la Semana Santa
la libertad	la Navidad	quinceañeras	el son
la Independencia	la palma	los Reyes Magos	

1. En muchos países, _____ les traen regalos a los niños el 6 de enero.

2. En los pueblos y ciudades de una región de Cuba central, hay grandes fiestas navideñas o

   _____.

3. José Martí fue un escritor y periodista que luchó (*fought*) por la independencia y

   _____ de Cuba.

4. Celia Cruz, una gran cantante cubana, llevó _____ por todo el mundo. Esa música

   tiene elementos musicales _____ y españoles.

5. En Cuba, el 10 de octubre se conoce como del Día de _____ Nacional. En este día,

   Carlos Manuel de Céspedes declaró libres a todos los esclavos.

6. Desde 1959 hasta 1998 el gobierno (*government*) de Fidel Castro no permitió la celebración oficial

   de _____ en Cuba.

7. _____, un tipo de árbol tropical, es uno de los símbolos nacionales de Cuba y es

   parte de su escudo (*coat of arms*).

PÓNGASE A PRUEBA

A. Irregular Preterites. Escriba las formas apropiadas de los verbos en el pretérito.

1. **estar:** yo _____

2. **poder:** tú _____

3. **poner:** Ud. _____

4. **querer:** nosotros _____

5. **saber:** ellos _____

6. **tener:** yo _____

7. **venir:** tú _____

8. **traer:** Ud. _____

9. **decir:** ellos _____

10. **ir:** nosotros _____

B. Preterite of Stem-Changing Verbs. Complete la siguiente tabla.

	DORMIR	PEDIR	PREFERIR	RECORDAR	SENTIRSE
él / ella / Ud.					
ellos / ellas / Uds.					

C. Double Object Pronouns. Sustituya (*Substitute*) los complementos directos e indirectos por sus respectivos pronombres.

MODELO: Alberto le sirvió café a Jimena. → Alberto se lo sirvió.

1. Ricardo le pidió dinero a su padre.   Ricardo _____ _____ pidió.

2. Clara le sugirió la idea a Enrique.   Clara _____ _____ sugirió.

3. Carmen les puso los suéteres a sus hijos.   Carmen _____ _____ puso.

PRUEBA CORTA

A. ¿Qué pasó? Complete las oraciones con la forma apropiada del pretérito de un verbo de la lista.

conseguir   dormir   reírse
despedirse   hacer   traer
divertirse   ponerse   vestirse

1. Cuando vimos esa película, todos (nosotros) _____ mucho.

2. Después de comer ese pescado, Martín _____ enfermo y se acostó, pero no

   _____ en toda la noche.

3. Yo _____ un boleto extra para el concierto de mañana. ¿Quieres ir?

4. Marcos _____ de sus amigos y volvió a su casa.

5. Para celebrar el Año Nuevo, Mirasol _____ con ropa elegante: pantalones negros y

   una blusa de seda. Ella _____ muchísimo bailando con sus amigos.

6. Para celebrar el Año Nuevo, nosotros _____ una fiesta y unos amigos nos

   _____ champán.

B. Preguntas y respuestas. Conteste las preguntas con la respuesta más apropiada.

1. ¿Cuándo nos traes el café?

   a. Se lo traigo en seguida (*right away*).
   b. Te los traigo en seguida.
   c. Te lo traigo en seguida.

2. ¿Cuándo me van a lavar el coche?

   a. Se lo vamos a lavar esta tarde.
   b. Me lo voy a lavar esta tarde.
   c. Te lo voy a lavar esta tarde.

3. ¿Quién te sacó estas fotos?

   a. Julio me los sacó.
   b. Julio te las sacó.
   c. Julio me las sacó.

4. ¿Quién les mandó estas flores a Uds.?

   a. Ceci nos los mandó.
   b. Ceci nos las mandó.
   c. Ceci se las mandó.

5. ¿A quién le vas a regalar esa camisa?

    a. Te la voy a regalar a ti.
    b. Se lo voy a regalar a Uds.
    c. Me las vas a regalar a mí.

6. ¿A quién le sirves ese vino?

    a. Se los sirvo a Uds.
    b. Se lo sirvo a Uds.
    c. Mario nos lo sirve.

C. Preparativos para la fiesta de Gilberto. Va a oír algunas preguntas sobre el cumpleaños de Gilberto. Escoja la letra de la mejor respuesta para cada pregunta. Preste (*Pay*) atención a los pronombres y los complementos directos que oye en las preguntas.

1. **a.** Sí, voy a mandártela.   **b.** Sí, voy a mandártelos.
2. **a.** Sí, se lo tengo que hacer.   **b.** Sí, te lo tengo que hacer.
3. **a.** Sí, nos los van a traer.   **b.** Sí, se los voy a traer.
4. **a.** No, no van a traértelas.   **b.** No, no van a traérmelas.
5. **a.** Sí, te las sirvo.   **b.** Sí, se las sirvo.

D. El cumpleaños de Gilberto. Imagine que Ud. le hizo una fiesta sorpresa para su cumpleaños a su amigo Gilberto. Cuando oiga el sujeto, forme oraciones con las palabras que se dan. Use el pretérito de los verbos. Luego escuche la respuesta correcta y repítala. ¡OJO! Si el sujeto es un pronombre de sujeto (*subject pronoun*), no lo use.

    MODELO: (Ud. ve)   **1.** hacerle una fiesta sorpresa a Gilberto
                     (Ud. oye)   **1.** yo
                   (Ud. dice)   Le hice una fiesta sorpresa a Gilberto.
       (Ud. oye y repite)   Le hice una fiesta sorpresa a Gilberto.

2. venir
3. querer venir, pero no poder
4. traer o mandar regalos
5. tener que preparar todo
6. servir los refrescos
7. contar chistes como siempre
8. divertirse y reírse
9. quejarse
10. tener que bailar con todas las muchachas
11. ¡ponerse muy nervioso!

PUNTOS PERSONALES

❖ **A. Ud. y las fiestas.** Conteste las preguntas con oraciones completas.

1. ¿Cómo celebra Ud. el Día de Acción de Gracias (*Thanksgiving*)?

_____

2. ¿Qué hace Ud. para celebrar la Nochevieja? ¿Se queda en casa o va a algún lugar?

_____

3. ¿Hace algo para celebrar el Día de San Patricio?

_____

(Continúa.)

4. ¿Celebra Ud. la Pascua?

_____

5. En su familia, ¿se gasta mucho dinero para los regalos de Navidad o Janucá?

_____

❖ **B.** **Reacciones.** ¿Cómo reacciona o cómo se pone Ud. en estas circunstancias? Use por lo menos uno de los verbos útiles en cada respuesta. Puede usar la forma enfática (**-ísimo/a**) de los adjetivos.

Verbos útiles

enojarse	quejarse
llorar	reírse
ponerse contento/a (enojado/a, feliz, rojo/a, triste)	sonreír

1. Alguien le hace una broma un poco pesada (_in bad taste_).

_____

2. Alguien le cuenta un chiste gracioso (_funny_).

_____

3. En un restaurante le traen a Ud. la cuenta y ve que no tiene su cartera.

_____

4. Ud. acaba de oír que su perro (gato) murió en un accidente.

_____

5. Le sirven una comida malísima en un restaurante muy caro.

_____

6. Ud. acaba de saber que recibió la nota más alta de la clase en el examen de historia.

_____

❖ **C.** **¿Qué pasó la última vez que... ?** Conteste estas preguntas con oraciones completas.

1. La última vez que Ud. cumplió años, ¿cómo celebró? ¿Con quién y dónde celebró? ¿Recibió un regalo especial? ¿Cómo se sintió ese día?

_____

2. La última vez que Ud. y su familia celebraron algo especial, ¿vinieron de lejos (_from far away_) algunos parientes (tíos, abuelos, hermanos)? ¿Quién vino y de dónde vino? ¿O no vino de lejos ningún pariente?

Para celebrar _____ , _____

_____

3. ¿Pudo Ud. contestar todas las preguntas del último examen de español? ¿Fue fácil o difícil el examen?

_____

4. ¿Conoció Ud. a alguien durante sus últimas vacaciones? ¿A quién conoció?

_____

D. Días de fiesta

Paso 1. Ud. va a escuchar una entrevista en la que (*in which*) Karina (de Venezuela), Rubén (de España) y Miguel René (de México) hablan de las fiestas que celebran. Primero, escuche el **Vocabulario útil,** luego escuche la entrevista una vez para tener una idea general de su contenido (*content*). Después, escuche la entrevista otra vez (*again*). Mientras la escucha, empareje la letra del nombre de cada persona (**K** = Karina, **R** = Rubén, **MR** = Miguel René) con la oración apropiada.

Karina

Rubén

Miguel René

Vocabulario útil

la boda	wedding
el bautizo	baptism
el Día de Muertos	Day of the Dead (Nov. 2)
festejar	**celebrar**
entregar	**dar**
la bendición	blessing

1. _____ Su familia celebra los carnavales.

2. _____ Su familia celebra el Día de los Muertos.

3. _____ En su país el Niño Jesús trae regalos.

4. _____ En su país, hay diferencias entre las tradiciones navideñas (*Christmas, adj.*) del norte y

   las del sur.

5. _____ En su país, en Nochebuena viene Papá Noel

6. _____ y _____ (**¡OJO!** dos personas) En sus países los Reyes Magos (*Magi*) vienen con

   regalos el 6 de enero.

❖ **Paso 2.** Ahora escuche la primera pregunta que se hace, y contéstela por escrito.

❖ **E. Guided Composition.** En hoja aparte (*On a separate sheet of paper*), conteste las siguientes preguntas sobre su último cumpleaños. Luego organice y combine sus respuestas en una composición. Recuerde usar palabras conectivas como, por ejemplo, **por eso, como... ,** (*since . . .*), **porque, aunque** (*although*) y **luego.**

1. ¿Cuántos años cumplió en su último (*last*) cumpleaños?
2. ¿Qué hizo para celebrarlo?
3. ¿Dio una fiesta? ¿Salió con su pareja (*partner*), amigos y/o con su familia?
4. ¿Qué comidas y bebidas se sirvieron?
5. ¿Se sirvió un pastel de cumpleaños?
6. ¿Qué le regalaron sus amigos y su familia?
7. ¿Se divirtió en el día de su cumpleaños?

❖ **F. Mi diario.** En su diario, escriba sobre el día festivo más importante para su familia o sus amigos. ¿Cuándo se celebra? ¿Se celebra con una cena especial o con una fiesta? ¿Dónde se celebra? ¿Quiénes asisten? ¿Qué comidas y bebidas se sirven? ¿Es una actividad cooperativa la preparación de la comida? ¿O lo prepara todo una sola persona? ¿Cuáles son las costumbres (*customs*) y tradiciones más importantes relacionadas con este día festivo?

Vocabulario útil

dar las doce	to strike twelve	**el globo**	balloon
decorar el árbol		**normalmente**	normally
los fuegos artificiales	fireworks		

❖ **G. Intercambios.** Escuche las siguientes preguntas y contéstelas por escrito.

1. _____
   _____

2. _____
   _____

3. _____
   _____

4. _____
   _____

5. _____
   _____

APPENDIX: ANSWER KEY

CAPÍTULO 1: Ante todo

PRIMERA PARTE

Saludos y expresiones de cortesía

A. **1.** I **2.** I **3.** F **4.** F **5.** I **6.** I

D. **1.** ¿Qué tal? (¿Cómo estás?) **2.** ¿Y tú? **3.** hasta **4.** Hasta luego. (Hasta mañana.)

E. **1.** Buenas **2.** está **3.** gracias **4.** se llama **5.** Me llamo **6.** gusto **7.** Mucho gusto (Igualmente./Encantado/a.)

G. (*Possible answers*) **1.** Gracias. **2.** Con permiso. **3.** Perdón. **4.** No hay de qué. (De nada.)

PRONUNCIACIÓN: Las vocales: a, e, i, o, u

B. Paso 1. **1.** ro<u>d</u>illa **2.** Mar<u>i</u>bel **3.** <u>uni</u>lateral **4.** s<u>a</u>lvav<u>idas</u> **5.** olvid<u>a</u>dizo

Paso 3. **1.** Muñoz **2.** Robles **3.** Garrido **4.** Peralta

El alfabeto español

C. **1.** ñ **2.** h **3.** v **4.** ll **5.** r

D. **1.** jota **2.** uve **3.** equis **4.** ye **5.** ceta (zeta) **6.** hache

Nota comunicativa: Los cognados

B. Paso 2. **1.** C **2.** F **3.** F **4.** C **5.** C **6.** C

¿Cómo es usted? (Part 1)

A. Paso 1. (*Possible answers*) **1.** N **2.** N **3.** P **4.** N **5.** P **6.** P **7.** N **8.** P

E. **1.** elegante **2.** responsable **3.** examen **4.** interesante **5.** liberal

¡Aquí se habla español!

A. **1.** Bolivia / Paraguay **2.** Venezuela **3.** Guatemala **4.** Chile **5.** Equatorial Guinea (Guinea Ecuatorial)

B. **1.** C **2.** C **3.** F **4.** C **5.** C **6.** F

SEGUNDA PARTE

Los números del 0 al 30; *Hay*

A. **1.** una **2.** cuatro **3.** siete **4.** trece **5.** once **6.** un **7.** veinte **8.** veintitrés (veinte y tres) **9.** veintiséis (veinte y seis) **10.** veintiún (veinte y un) **11.** veintiuna (veinte y una) **12.** treinta

B. **1.** 8 / ocho **2.** 11 / once **3.** 5 / cinco **4.** 6 / seis **5.** 7 / siete **6.** 22 / veintidós (veinte y dos) **7.** 30 / Treinta

C. Paso 1. **1.** 8 (ocho) **2.** 22 (veintidós; veinte y dos) **3.** 14 (catorce) **4.** 3 (tres) **5.** 13 (trece)

D. Paso 1. **1.** 3 (tres) **2.** 2 (dos) **3.** 1 (un) **4.** 1 (una)

E. Paso 1. **a.** 20 **b.** 13 **c.** 18 **d.** 19 **e.** 6 **f.** 24 **g.** 22 **h.** 16

Los gustos y preferencias (Part 1)

A. **1. a.** Me **b.** me **2. a.** Te **b.** le **3. a.** Te **b.** Le

B. **1.** le gusta / me gusta **2.** le gusta / me gusta **3.** te gusta / me gusta **4.** te gusta / me gusta

¿Qué hora es?

A. **1.** c **2.** f **3.** d **4.** a **5.** e **6.** b

B. **1.** Son las doce y veinte de la mañana. **2.** Es la una y cinco de la tarde. **3.** Son las siete y media (treinta) de la noche (tarde). **4.** Son las once de la mañana en punto. **5.** Son las diez menos cuarto (quince) de la noche. **6.** Es la una y media (treinta) de la mañana.

PÓNGASE A PRUEBA

A. **1.** Hola **2.** Buenos / Buenas / Buenas **3.** te llamas **4.** De nada. / No hay de qué.

B. **1.** soy **2.** eres **3.** es

C. **1.** gusta **2.** me gusta **3.** le **4.** gusta

D. **1.** ¿Qué hora es? **2.** Es / Son

PRUEBA CORTA

A. **1.** e **2.** h **3.** a **4.** b **5.** d **6.** g **7.** f **8.** c

CAPÍTULO 2: En la universidad

VOCABULARIO: PREPARACIÓN

En el salón de clase

A. **1.** el edificio **2.** la librería **3.** el lápiz **4.** el bolígrafo **5.** la oficina **6.** la secretaria **7.** el escritorio **8.** el papel **9.** el estudiante **10.** la computadora (portátil) **11.** la ventana **12.** el diccionario **13.** la mochila **14.** el salón de clase **15.** la silla **16.** la profesora **17.** el pizarrón (blanco) **18.** la puerta **19.** el libro (de texto) **20.** la biblioteca **21.** la mesa **22.** la bibliotecaria **23.** el teléfono celular (la calculadora)

B. Paso 1. 1. la calculadora 2. la mochila 3. el hombre 4. el salón de clase 5. la bibliotecaria **Paso 2.** PERSONA: el hombre, la bibliotecaria; LUGAR: el salón de clase; OBJETO: la calculadora, la mochila

D. *The following items are mentioned:* bolígrafos (3); calculadora (1); cuadernos (5); lápiz (1); libros de texto (7); mochila (1).

Las materias

A. **1.** Francés 304, Gramática alemana, La novela moderna **2.** Álgebra, Cálculo 1, Economía, Trigonometría **3.** Antropología, Sicología del adolescente, Sociología urbana **4.** Astronomía, Biología 2, Física, Química orgánica

B. **1.** b **2.** a **3.** d **4.** f **5.** c **6.** e

C. Paso 1. *You should have checked:* RUBÉN: informática, inglés, literatura; TANÉ: computación, historia del teatro, historia universal, inglés, literatura

Nota comunicativa: Las palabras interrogativas

A. **1.** Cuánto **2.** A qué hora **3.** Cómo **4.** Cuál **5.** Dónde **6.** Quién **7.** Cuándo **8.** Qué

B. **1.** Cómo **2.** Quién **3.** Qué **4.** Cuánto **5.** Dónde **6.** A qué hora (Cuándo) **7.** Qué

GRAMÁTICA

1. Naming People, Places, Things, and Ideas (Part 1) • Singular Nouns: Gender and Articles

A. **1.** la **2.** la **3.** la **4.** el **5.** el **6.** la **7.** la **8.** el

B. **1.** un **2.** una **3.** un **4.** una **5.** un **6.** una **7.** una **8.** un

C. **1.** La bibliotecaria es una persona. **2.** El lápiz es un objeto. **3.** La puerta es un objeto. **4.** La administración de empresas es una materia. **5.** El alemán es una materia. **6.** El compañero es una persona. **7.** La librería es un edificio. **8.** El teléfono celular es un objeto. **9.** La biblioteca es un edificio.

D. Paso 1. (*Answers for each item may be in any order.*) **1.** un diccionario, el escritorio **2.** una silla, el cuarto **3.** un profesor, el salón de clase **4.** un estudiante, la biblioteca

2. Naming People, Places, Things, and Ideas (Part 2) • Nouns and Articles: Plural Forms

A. **1.** las amigas **2.** los bolígrafos **3.** las clases **4.** unos profesores **5.** los lápices **6.** unas extranjeras **7.** las universidades **8.** unos programas

B. **1.** el edificio **2.** la fiesta **3.** un cliente **4.** un lápiz **5.** el papel **6.** el lugar **7.** un problema **8.** una mujer

C. **1.** Hay unos escritorios. **2.** Hay unas sillas. **3.** Hay unas computadoras portátiles. **4.** Hay unos estudiantes. **5.** Hay unos cuadernos.

3. Expressing Actions • Subject Pronouns (Part 1); Present Tense of -ar Verbs; Negation

A. **1.** ellas **2.** él **3.** yo **4.** ellos **5.** ellos **6.** nosotros/nosotras

B. **1.** tú **2.** vosotros / Uds. **3.** Uds. **4.** Ud. **5.** tú

D. Paso 1. **1.** hablamos / tomamos / bailan / tocan **2.** necesito / busco / trabaja / pago **3.** enseña / practican / estudian / regresa **Paso 2.** **1.** Yo no canto en la discoteca. **2.** Nosotros no bailamos en la discoteca. **3.** El dependiente no trabaja en la discoteca. **4.** Ella no enseña francés. **5.** Ellos no escuchan música.

Nota comunicativa: El verbo *estar*

A. **1.** Raúl y Carmen están en el salón de clase. **2.** Yo estoy en la biblioteca. **3.** Tú estás en la clase de biología. **4.** Uds. están en la residencia.

B. Paso 2. *Answers will vary. Possible answers:* **1.** Héctor y Juan hablan en el salón de clase. **2.** Julio y Juana hablan (trabajan) en la oficina. **3.** María compra libros en la librería. **4.** Bailamos en la fiesta.

4. Getting Information (Part 1) • Asking Yes/No Questions

A. **1.** (Martín) Compra libros en la librería. **2.** Sí, hay libros en italiano. **3.** Hay cuadernos y bolígrafos (lápices). **4.** Compra dos libros. **5.** Hablan inglés. **6.** Paga veintidós dólares.

UN POCO DE TODO

A. **1.** somos **2.** la **3.** la **4.** enseña **5.** necesitamos **6.** Escuchamos **7.** practicamos **8.** cantamos **9.** Regresa **10.** a **11.** las **12.** los **13.** necesitan **14.** la

B. Después de escuchar. **1.** especialización / carrera **2.** semestres **3.** ciencias políticas **4.** el inglés **5.** extranjeros

C. Paso 1. **1.** Eduardo **2.** Juan Carlos **3.** los dos **4.** los dos **5.** Eduardo
Paso 2. **1.** economía **2.** Qué **3.** hora **4.** tomas / sociología **5.** qué / hora / sociología **6.** la / una / media **7.** A / qué **8.** qué / es

CULTURA

A. **1.** San Francisco **2.** Los Ángeles **3.** San Diego **4.** Santa Fe **5.** El Paso 6. San Antonio

B. **1.** preuniversitaria **2.** España **3.** latinos **4.** conferencias **5.** prestigiosas

PÓNGASE A PRUEBA

A. **1.** el / los **2.** la / las **3.** un / unos **4.** una / unas

B. **1.** busco **2.** buscas **3.** busca **4.** buscamos **5.** buscan

C. **1.** Yo no deseo tomar café. **2.** No hablamos alemán en la clase. **3.** Marta no baila el tango.

D. **1.** nosotros estamos **2.** están **3.** ellos están **4.** ellas están

E. **1.** ¿Dónde? **2.** ¿Cómo? **3.** ¿Cuándo? **4.** ¿Quién? **5.** ¿Qué? **6.** ¿Por qué?

PRUEBA CORTA

A. **1.** el **2.** la **3.** la **4.** el **5.** la **6.** los **7.** los **8.** los

B. **1.** una **2.** unos **3.** unos **4.** un **5.** una **6.** unas **7.** una **8.** unas **9.** un

C. **1.** estudian **2.** escucho **3.** hablamos **4.** Toca **5.** enseña **6.** Necesito **7.** regresa **8.** manda

CAPÍTULO 3: La familia

VOCABULARIO: Preparación

La familia y los parientes

A. **1.** Tulia es la madre de Enrique. **2.** Héctor es el tío de Enrique. **3.** Alberto y Carmen son los abuelos de Enrique. **4.** Angélica es la hermana de Enrique. **5.** Luis es el primo de Enrique. **6.** Ana María es la prima de Enrique. **7.** Daniel y Alejandra son los tíos de Enrique.

B. **1.** sobrino **2.** tía **3.** abuelos **4.** abuela **5.** nieta **6.** parientes **7.** mascota

E. (*In order from left to right*) *Top row:* Roberto (el abuelo), Julia (la abuela). *Middle row:* Elena (la madre), Juan (el padre), Lisa (la tía), Rosa (la tía), Pablo (el tío). *Bottom row:* Sara, Manolo y Juanito (los hermanos), Andrés y Julio (los primos)

Nota cultural: Los apellidos hispanos

1. c **2.** b

Los números del 31 al 100

A. **1.** cien   **2.** treinta y una   **3.** cincuenta y siete   **4.** noventa y un   **5.** setenta y seis

B. **Paso 1.** **a.** 45 (cuarenta y cinco)   **b.** 99 (noventa y nueve)   **c.** 52 (cincuenta y dos)   **d.** 74 (setenta y cuatro)   **e.** 31 (treinta y una)   **f.** 100 (cien)

C. **Paso 1.** **a.** 40 (cuarenta)   **b.** 35 (treinta y cinco)   **c.** 100 (cien)   **d.** 78 (setenta y ocho)   **e.** 92 (noventa y dos)   **f.** 86 (ochenta y seis)

Los adjetivos

A. (*Possible answers*)   **1.** grande / nuevo   **2.** pequeño / viejo   **3.** joven / perezoso   **4.** joven / moreno / trabajador

C. **1.** bajo / feo / inteligente (listo) / trabajador   **2.** delgado / viejo / simpático / moreno

D. **1.** joven y morena.   **2.** tiene 48 (cuarenta y ocho) años.   **3.** listo (inteligente) y delgado.   **4.** le gusta la música clásica.   **5.** el siete, catorce, veintiuno, setenta y siete.

PRONUNCIACIÓN: Stress and Written Accent Marks (Part 1)

C. (*The stressed syllables are underlined.*)   **1.** con-<u>trol</u> (aguda)   **2.** e-le-<u>fan</u>-te (llana)   **3.** mo-nu-men-<u>tal</u> (aguda)   **4.** com-pa-<u>ñe</u>-ra (llana)   **5.** <u>bue</u>-nos (llana)   **6.** us-<u>ted</u> (aguda)

D. **Paso 1.** **1.** doc-<u>tor</u>   **2.** mu-<u>jer</u>   **3.** mo-<u>chi</u>-la   **4.** ac-<u>tor</u>   **5.** per-<u>mi</u>-so   **6.** po-<u>si</u>-ble   **7.** lo-<u>cal</u>   **8.** pro-fe-<u>so</u>-res   **9.** u-ni-ver-si-<u>dad</u>   **10.** <u>Car</u>-men   **11.** I-sa-<u>bel</u>   **12.** bi-blio-<u>te</u>-ca   **13.** us-<u>ted</u>   **14.** li-ber-<u>tad</u>   **15.** o-<u>ri</u>-gen   **16.** a-ni-<u>mal</u>

GRAMÁTICA

5. Describing Adjectives: Gender, Number, and Position

A. **1.** María es alta, bonita, trabajadora y tonta.   **2.** Javier es delgado, guapo, listo, moreno y simpático.   **3.** Los Sres. Cruz son bajos, gordos, inteligentes, jóvenes, pobres y rubios.

B. Paso 1. *For each person you should have written:* SU PADRE: bajo; SU TÍO: bajo; SU HERMANA: alta; LOS ABUELOS: activos; SUS PRIMOS: activos, jóvenes.

C. Paso 2. **1.** delgado   **2.** mediana   **3.** altas   **4.** morena   **5.** joven   **6.** rubia

E. **1.** alemana   **2.** costarricense   **3.** argentinos   **4.** inglesa   **5.** mexicana   **6.** colombianos   **7.** francesas   **8.** ruso   **9.** iraquí   **10.** japonesa

G. **1.** Buscamos otra motocicleta alemana.   **2.** Pablo busca otros bolígrafos franceses.   **3.** Busco al gran escritor Mario Vargas Llosa.   **4.** Jorge busca dos perros pequeños.

¿Recuerda Ud.? **1.** soy   **2.** eres   **3.** es   **4.** somos   **5.** son

6. Expressing *to be* • Present Tense of *ser,* Summary of Uses (Part 2)

A. **1.** c   **2.** e   **3.** a   **4.** b   **5.** f   **6.** d

B. **1.** soy   **2.** son   **3.** es   **4.** son   **5.** eres   **6.** somos

C. **1.** El programa de *Weight Watchers* es para mi tía. Es gorda.   **2.** La casa grande es para los Sres. Walker. Tienen cuatro niños.   **3.** El dinero es para mis padres. Necesitan comprar una computadora nueva.   **4.** Los bolígrafos son para mi hermana Ana. Le gusta escribir.

D. **1.** es de Cuba   **2.** son de España   **3.** es de Chile   **4.** eres de Costa Rica

E. **1.** ¿De quién son los libros (de texto)? Son de la profesora.   **2.** ¿De quién es la mochila? Es de Cecilia.   **3.** ¿De quién son los bolígrafos? Son del Sr. (señor) Alonso.   **4.** ¿De quién es la casa? Es de la familia Olivera.

7. Expressing Possession • Unstressed Possessive Adjectives (Part 1)

¿Recuerda Ud.?   **1.** (Ella) Es la hermana de Isabel.   **2.** (Ellos) Son los parientes de Mario.   **3.** (Ellos) Son los abuelos de Marta.

A. **Paso 1.**   **1.** su   **2.** sus   **3.** su   **4.** sus   **5.** su   **Paso 2.**   **1.** mi familia   **2.** sus parientes   **3.** mis abuelos   **4.** nuestros padres   **5.** su hermano

B.   **1.** Sí, es su suegra.   **2.** Sí, es nuestro hermano.   **3.** Sí, son sus padres.   **4.** Sí, somos sus primos.   **5.** Sí, es su sobrina.   **6.** Sí, soy su nieto/a.

E. **Paso 1.**   **1.** su   **2.** tu   **Paso 2.** D (la Sra. Dolores): numerosa, bonita, unida; T (Tané): pequeña, bonita

¿Recuerda Ud.?   **1.** -amos   **2.** -o   **3.** -as   **4.** -an   **5.** -a

8. Expressing Actions • Present Tense of -er and -ir Verbs; Subject Pronouns (Part 2)

A.   **1.** come   **2.** estudia   **3.** beben   **4.** escribe   **5.** lee

B.   **1.** vivimos   **2.** asisto   **3.** hablamos   **4.** leemos   **5.** escribimos   **6.** aprendemos   **7.** abren   **8.** comemos   **9.** debemos   **10.** prepara

C. Paso 2.   **1.** Vivo   **2.** Asisto   **3.** como   **4.** debo   **5.** estudio / recibo   **6.** comprendo

UN POCO DE TODO

A.   **1.** mi   **2.** somos   **3.** somos   **4.** vivimos   **5.** una   **6.** bonita   **7.** Mi   **8.** trabaja   **9.** asistimos   **10.** tiene   **11.** tengo   **12.** vive   **13.** sesenta y siete   **14.** baja   **15.** simpática   **16.** trabajadora   **17.** Estamos   **18.** extrañamos   **19.** nuestros   **20.** chilenos

B. Después de escuchar. Paso 1.   **1.** C   **2.** F (*Possible answer*) En general, los abuelos (sí) participan activamente en el cuidado de sus nietos.   **3.** F (*Possible answer*) Por lo general, las personas viejas no viven en asilos. Viven con sus familias.   **4.** C   **5.** C   **Paso 2.**   **1.** materna   **2.** grandes   **3.** esposos   **4.** viejos

C. Paso 1.   **1.** F   **2.** F   **3.** C   **Paso 2.**   **1.** Sí, mucho.   **2.** Tengo dos hermanos, Miguel y Mateo.   **3.** Miguel tiene veinte años y es muy alto.   **4.** Tiene 17 años y es muy simpático.

CULTURA

A.   **1.** Monterrey   **2.** Guadalajara   **3.** la Ciudad de México   **4.** Puebla   **5.** Oaxaca

B.   **1.** b   **2.** a   **3.** a   **4.** a   **5.** b   **6.** a

PÓNGASE A PRUEBA

A.   **1. a.** guapa **b.** guapos   **2. a.** grandes **b.** sentimentales   **3.** mexicano / mexicanas / mexicanos // francesa / francés / francesas // española / español / españoles

B.   **1.** c   **2.** a   **3.** b   **4.** d

C.   **1.** mi hermano   **2.** su tío   **3.** nuestros abuelos   **4.** su casa

D. *leer:* yo leo, él lee, nosotros leemos; *escribir:* tú escribes, ella escribe, Uds. escriben

PRUEBA CORTA

A.   **1.** italiano   **2.** francesa   **3.** alemán   **4.** inglesas

B.   **1.** es   **2.** soy   **3.** son   **4.** eres   **5.** somos

C. **1.** mi **2.** mi **3.** Mis **4.** nuestros **5.** su **6.** nuestra **7.** sus **8.** tu

D. **1.** comprendemos / habla **2.** Escuchas / estudias **3.** lee **4.** venden **5.** recibe **6.** bebo **7.** asistimos

CAPÍTULO 4: De compras

VOCABULARIO: Preparación

De compras: La ropa

A. **1. a.** una chaqueta **b.** unos pantalones **c.** una corbata **d.** una camisa **e.** unos zapatos **f.** un cinturón **2. a.** un vestido **b.** unas botas **c.** un abrigo **d.** un bolso **e.** unos aretes

B. **1.** centro **2.** almacén **3.** venden de todo **4.** fijos **5.** de última moda **6.** tiendas **7.** rebajas (gangas) **8.** mercado **9.** regatear **10.** gangas (rebajas)

C. **1.** algodón **2.** corbatas / seda **3.** suéteres / faldas / lana **4.** cuero

D. **1.** Necesitas una sudadera nueva, ¿verdad? (¿no?) **2.** Buscas una camisa de seda, ¿verdad? (¿no?) **3.** Tus sandalias son cómodas ¿verdad? (¿no?) **4.** No necesito llevar corbata, ¿verdad? **5.** Esta chaqueta es perfecta, ¿verdad? (¿no?)

F. Paso 2. *Order of* questions is: 4, 3, 1, 2.

Los colores: ¿De qué color es?

A. **1.** verdes **2.** azul / blanca / azul **3.** roja / blanca / azul **4.** anaranjada / amarillo **5.** gris **6.** morado **7.** rosado **8.** color café

B. Paso 1. *For each person you should have checked*: LUIS: calcetines, camisa, pantalones, cinturón, corbata; ANA: tenis, calcetines, pantalones, camiseta; JUAN: tenis, pantalones, camiseta.
Paso 2. corbata: amarilla; camisa: azul; cinturón: negro; pantalones: grises, negros, azules; camiseta: morada, blanca; tenis: blancos; calcetines: grises, morados.

Los números a partir del 100

A. **1.** 11 **12.** 476 **3.** 15.714 **4.** 700.500 **5.** 1.965 **6.** 1.000.013

B. **1.** quinientos **2.** mil; veinticinco **3.** siete; trescientos **4.** setecientos ochenta **5.** ochocientas; tres **6.** novecientas

C. Paso 1. pares de medias: 1.136; camisas blancas: 567; suéteres rojos: 9.081; pares de zapatos: 3.329; blusas azules: 111; faldas negras: 843

PRONUNCIACIÓN: Stress and Written Accent Marks (Part 2)

D. *The following words require an accent:* **1.** métrica, **4.** Rosalía, **6.** sabiduría, **7.** jóvenes, **8.** mágico

E. Paso 1. **1.** doctor **2.** mujer **3.** mochila **4.** inglés **5.** actor **6.** permiso **7.** posible **8.** Tomás **9.** general **10.** profesores **11.** universidad **12.** Bárbara **13.** lápices **14.** Carmen **15.** Isabel **16.** López **17.** Ramírez **18.** biblioteca **19.** sicología **20.** usted **Paso 2.** The following words require an accent: **3.** matrícula, **4.** bolígrafo, **7.** Pérez, **9.** alemán

GRAMÁTICA

¿Recuerda Ud.?   **1.** Este   **2.** Estos   **3.** esta   **4.** estas

9. Pointing Out People and Things • Demonstrative Adjectives (Part 2) and Pronouns

A.   **1. a.** este / estos **b.** esta / estas   **2. a.** ese / esos **b.** esa / esas   **3. a.** aquel / aquellos **b.** aquella / aquellas

B.   **1.** Este   **2.** falda   **3.** abrigo   **4.** Ese   **5.** traje   **6.** Aquel   **7.** pantalones cortos   **8.** camiseta

C.   **1.** Sí, esta chaqueta es de Miguel.   **2.** Sí, esos calcetines son de Daniel.   **3.** Sí, aquellos impermeables son de Margarita.   **4.** Sí, estas chanclas son de Ceci.   **5.** Sí, aquel reloj es de Pablo.   **6.** Sí, esos papeles son de David.

D. Paso 1.   **1.** Este   **2.** Aquellas   **3.** Esas

¿Recuerda Ud.?   **1.** tienes   **2.** tengo   **3.** tiene

10. Expressing Actions and States • *Tener, venir, preferir, poder* and *querer*; Some Idioms with *tener*

A. *tener*: tienes / tiene / tienen   *venir*: vengo / viene / venimos   *preferir*: prefiero / preferimos / prefieren   *poder*: puede / podemos / pueden   *querer*: quiero / quieres / quieren

B.   **1.** Quieres   **2.** puedo   **3.** tengo   **4.** Podemos   **5.** Creo   **6.** quieren   **7.** vengo   **8.** quiero
9. prefiero

C.   **1.** Tengo   **2.** ganas   **3.** miedo   **4.** razón   **5.** sueño

D. Paso 1.   **1.** queremos   **2.** puedo   **3.** Prefieres   **4.** vienen   **5.** tiene

G. Paso 2.   **1.** ... tienen un aniversario.   **2.** ... pueden ir a un centro comercial o al centro.   **3.** ... quiere ir de compras al centro.   **4.** ... tienen cosas elegantes.   **5.** ... tiene el coche.   **6.** ... no puede esperar más.

11. Expressing Destination and Future Actions • *Ir;* The Contraction *al; Ir +a + Infinitive*

A.   **1.** va   **2.** van   **3.** vas   **4.** vamos   **5.** voy

B.   **1.** David va a comprar...   **2.** Ignacio y Pepe van a ir...   **3.** Por eso vamos a necesitar...
4. Afortunadamente no voy a tener...

D. Paso 2. *Answers may vary slightly.*   **1.** Gilberto va a ir al centro comercial con sus amigos.   **2.** Gilberto va a jugar al basquetbol con su amigo David.   **3.** Gilberto va a cenar en un restaurante con su familia.
4. Gilberto va a estudiar para un examen de ciencias.

E.   **1.** ... va a hacer una fiesta en su casa ...   **2.** ... va a ir a la fiesta.   **3.** ... van a ir al cine.   **4.** ... va a comprar *jeans*.   **5.** ... va a comprar nada.

UN POCO DE TODO

A.   **1.** la   **2.** quiere   **3.** ir   **4.** pequeñas   **5.** venden   **6.** especiales   **7.** grandes   **8.** prefiere
9. españolas   **10.** esta   **11.** especializadas   **12.** populares   **13.** existen   **14.** elegantes   **15.** famosos

C. Paso 1. You should have checked the following sentences: Las chaquetas son de pura lana. ¡El precio es una ganga! Muchas gracias, muy amable. ¿Qué colores prefiere? **Paso 2.** *Answers may vary slightly:*   **1.** Las chaquetas son de pura lana.   **2.** Mariela quiere comprar la chaqueta para su hermana.   **3.** Sí, es posible regatear en ese mercado.   **4.** Mariela va a pagar cuatro mil quinientos colones.   **5.** El precio original de las chaquetas es cinco mil colones.

CULTURA

A.   **1.** Guatemala   **2.** La Ciudad de Guatemala   **3.** Honduras   **4.** Tegucigalpa

B.   **1.** a   **2.** e   **3.** d   **4.** c   **5.** b

PÓNGASE A PRUEBA

A. **1.** este **2.** estos **3.** ese **4.** aquellos **5.** aquella **6.** esos

B. **1.** *poder:* puedo / puede / podemos / *querer:* quiero / quiere / queremos / *venir:* vengo / viene / venimos **2.** **a.** tener miedo (de) **b.** tener razón **c.** no tener razón **d.** tener ganas (de) **e.** tener que

C. **1.** van **2.** vas **3.** vamos **4.** voy; ir

PRUEBA CORTA

A. **1.** Quiero comprar ese impermeable negro. **2.** ¿Buscas este traje gris? **3.** Juan va a comprar esa chaqueta blanca. **4.** Mis padres trabajan en aquella tienda nueva.

B. **1.** venimos / tenemos **2.** prefieres (quieres) / prefiero (quiero) **3.** tienen **4.** pueden

C. **1.** Roberto va a llevar traje y corbata. **2.** Voy a buscar unas chanclas baratas. **3.** Vamos a hablar por teléfono. **4.** ¿Vas a venir a casa esta noche?

CAPÍTULO 5: En casa

VOCABULARIO: Preparación

Los muebles, los cuartos y otras partes de la casa (Part 1)

A. **2.** el comedor **3.** la cocina **4.** la alcoba **5.** el baño **6.** el garaje **7.** el estudio **8.** el jardín

B. *En la sala hay...* **2.** una mesita **3.** un sillón **4.** una alfombra **5.** un sofá
En la alcoba hay... **1.** una cama **2.** una cómoda **3.** un armario **4.** una lámpara

D. *You should have checked:* 1, 5, 6.

¿Qué día es hoy?

A. **1.** lunes / miércoles / martes **2.** lunes / miércoles / viernes / viernes **3.** sábado **4.** domingo **5.** miércoles **6.** martes

B. **1.** fin / sábado / domingo **2.** lunes **3.** miércoles **4.** jueves **5.** pasado mañana **6.** el / los **7.** próxima

¿Cuándo? Las preposiciones (Part 1)

B. **1.** Tengo sueño antes de descansar. **2.** Regreso a casa después de asistir a clases. **3.** Tengo ganas de comer después de practicar un deporte. **4.** Entro en una fiesta antes de bailar. **5.** Lavo los platos después de comer.

GRAMÁTICA

12. Expressing Actions • *Hacer, oír, poner, salir, traer, ver*

A. **hacer:** hago, hace, hacen; **oír:** oigo, oyes, oyen; **poner:** pongo, ponemos, ponen; **salir:** salgo, sale, salimos; **traer:** traigo, traes, traen; **ver:** veo, ve, vemos, ven

B. **1.** veo (pongo) **2.** salimos **3.** Pongo (Veo) **4.** traigo **5.** oímos **6.** hago

13. Expressing Actions • Present Tense of Stem-Changing Verbs (Part 2)

¿Recuerda Ud.? **querer:** quiero, quieres, quiere, quieren; **preferir:** prefiero, prefiere, preferimos, prefieren; **poder:** puedo, puedes, podemos, pueden

A. **1.** duermo **2.** volvemos **3.** pienso **4.** jugamos **5.** empiezo **6.** pedimos

B. **1.** piensan / pensamos / piensas **2.** volvemos / vuelve / vuelven **3.** pide / piden / pedimos

C. **1.** Sale de (la) casa a las siete y cuarto (quince). **2.** Su primera clase empieza a las ocho (en punto). **3.** Si Bernardo no entiende la lección, hace muchas preguntas. **4.** Con frecuencia almuerza en la cafetería. **5.** A veces pide una hamburguesa y un refresco. **6.** Los lunes y (los) miércoles juega al tenis con un amigo. **7.** Su madre sirve la cena a las seis. **8.** Por la noche, Bernardo hace la tarea y duerme siete horas.

D. **1.** cierra **2.** almuerza **3.** entiende **4.** pide **5.** vuelve **6.** juega

14. Expressing *-self/-selves* • **Reflexive Pronouns (Part 1)**

A. **1.** se **2.** nos **3.** se **4.** se **5.** te **6.** me **7.** se **8.** se

B. **1.** me / se **2.** se **3.** te **4.** se (despertarse) **5.** nos / nos **6.** te

C. Paso 1. **a.** 6: se viste **b.** 5: se cepilla **c.** 4: se levanta **d.** 3: se despierta **e.** 1: se baña **f.** 7: se peina **g.** 2: se acuesta

D. **1.** Nos despertamos temprano. **2.** Nos vestimos después de ducharnos. **3.** Nunca nos sentamos para tomar el desayuno. **4.** En la universidad, asistimos a clases y nos divertimos. **5.** Después de volver a casa, hacemos la tarea. **6.** A las doce tenemos sueño, nos cepillamos los dientes y nos acostamos. **7.** Nos dormimos a las doce y media.

E. (*Possible answers*) **1.** Carlos y Daniel se despiertan en la alcoba a las seis y cuarto (quince). Daniel se levanta. **2.** Daniel se afeita en el cuarto de baño. Carlos se ducha en el cuarto de baño. **3.** Daniel se sienta en un café. Se divierte con unas amigas. **4.** Daniel se quita la chaqueta en la sala. Carlos duerme en el sofá.

F. Paso 1. **1.** J **2.** A **3.** D **4.** J, A, D **5.** A, D **6.** A, J **7.** J
Paso 2. **1.** Gracias **2.** Quién **3.** por la tarde **4.** especial

UN POCO DE TODO

A. **1.** me levanto **2.** tengo **3.** despertarme **4.** quiero **5.** jugar **6.** empezamos **7.** pongo **8.** salgo **9.** puedo **10.** almorzamos **11.** pierde **12.** tiene **13.** pierdo **14.** tengo **15.** vuelvo

B. Después de escuchar. **1.** ND **2.** F: Vive en las afueras. **3.** F: Es bastante grande. **4.** C **5.** F: Sí, tiene patio.

C. **1.** Miguel René se levanta a las seis de la mañana. **2.** Se baña por la mañana. **3.** Va a la universidad y tiene clases. **4.** Almuerza con sus amigos. **5.** Va al trabajo. **6.** Sale del trabajo a las ocho de la noche. **7.** Vuelve a casa después de ir al gimnasio.

CULTURA

A. **1.** El Salvador **2.** San Salvador **3.** Nicaragua **4.** Managua

B. **1.** Centroamérica **2.** bajareque **3.** costa **4.** jardín **5.** formales **6.** volcanes

PÓNGASE A PRUEBA

A. hacer: hago, haces, hacen **traer:** traigo, traes, traemos **oír:** oigo, oímos, oyen **poner:** pongo, pones, ponemos, ponen **ver:** veo, ves, vemos, ven **salir:** salgo, sales, salimos, salen

B. **1. a.** ie **b.** ue **c.** i **2.** nosotros/as, vosotros/as **3. a.** piensas / servir **b.** empiezo / a **c.** volver / a **d.** pedir

C. **1. a.** me **b.** te **c.** se **d.** nos **e.** se **2. a.** Me acuesto tarde. **b.** ¿Cuándo te sientas a comer? **c.** Me visto en cinco minutos.

PRUEBA CORTA

A. **1.** se duermen   **2.** sentarme / oigo   **3.** me divierto   **4.** levantarte (salir)   **5.** se pone   **6.** haces
7. salimos

E. **1.** cuatro   **2.** dos   **3.** cuatro metros por cinco metros   **4.** muchas escuelas / un parque   **5.** Miraflores
/ 246

CAPÍTULO 6: Las estaciones y el tiempo

VOCABULARIO: Preparación

¿Qué tiempo hace hoy?

B. **1.** Llueve. (Hace [muy] mal tiempo.)   **2.** Hace (mucho) frío.   **3.** Hace (mucho) calor.   **4.** Hace
fresco.   **5.** Hace buen tiempo. (Hace fresco.)   **6.** (*Possible answer*) Hay (mucha) contaminación.

C. (*Possible answers*)   **1.** Hace sol. (Hace calor.)   **2.** Hace (mucho) calor.   **3.** Está nublado.   **4.** Llueve.
(Está lloviendo.)   **5.** Hace (mucho) viento.   **6.** Hace (mucho) frío.   **7.** Hay mucha contaminación.

Los meses y las estaciones del año

A. **1.** junio / julio / agosto   **2.** invierno   **3.** otoño   **4.** llueve   **5.** cuatro de julio   **6.** nieva
7. primero de abril   **8.** enero / mayo   **9.** catorce de febrero

B. **1.** el catorce de junio de mil novecientos veinticinco (veinte y cinco)   **2.** el quince de septiembre de
mil quinientos sesenta y seis   **3.** el siete de diciembre de dos mil quince   **4.** el primero de enero de mil
setecientos setenta y siete   **5.** el veintiocho (veinte y ocho) de agosto de mil novecientos noventa y cuatro

D. Paso 1. **1.** el verano / no hay frío   **2.** la primavera / verde / llueve   **3.** el verano   **4.** el otoño /
marrones / todo

¿Dónde está? Las preposiciones (Part 2)

A. **1.** delante de (a la izquierda de)   **2.** encima de   **3.** detrás de (cerca de)   **4.** cerca del   **5.** debajo de
6. a la izquierda de (cerca de)   **7.** a la derecha de (cerca de)   **8.** entre

C. Paso 1. *You should have checked items 2, 4, 6, 7.*

PRONUNCIACIÓN: *r* and *rr*

D. Paso 1. **1.** Rosa   **3.** guitarra   **4.** Rigoberta   **5.** rojo   **6.** un error horrible   **7.** un aroma raro
8. Raquel es rubia.   **9.** Federico es rico.

GRAMÁTICA

15. ¿Qué están haciendo? • Present Progressive: *Estar* + *-ndo*

A. **1.** nevando   **2.** lloviendo   **3.** haciendo   **4.** leyendo   **5.** oyendo   **6.** durmiendo   **7.** prefiriendo

B. **1.** durmiendo   **2.** pidiendo   **3.** sirviéndose   **4.** leyendo   **5.** almorzando / divirtiéndose

C. **1.** está jugando / está escuchando   **2.** está mirando / está vistiéndose (se está vistiendo)   **3.** está
leyendo / está haciendo   **4.** está acostándose (se está acostando) / está comiendo

16. *Ser o estar* • Summary of the Uses of *ser* and *estar*

¿Recuerda Ud.? **1.** b   **2.** d   **3.** c   **4.** a

A. Paso 1. **a.** es   **b.** son   **c.** es   **d.** es   **e.** está   **f.** es   **g.** Son   **h.** estás   **i.** Están   **j.** están   **k.** somos

Paso 2. **1.** j (estar) **2.** a (ser) **3.** f, c (ser) **4.** b, d (ser) **5.** e, h, i (estar) **6.** c, k (ser) **7.** g (ser)

B. **1.** eres / Soy **2.** son / son **3.** son / están **4.** es / estar / es **5.** está / Estoy / está **6.** es / es

D. **1.** estás **2.** estoy **3.** son **4.** están **5.** Son **6.** Son **7.** es **8.** es **9.** estar

17. Describing • Comparisons

A. **1.** que **2.** como **3.** como **4.** que **5.** como

B. **1.** Briana es tan delgada como Petra. (Briana no es más/menos delgada que Petra.) **2.** Briana es más simpática que Petra. (Briana no es menos simpática que Petra.) **3.** Ernesto es más alto que José. (Ernesto no es menos alto que José.) **4.** Carlitos es más bajo que Julio. (Carlitos no es menos bajo que Julio.) **5.** Carmen es tan extrovertida como Mónica. **6.** José es menos delgado que Ernesto. (José no es tan delgado como Ernesto.) **7.** Inés es menor que Carlitos. (Inés es más joven que Carlitos.) **8.** Carmen es tan alegre como José. (Carmen es más alegre que José. Carmen no es menos alegre que José.)

D. **1.** Sí, el cine es tan alto como la tienda (Casa Montaño). **2.** El café es más pequeño que todos los otros edificios. **3.** El hotel es más alto que todos los otros edificios. **4.** No, el cine es más alto que el café. **5.** No, el hotel es más grande que el cine.

E. **1.** menos que / mejor que **2.** más que / más de **3.** mejor que **4.** tantas / como

G. Paso 2. **1.** más que **2.** menos / que **3.** menos que **4.** más / que

UN POCO DE TODO

A. **1.** veintiún (veinte y un) **2.** diecinueve **3.** ese **4.** que **5.** que **6.** que **7.** tanto **8.** como **9.** de **10.** doscientos **11.** porque **12.** estar **13.** de **14.** ciento cincuenta **15.** pagar

B. Después de escuchar. **1.** F (*Possible answer*) Nicanor vive en Vermont pero es de la República Dominicana, en el Caribe. **2.** F (*Possible answer*) A Nicanor le gusta la nieve (porque es una experiencia nueva para él) pero no le gusta el frío. **3.** C **4.** C **5.** F (*Possible answer*) En Sudamérica hace frío en el sur de Chile y la Argentina y en las montañas de los Andes. **6.** F (*Possible answer*) Cuando es verano en el hemisferio norte, es invierno en el hemisferio sur.

C. Paso 1. **1.** T **2.** R **3.** M **4.** R **5.** M **6.** T **7.** M **8.** T **9.** R **Paso 2.** **1.** En mi país **2.** llueve **3.** me encantan las vacaciones **4.** Es en otoño.

CULTURA

A. **1.** Costa Rica **2.** San José

B. **1.** temperaturas **2.** democracia **3.** capital, habitantes **4.** lluviosa **5.** transporte, colores **6.** desierto **7.** diversidad, sur

PÓNGASE A PRUEBA

A. cepillándose / divirtiéndose / escribiendo / estudiando / leyendo / poniendo / sirviendo

B. **1.** f **2.** a **3.** c **4.** i **5.** h **6.** b **7.** g **8.** e **9.** d

C. **1.** más / que **2.** tantos / como **3.** mejor **4.** tan / como **5.** menos / que **6.** de

PRUEBA CORTA

A. **1.** Estoy mirando el/un programa. **2.** Juan está leyendo el/un periódico. **3.** Marta está sirviendo (el) café ahora. **4.** Los niños están durmiendo. **5.** ¿Estás almorzando ahora?

B. **1.** está / Estoy **2.** eres / Soy **3.** están / Estamos **4.** Estás / estoy **5.** está

C. **1.** Arturo tiene más perros que Roberto. **2.** Arturo es más gordo que Roberto. **3.** Arturo no es tan moreno como Roberto. (Arturo no es más moreno que Roberto.) **4.** Roberto es menor que Arturo. **5.** Los perros de Arturo son más grandes que el perro de Roberto.

CAPÍTULO 7: ¡A comer!

VOCABULARIO: Preparación

La comida y las comidas

A. **1.** huevos / pan / jugo / té / leche **2.** camarones / langosta **3.** papas fritas **4.** agua **5.** helado **6.** carne / verduras **7.** queso **8.** lechuga / tomate **9.** hambre **10.** sed

E. Paso 1. **1.** Panamá **2.** restaurante / (típica) panameña **3.** arroz / tamales / tortillas **4.** sancocho (de gallina) **Paso 2.** *You should have checked:* ajíes, ajo, otoe, cebolla, pimientos, gallina, ñame, yuca

¿Qué sabe Ud. y a quién conoce?

A. **1.** saber **2.** conocer **3.** conocer **4.** saber **5.** saber **6.** saber **7.** saber

B. **1.** Sabes **2.** conocemos **3.** conozco **4.** sé **5.** saben **6.** sabe **7.** conocer

C. **1.** conocen **2.** sé **3.** Sabes **4.** saber **5.** Conocemos / conozco **6.** conocer

D. Paso 1. *You should have checked:* ENRIQUE: a los padres de Rosa; ROBERTO: bailar, jugar al tenis, a los padres de Rosa; SUSANA: jugar al tenis, a los padres de Rosa, la ciudad

Pronunciación: *d*

D. Paso 1. *You should have underlined:* **2.** a<u>d</u>ónde; **3.** uste<u>d</u>es; **4.** personali<u>d</u>ad; **5.** ver<u>d</u>ad; **6.** ven<u>d</u>en de to<u>d</u>o; **7.** Per<u>d</u>ón, Diego.; **8.** Buenos <u>d</u>ías, A<u>d</u>ela. **9.** ¿<u>D</u>ónde está el <u>d</u>octor?

GRAMÁTICA

18. Expressing *what* or *whom* • Direct Objects: The Personal *a*; Direct Object Pronouns

A. **1.** b **2.** c **3.** a **4.** f **5.** d **6.** c **7.** b **8.** e **9.** g

B. Paso 1. *You should have underlined the following direct objects (the number refers to the numbered blank that precedes them):* **1.** el dueño **2.** los camareros **3.** quién **4.** la Srta. Estrada **5.** nuestra amiga **6.** este restaurante **7.** el camarero **8.** el menú **9.** Marilena **Paso 2.** **1.** al **2.** a **3.** A **4.** a **5.** a **6.** ø **7.** al **8.** ø **9.** a

C. Paso 1. **1.** c **2.** d **3.** a **4.** b **Paso 2.** **1.** He eats them frequently (often). **2.** He likes to drink (have) it only on special occasions. **3.** He prefers to eat them raw. **4.** He drinks it every day.

D. **1.** Yo lo preparo. **2.** Yo voy a comprarlos. / Yo los voy a comprar. **3.** Dolores va a hacerlas. / Dolores las va a hacer. **4.** Juan los trae. **5.** Yo los invito.

E. **1.** te ayudamos **2.** me, ayudar **3.** la ayudo **4.** los ayudan

H. Paso 1. **1.** No, no lo necesita. **2.** No, no lo necesita. **3.** Sí, los necesita. Los necesita para el ceviche. **4.** Sí, las necesita. Las necesita para las chuletas de cerdo. **5.** No, no la necesita. **6.** Sí, las necesita. Las necesita para el ceviche. **7.** No, no lo necesita. **8.** Sí, los necesita. Los necesita para el ceviche. **Paso 2.** **1.** los padres de su novio. **2.** pescado frito **3.** camarones **4.** chuletas de cerdo **5.** chuletas de cerdo **6.** espárragos / los

I. **1.** Los despierta a las seis y media. **2.** El padre lo levanta. **3.** La madre lo baña. **4.** Su hermana lo divierte. **5.** Lo sienta en la silla. **6.** El padre lo acuesta.

J. (*Possible answers*) **1.** Acaban de escuchar música y bailar. **2.** Acaba de celebrar su cumpleaños. **3.** Acaban de comer. **4.** Acaba de traer la cuenta. **5.** Acaba de pagar la cuenta.

19. Expressing Negation • Indefinite and Negative Words

¿Recuerda Ud.? **1.** siempre **2.** también **3.** Nunca

A. **1.** c **2.** d **3.** b **4.** e **5.** a

B. Paso 1. **1.** no voy a hacer nada interesante **2.** nunca/jamás salgo con nadie **3.** no tengo ninguno (no tengo ningún amigo nuevo.) **4.** Ninguna (de esas chicas) es mi amiga **5.** nadie cena conmigo nunca/ jamás **Paso 2.** **1.** quiero (comer) algo. La comida aquí es buena. **2.** alguien (a atendernos). **3.** siempre cenamos en un restaurante bueno. **4.** algunos platos sabrosos (en el menú).

20. Influencing Others • Commands (Part 1): Formal Commands

¿Recuerda Ud? **2.** Read the sentences. / leer **3.** Answer the questions. / contestar **4.** Write a paragraph. / escribir

A. *comer:* como / coman; *escribir:* escriba / escriban; *buscar:* busco / busquen; *conocer:* conozco / conozca / conozcan; *dar:* doy / dé / den; *divertir:* divierta / diviertan; *empezar:* empiece / empiecen; *estar:* estoy / esté / estén; *ir:* vaya / vayan; *oír:* oigo / oiga; *perder:* pierda / pierdan; *saber:* sé / sepa / sepan; *ser:* soy / sean; *salir:* salgo / salga / salgan; *traer:* traigo / traiga; *volver:* vuelvo / vuelvan

B. Paso 1. **1.** compruebe **2.** encargue **3.** no lo haga **4.** déjelas **5.** no comente **6.** no deje **7.** no los deje **Paso 2.** **1.** e **2.** a **3.** d **4.** b **5.** c

D. (*Possible answers*) **1.** Entonces, coman algo. **2.** Entonces, beban (tomen) algo. **3.** Entonces, estudien. **4.** Entonces, ciérrenlas. **5.** Entonces, lleguen (salgan) (más) temprano. **6.** Entonces, no sean impacientes. (Entonces, sean pacientes.)

E. **1.** córtenlo ahora **2.** no la preparen todavía **3.** no la sirvan todavía **4.** llámenlo ahora **5.** no lo hagan todavía **6.** tráiganlas ahora

H. **1.** sí **2.** no **3.** sí **4.** no **5.** sí **6.** sí **7.** sí

UN POCO DE TODO

A. **1.** conoces **2.** al **3.** lo **4.** conozco **5.** sé **6.** siempre **7.** tampoco **8.** El

B. Después de escuchar. **1.** bar (café) / café (bar) / amigos **2.** familia **3.** estilos / música / tradicionales **4.** calle **5.** tapas

C. Paso 1. (*Answers may vary slightly*) **1.** (una botella de) vino tinto (Rioja) / agua mineral (con gas) **2.** una sopa (de ajo) / gambas (camarones) al limón con arroz **3.** una sopa (de ajo) / el bistec (estilo argentino, poco asado). **4.** no piden nada (no piden [ningún] postre) **5.** copa **6.** excelente / deliciosa **Paso 2.** **1.** los tacos de pollo **2.** un coctel de camarones **3.** el flan de naranja **4.** un vino blanco

CULTURA

A. **1.** Panamá **2.** la Ciudad de Panamá **3.** el canal de Panamá

B. **1.** El arroz **2.** salsa **3.** la arquitectura **4.** los emberás **5.** sopa / verduras **6.** frutas **7.** Las empanadas **8.** El canal de Panamá

PÓNGASE A PRUEBA

A. **1.** te / lo / la / nos / las **2. a.** Yo lo traigo. **b.** ¡Tráigalo! **c.** ¡No lo traiga! **d.** Estamos esperándolo. / Lo estamos esperando. **e.** Voy a llamarlo. / Lo voy a llamar.

B. **1.** nadie **2.** tampoco **3.** nunca (jamás) **4.** nada **5.** ningún detalle

C. piense / vuelva / dé / vaya / busque / esté / sepa / diga

PRUEBA CORTA

A. **1.** conozco **2.** conoces **3.** sé **4.** sabe

B. **1.** Quiero comer algo. **2.** Busco a alguien. **3.** Hay algo para beber. **4.** Yo conozco a algunos de sus amigos. / Yo también.

C. **1.** no voy a pedirla. (no la voy a pedir.) **2.** las quiero. **3.** no lo tomo. **4.** la preparo.

D. **1.** Compren **2.** hagan **3.** Traigan **4.** pongan **5.** Llámenlo **6.** lo sirvan

PUNTOS PERSONALES

B. Paso 1. Karina: **1.** las arepas **2.** su mamá **3.** pabellón criollo **4.** a las ocho **5.** a las doce (del mediodía) **6.** a las ocho (de la noche) **7.** Venezuela; Tané: **1.** los mariscos **2.** su abuela **3.** el arroz con gris y la carne de puerco asada **4.** a las ocho a nueve (de la mañana) **5.** de doce a una o una y media **6.** de siete y media a nueve (de la noche) **7.** Cuba; Rubén: **1.** los huevos fritos **2.** su madre y él **3.** n/a **4.** cuando te levantas **5.** a las dos (de la tarde) **6.** a las nueve (de la noche) **7.** España

---

CAPÍTULO 8: De viaje

VOCABULARIO: Preparación

De Viaje

A. **1.** ida y vuelta **2.** escala / bajarme **3.** extranjero / pasaporte **4.** equipaje **5.** control de seguridad **6.** pasajeros **7.** vuelo / demora **8.** salida / cola / subir **9.** asistentes de vuelo

B. **1.** boleto, tarjeta **2.** equipaje, embarque **3.** control, seguridad **4.** cola, embarque **5.** asientos **6.** aduana, pasaporte

E. Paso 2. **1.** trenes **2.** pide **3.** billete **4.** ida **5.** vuelta **6.** sale **7.** atrasado **8.** cambia

De Vacaciones

A. Paso 1. **1.** las montañas **2.** la tienda (de campaña) **3.** la playa **4.** la camioneta **5.** el mar / el océano **Paso 2.** (*Possible answers*) **1.** está tomando el sol (en la playa). **2.** están jugando (en la playa). **3.** está nadando (en el mar/océano). **4.** está haciendo *camping* (está divirtiéndose).

B. **1.** F **2.** F **3.** C **4.** C

Nota comunicativa: Other Uses of *se* (For Recognition)

1. Se habla **2.** Se factura **3.** se permite **4.** Se muestra **5.** Se come

Pronunciación: *g, gu,* and *j*

E. **1.** Don Guillermo es viejo y generoso. **2.** Por lo general, los jóvenes son inteligentes. **3.** Juan estudia geografía y geología. **4.** A mi amiga Gloria le gustan los gatos.

F. Paso 1. 1. [x] 2. [g] 3. [x] 4. [g] 5. [g] 6. [x] 7. [g] 8. [x]

GRAMÁTICA

¿Recuerda Ud.? 1. las sillas 2. Carlos 3. Ana

21. Expressing to who(m) or for who(m) • Indirect Object Pronouns; *Dar* and *decir*

A. te / le / nos / les

B. 1. me 2. Le 3. nos 4. Les 5. Le 6. te

C. 1. damos 2. da 3. dan 4. das 5. doy 6. digo 7. dice 8. dicen 9. dices 10. decimos

D. 1. ¿Le presto (el) dinero? 2. ¿Le cuento un chiste? 3. ¿Les ofrezco mi maleta? 4. ¿Le pido ayuda al profesor? 5. ¿Les sirvo más?

E. Paso 1. 2. les / a sus padres (a ellos) 3. le / a su esposo (al padre de Javier) 4. le / a Javier (a él / a su hijo)

H. Paso 2. (*Answers will vary. Sample answers.*) 1. Elisa le pregunta al Sr. Gómez cuánto cuesta el boleto de avión. 2. El Sr. Gómez le pregunta a Elisa qué días quiere viajar. 3. El Sr. Gómez le pregunta a Elisa cuánto tiempo piensa quedarse allí. 4. El Sr. Gómez le hace a Elisa una reservación de avión para las Islas Galápagos. 5. Elisa le pregunta al Sr. Gómez si él conoce las Galápagos. 6. El Sr. Gómez le dice a Elisa que el viaje a las Galápagos con su esposa fue inolvidable. 7. El Sr. Gómez le pregunta a Elisa si ella necesita una reservación de hotel también.

¿Recuerda Ud.? 1. me gusta (la leche). 2. me gusta (viajar al extranjero). 3. me gusta (nadar en el mar). 4. me gusta (hacer *camping*).

22. Expressing Likes and Dislikes • *Gustar* (Part 2)

A. 1. me gusta 2. te gustan 3. le gusta 4. nos gusta 5. les gusta 6. les gustan

B. 1. te gusta 2. les gusta 3. me gustan 4. nos gusta / le gusta 5. les gusta

C. 1. A su padre le gustan las vacaciones en las montañas. 2. A su madre le encantan los cruceros. 3. A sus hermanos les gustan los deportes acuáticos. 4. A nadie le gusta viajar en autobús. 5. A Ernesto le encanta sacar fotos.

F. (*Answers will vary. Sample possible answers.*) 1. A Heidi le encanta su trabajo. 2. A sus clientes les gusta viajar a *Disney World*. 3. A sus clientes les gustan algunos destinos de México y Sudamérica. 4. A Heidi le encanta viajar. 5. A Heidi le gusta Canadá como destino turístico.

23. Talking about the Past (Part 1) • Preterite of Regular Verbs and of *dar, hacer, ir,* and *ser*

A. *hablar:* hablaste / habló / hablamos / hablaron; *volver:* volví / volvió / volvimos / volvieron; *vivir:* viví / viviste / vivimos / vivieron; *dar:* di / diste / dio / dieron; *hacer:* hice / hiciste / hizo / hicimos; *ser/ir:* fuiste / fue / fuimos / fueron; *jugar:* jugué / jugó / jugamos / jugaron; *sacar:* saqué / sacaste / sacamos / sacaron; *empezar:* empecé / empezaste / empezó / empezaron

B. *yo:* 1. volví 2. Me hice 3. comí 4. terminé 5. metí 6. di *tú:* 1. asististe 2. Te acostaste 3. empezaste 4. fuiste 5. Saliste 6. volviste *Eva:* 1. fue 2. se matriculó 3. empezó 4. regresó 5. viajó 6. vio 7. pasó *Mi amiga y yo:* 1. pasamos 2. Vivimos 3. asistimos 4. hicimos 5. Visitamos 6. caminamos 7. comimos 8. vimos *Dos científicos:* 1. fueron 2. Salieron 3. llegaron 4. viajaron 5. vieron 6. sacaron 7. gustaron 8. volvieron

E. Paso 2. (*Possible answers*) 1. Caminaron por las islas. 2. Observaron los animales. 3. Sacaron muchas fotos. 4. La Sra. Gómez nadó y tomó el sol. 5. Descansaron mucho.

UN POCO DE TODO

A. **1.** fui **2.** compré **3.** pagué **4.** costó **5.** doscientos veintitrés (veinte y tres) **6.** poca **7.** llevé **8.** pasamos **9.** ningún **10.** fuimos **11.** hicimos **12.** Saqué **13.** algunas **14.** salimos **15.** comimos (comieron) **16.** comimos (comieron) **17.** Nos

B. Antes de escuchar. **1.** *You should have checked:* la Basílica de Guadalupe, Guadalajara, Isla Mujeres, el Museo Nacional de Antropología, las pirámides de Teotihuacán, ruinas mayas, Taxco, el Yucatán. **2.** b **3.** d **Después de escuchar.** *You should have checked the numbers 1, 2, 4, 5, 7 and 8.*

C. Paso **1.** (*Answers may vary slightly.*)

1. ¿Adónde vas a ir de vacaciones este año? **2.** ¿Qué te gusta hacer durante las vacaciones? **3.** ¿Adónde fuiste en tu último viaje y qué hiciste?

CULTURA

A. **1.** República Dominicana **2.** Santo Domingo **B.** **1.** los colmados **2.** El casabe **3.** las Mariposas **4.** Punta Cana **5.** monumentos **6.** música, el güiro

PÓNGASE A PRUEBA

A. **1. a.** le **b.** Le / diciéndole **c.** Le / decirle **d.** Dígale **e.** No le diga **2.** *dar:* doy / da / damos / dan; *decir:* digo / dices / dice / dicen

B. **1.** ¿Les gusta viajar? **2.** A mí no me gusta quejarme. **3.** A Juan le gustan los aeropuertos.

C. *dar:* di / dio / dimos / dieron; *hablar:* hablé / hablaste / hablamos / hablaron; *hacer:* hice / hiciste / hizo / hicieron; *ir/ser:* fuiste / fue / fuimos / fueron; *salir:* salí / saliste / salió / salimos

PRUEBA CORTA

A. **1.** le **2.** nos **3.** les **4.** me **5.** te

B. **1.** le gustan **2.** les gusta **3.** me gusta **4.** nos gustan **5.** te gusta

C. **1.** mandaste **2.** empecé **3.** hizo **4.** Fueron **5.** Oíste **6.** volvieron **7.** dio

CAPÍTULO 9: Los días festivos

VOCABULARIO: Preparación

Una fiesta de cumpleaños para Javier

A. **1.** d **2.** b **3.** i **4.** e **5.** l **6.** k **7.** f **8.** g **9.** c **10.** h

B. **1.** la Nochevieja **2.** la Navidad **3.** La Pascua Judía **4.** la Nochebuena **5.** El Día de los Muertos **6.** El Día de la Raza

E. (*Possible answers*) **1.** Van a hacerle una fiesta porque es su cumpleaños. **2.** Se llama la quinceañera. **3.** Va a ser en la casa de Amanda. **4.** Decidieron hacerla en casa para no gastar tanto dinero. **5.** Van a ir cien invitados. **6.** Todos van a regarle a Amanda algo. **7.** Todos los parientes van a prepararla. **8.** Los botanas que van a preparar son empanadas y croquetas de jamón.

F. **1.** La Habana **2.** Cuba **3.** México **4.** tienda **5.** típicos **6.** fiesta **7.** cumpleaños **8.** refrescos **9.** Navidad **10.** fiesta **11.** comida **12.** asada

Las emociones y los estados afectivos

A. **1.** a **2.** c **3.** d **4.** f **5.** e **6.** b

B. (*Possible answers*) **1.** recuerdo / me pongo avergonzado/a   **2.** se enojan (se ponen irritados)
3. se enferman / se quejan   **4.** se portan   **5.** discutir

C. **1.** larguísima   **2.** riquísimos   **3.** cansadísimo/a   **4.** carísima   **5.** dificilísimas

PRONUNCIACIÓN: *c* and *qu*

B. **1.** quemar   **2.** quince   **3.** campaña   **4.** compras   **5.** coqueta   **6.** comedor

GRAMÁTICA

24. Talking about the Past (Part 2) • Irregular Preterites

¿Recuerda Ud.? **hablar:** hablé / hablamos / habló / hablaron; **comer:** comí / comimos / comió / comieron;
vivir: viví / vivimos / vivió / vivieron; **hacer:** hice / hicimos / hizo / hicieron

A. estar: estuve / estuvo / estuvieron; **tener:** tuviste / tuvo / tuvimos; **poder:** pude / pudiste / pudieron;
poner: pusiste / puso / pusieron; **querer:** quise / quisimos; **saber:** supe / supiste / supo / supimos; **venir:** vine
/ vino / vinimos / vinieron; **decir:** dije / dijiste / dijeron; **traer:** trajiste / trajo / trajimos

B. Paso 1.   a. 4 (Antonio y Mario)   **b.** 2 (Laura y Marcos)   **c.** 5 (Norma)   **d.** 3 (María)   **e.** 1 (Ricardo)

C. *Durante la Navidad:* **1.** tuvo   **2.** estuvieron   **3.** Vinieron   **4.** trajeron   **5.** dijeron   **6.** fueron
7. comieron   **8.** pudieron   **9.** lo pasaron   *Otro terremoto en California:* **1.** supimos   **2.** hubo   **3.** oí
4. leí   **5.** se dañaron   **6.** hizo   **7.** dijo   **8.** fue

D. **1.** estuvo   **2.** pude   **3.** tuve   **4.** fuiste   **5.** Quise   **6.** estuve   **7.** hizo   **8.** Supiste   **9.** tuvo
10. fue   **11.** dijo   **12.** puse   **13.** trajiste   **14.** traje

25. Talking About the Past (Part 3) • Preterite of Stem-Changing Verbs

A. divertirse: me divertí / se divirtió / se divirtieron; **sentir:** sentí / sentiste / sintieron; **dormir:** dormiste /
durmió / dormimos / durmieron; **conseguir:** conseguí / consiguió / conseguimos / consiguieron; **reír:** me reí
/ te reíste / nos reímos / se rieron; **vestir:** vestiste / vistió / vestimos

B. **1.** me senté / me dormí   **2.** se sentaron / nos dormimos   **3.** se durmió   **4.** nos reímos / se rio
5. sintieron / se sintió

C. Paso 1. **2.** se sentó   **3.** Pidió   **4.** sirvió   **5.** se sintió   **6.** se levantó   **7.** se despidió   **8.** Volvió
9. durmió   **Paso 2.** **1.** entré   **2.** me senté   **3.** Pedí   **4.** me sirvió   **5.** me sentí   **6.** me levanté   **7.** me
despedí   **8.** Volví   **9.** dormí

D. Paso 1. *Vestirse elegantemente:* Julia, Verónica, Ernesto; *sentirse mal:* Tomás; *dormir toda la tarde:*
Tomás; *preferir quedarse en casa:* Tomás

26. Avoiding Repetition • Expressing Direct and Indirect Object Pronouns Together

¿Recuerda Ud.? **1.** Yo le traigo el café. (C.I.)   **2.** Yo lo traigo ahora. (C.D.)   **3.** Ellos nos compran los
boletos hoy. (C.I.)   **4.** Ellos los compran hoy. (C.D.)   **5.** No les hablo mucho. (C.I.)   **6.** No las conozco
bien. (C.D.)   **7.** Queremos darles una fiesta. (Les queremos dar una fiesta.) (C.I.)   **8.** Pensamos darla en
casa. (C.D.)

A. Paso 1. **1.** a   **2.** c   **3.** d   **4.** b   **Paso 2.**   **1.** nos las   **2.** Te lo   **3.** Se los   **4.** Se las

C. Paso 1. **1.** se las   **2.** me lo   **3.** nos la   **4.** se las   **5.** se los

D. (*Possible answers*) **1.** Se lo dejó a Memo.   **2.** Se la dejó a Marta.   **3.** Se los dejó a la biblioteca.
4. Se los dejó a la Cruz Roja.   **5.** ¡Me la dejó a mí!   **6.** Se los dejó a Ana y Ernesto

G. **1.** Me las dio   **2.** Se las mandé   **3.** pedírmelo   **4.** dénmela

UN POCO DE TODO

A. Paso 1. **1.** hice **2.** nuestra **3.** Fue **4.** fue **5.** larga **6.** invitó **7.** tuve **8.** también **9.** terminaron **10.** supe **11.** me encontré **12.** di **13.** estuvimos **14.** le **15.** pedí **16.** las **Paso 2.** (*Possible answers*) **1.** Fue para reunirse con un director de su compañía. **2.** No pudo verlo porque la reunión fue muy larga. **3.** Lo supo porque se lo dijo su amigo Luis Dávila. **4.** Se las dio a Luis.

B. Antes de escuchar. UNA FIESTA AL AIRE LIBRE: 1, 5, 6 UNA CELEBRACIÓN RELIGIOSA SOLEMNE: 2, 3, 4 **Después de escuchar** **1.** C **2.** F **3.** C **4.** C **5.** F **6.** F **7.** C.

C. Paso 2. **1.** le va a encantar **2.** celebra tu familia la Navidad **3.** gastamos mucho dinero **4.** comemos las doce uvas de la suerte

CULTURA

A. **1.** Cuba **2.** La Habana

B. **1.** los Reyes Magos **2.** parrandas **3.** la libertad **4.** el son, africanos **5.** la Independencia **6.** la Navidad **7.** La palma

PÓNGASE A PRUEBA

A. **1.** estuve **2.** pudiste **3.** puso **4.** quisimos **5.** supieron **6.** tuve **7.** viniste **8.** trajo **9.** dijeron **10.** fuimos

B. él/ella/Ud.: durmió / pidió / prefirió / recordó / se sintió; **ellos/ellas/Uds.:** durmieron / pidieron / prefirieron / recordaron / se sintieron

C. **1.** se lo **2.** se la **3.** se los

PRUEBA CORTA

A. **1.** nos reímos (nos divertimos) **2.** se puso / durmió **3.** conseguí (traje) **4.** se despidió **5.** se vistió / se divirtió **6.** hicimos / trajeron (consiguieron)

B. **1.** a **2.** a **3.** c **4.** b **5.** a **6.** b

PUNTOS PERSONALES

D. Paso 1. **1.** K **2.** MR **3.** K **4.** MR **5.** R **6.** MR y R